Shameful Admissions

Many things indicate that we are going through a transitional period, when it seems that something is on the way out and something else is painfully being born. It is as if something were crumbling, decaying and exhausting itself, while something else, still indistinct, were arising from the rubble.

The distinguishing features of transitional periods are a mixing and blending of cultures and a plurality or parallelism of intellectual and spiritual worlds. These are periods when all consistent value systems collapse, when cultures distant in time and space are discovered or rediscovered. New meaning is gradually born from the encounter, or the intersection, of many different elements.

Vaclav Havel, President of the Czech Republic, upon receiving the Philadelphia Liberty Medal at Independence Hall, July 4, 1994

Freeman and slave, patrician and plebeian, lord and serf, guildmaster and journeyman, in a word, oppressor and oppressed, stood in constant opposition to one another, carried on an uninterrupted, now hidden, now open fight, a fight that each time ended, either in a revolutionary reconstitution of society at large, or in the common ruin of the contending classes.

Karl Marx and Friedrich Engels
The Communist Manifesto
English Translation by Samuel Moore, 1888

We hold these Truths to be self-evident, that all Men are created equal . . .

The Declaration of Independence, July 4, 1776

Angela Browne-Miller

Shameful Admissions

· ·

The Losing Battle to Serve
Everyone in Our Universities

Jossey-Bass Publishers
San Francisco

• • • • • • • • • • • • • •

Substantial discounts on bulk quantities of Jossey-Bass books are available to corpora-
tions, professional associations, and other organizations. For details and discount
information, contact the special sales department at Jossey-Bass Inc., Publishers
(415) 433-1740; Fax (800) 605-2665.

For sales outside the United States, please contact your local Simon & Schuster International Office.

Frontispiece quote excerpted from Vaclav Havel, "The New Measure of Man" (entire
transcript of speech delivered July 4, 1994). *The New York Times*, Op-Ed Section, Friday
July 8, 1994. Reprinted by permission.

 Manufactured in the United States of America on Lyons Falls Pathfinder
Tradebook. This paper is acid-free and 100 percent totally chlorine-free.

Library of Congress Cataloging-in-Publication Data

Browne-Miller, Angela, date.
 Shameful admissions : the losing battle to serve everyone in our universities / Angela
Browne-Miller. — 1st ed.
  p. cm. —(The Jossey-Bass higher and adult education series)
 Includes bibliographical references and index.
 ISBN 0-7879-0182-2
 1. Universities and colleges—United States—Admission. 2. Minorities—Education
(Higher)—United States 3. Affirmative action programs—United States. 4. Education,
Higher—Political aspects—United States. 5. University of California, Berkeley—
Admission. I. Title. II. Series.
LB2351.2.B76   1996
378.1'051'0973—dc20   95-32120
                                                              CIP

FIRST EDITION
HB Printing 10 9 8 7 6 5 4 3 2

Contents

*To the
underground
rising*

• • • • • • •

*subterra
surgit*

Preface

§§§§§§§§§§§§§§§§§§§§§§§§§§§§§§§§§§§

Shameful Admissions is about who gets through the gate of college admissions and what happens next. *Shameful Admissions* is also about why this information is critically important to all of us—taxpayers, parents, students, administrators, educators, citizens from all cultural and ethnic groups and from all walks of life. No one can honestly say: this situation has nothing to do with me. The quality of our lives, the future of our freedoms, the strength of our economy, the well-being of our children, are at stake.

Our young people, who are society's future and its great store of energy, are on the front lines of this crisis. They are struggling to decide how, where, when, how long, at what price, with what major, and even *whether* to go to college. Yet ultimately, every one of us, of college age or any age, is affected by the mounting economic, political, multicultural, and ideological pressures that are exerting themselves upon the gates of our colleges and universities. The survival of our democratic process depends upon our maintaining an educated, well-informed public. The continuing of our economic strength depends upon the ongoing production of an increasingly competent workforce, which taxpayers assume is ensured by the system of education they support. So far, as a relatively new nation, we have done at least moderately well. Yet today, the very fabric of our society may unravel unless its primary institutions, such as colleges and universities, either stretch or entirely transform to incorporate the demands of the many subcultures now claiming their rights to the all-American opportunity. In this sense, the affirmative action debate which emerged in the mid-1990s represents only the tip of the iceberg, a mere foreshadowing of the increasing, unprecedented competition among the ethnic, socioeconomic, and, most importantly, ideological constituencies to come.

Higher education is now center stage. To understand what this focus on higher education and the right to it means, we have to look far beyond affirmative action debates and ask difficult and daring questions such as: Should everyone really go to college? And we must focus beyond the veil of human politics and wonder: What are our colleges and universities not telling us about any less-than-positive changes in the quality of the education they offer? Is a college education really all it is cracked up to be? What is higher education really about?

Decisions regarding whether or not to go to college, which college to apply to and to attend, the worth of a tuition bill, the number of years to spend in school, which and how many degrees to earn, and to what extent these factors will enhance the return on students' and parents' and taxpayers' investments are difficult. Will today's college degree have any value tomorrow? Will it make any difference when today's college graduates are in the midlife prime of their working and earning lives? Are students learning useful skills, applicable knowledge, and the techniques for learning new things quickly in a rapidly changing environment and a fiercely competitive world—a world that will, within two or three decades, differ vastly from today's?

We must seek the truth: what should parents, college applicants, and all of us know about the hidden trends in, as well as the less-visible-but-profound effects of, changing admissions policies and academic tracking procedures? We should know at least what is disclosed in the chapters that follow. We must gain some perspective on the tension between standards of academic merit and standards of politically or multiculturally sensitive admissions policies. Are admissions standards remaining about the same; are they relaxing, or are they becoming more restrictive? How can we be certain? Should admissions standards be adapted to fit the changing profile of America's population? Who should decide? How have the minor and major dramas of college admissions, affirmative actions, special educational arrangements, and the altering of classroom standards affected the meaning of and value placed upon an undergraduate college degree? How have these dramas affected all members of our modern, highly diversified, representative democracy? Does excellence mean something different today than it did in the middle of the twentieth century?

I have asked these questions around the country, and I have been unsettled by the answers. These are answers that demand we take notice. They insist that we not look away or fool ourselves into thinking that today's college degree is a guarantee that a "higher" education has taken place. The stories in this book unfolded themselves to me as if waiting to be heard, leading me into the perceptions, realities, and lives of so many different players in the university system. Real people—college applicants, college students and professors, parents and counselors, members of government, and of the media—emerged from an invisible background, coming to the forefront with their comments, grievances, triumphs, observations, and individual cases for me to consider as I wrote this book. I have collected these stories from the broken gate—the gate that was once a highly selective but culturally restrictive college admissions process—and have imprinted my own overview upon this colorful, collagelike image.

Yet, this image is a still shot of what is actually a moving picture. Even as I write these words, the world about which I write is in tremendous flux. Just prior to *Shameful Admissions* going to press, the University of California regents voted to eliminate the use of affirmative action preferences in admissions, hiring, and contracting, thus intensifying an already heated debate: who has a right to be on campus? Shortly thereafter, U.S. Senator Robert Dole proposed that the Equal Opportunity Act of 1995, which would terminate affirmative action policies, be adopted by the federal legislature.

College students are sitting on the front lines of an almost ubiquitous debate about rights to education, to knowledge, and to the quality of life and power these bring. And this is a shame. The real problems with higher education are being overlooked. Too many of our college students are getting lost in the shuffle. They are being caught up in a sort of pseudo paper chase for a hollow baccalaureate degree—being awarded A's and B's for C and D work, being told they are becoming well educated and believing this is true because they know no better, and graduating about as competent as they should have been when they completed high school, if that. Far too many college students graduate without the writing, speaking, organizational, analytical, mathematical, practical, and intellectual skills that taxpayers, parents, and employers like to assume college graduates acquire, especially after having invested $20,000 to $100,000 (at least) and four or five (or more) years in post–high school education.

Despite efforts to distract us from the core issues and to convince us otherwise, efforts made by those employed within the higher education industry and by colleges trying to recruit applicants, the quality of higher education is being compromised. We know this; yet, we would like to ignore this dangerous reality. Students are being shortchanged, and the institutions that teach them are disintegrating. Eventually, the sham of the hollow degrees they confer will bring them down. So it is that the hallowed halls of learning are themselves struggling to learn, at almost light speed, merely how to survive as major social institutions. If a college, or a college system, degenerates or collapses, what does a degree from it mean? Certainly, colleges may manage to exist for some time into the future, appearing to educate and sounding their horns when they do achieve some successes, but they are increasingly becoming masks behind which major neglect and abuse of the American intellect is taking place.

Without a transformation in their most fundamental and long-held goals and policies, these institutions of higher education will die. At the same time, if a forceful attempt is not made to preserve the central intellectual traditions that have served us so well for so long, these traditions will be lost to history, and the forms of intellect they represent will be rendered impotent, and, ultimately, irretrievable. Only a complete restructuring of the higher education process can meet these polarized demands. Only a radical revision can preserve what is valuable about democratic higher education as well as what is valuable within established and, at least predominantly White, Western intellectual traditions. Only an understanding of these larger issues can provide parents and students an opportunity to make intelligent decisions regarding college application, college choice, and the amount of higher education in which it is worthwhile investing.

I have written *Shameful Admissions* to help college-bound and college students and their parents make decisions regarding higher education; to report on the wide range of perceptions about what higher education is becoming; and to offer citizens—voters, who should have a say in the use of their tax dollars—my reasons for advocating massive change. This is a troubled but exciting juncture in human history. Our lives have been forever altered by the shifts in American society that took place during the latter half of the twentieth century. Whether or not affirmative action policies become entirely a thing of the past, struggles over equal opportunity or fair access to equal opportunity are here to stay and most definitely will escalate. No American remains untouched by the coming of age of the melting pot. Racial integration has increased in many parts of American life. But so has racial tension. Have we fairly evaluated the impact of affirmative action on college admissions? No, because we have not had enough time to study its long-range impact. Perhaps we instinctively feel that there is little time to wait. Maybe we just do not know what works.

Only time will tell what the outcome of the massive integration— or "heterogenization"—of society and its major institutions will be. And that time may be too far in the future to provide us the wisdom to make today's choices. It is, therefore, best that we keep an honest and open eye on ourselves and our decisions regarding the inevitable multicultural pressures arising in our modern world. It is best that we view diversification as a great adventure, an opportunity for humanity to evolve to new heights. We stand at the threshold of what some political leaders have called a "new world order," one in which our traditional definitions of both diversity and unity will be entirely remodeled. As I propose in the last chapter of this book, the challenge is to move bravely into the future, ready to embrace change with wisdom, actively rather than on a continually ad hoc basis.

I have chosen to look at the reflection of our society that higher education provides us by examining many types of colleges and universities and focusing upon one that I take to be an extreme example as well as a foreshadowing of things to come. I have selected this university because it is large, public, and world renowned, and because it has been grappling with the difficulties of diversity in advance of most major institutions, and it has been doing so in a large, culturally diverse state where the first state-level challenge to affirmative action was launched in 1995. The nation is and has been watching the University of California, Berkeley and the State of California's management of the conflicts that have arisen there. It was at this university that one of the most visible backlashes against diversity was born. And it was at this university that some of the most potent backlashes against this backlash are already under way.

The University of California, Berkeley maintains a marked presence in the higher education scene. It looms like a vast planet on the horizon of the broadest of global social change. It is a pioneer, persisting in its forward-looking, determined, and elaborate intermixing of diverse and competing intelligences and ethnic constituencies, a type of intermixing that is emerging around the globe.

The lessons learned by this institution are important lessons for us all. I believe that we can learn enough from its experiments to plan for the future.

I have spent many years in the halls of this institution, working on graduate degrees, completing a postdoctoral fellowship, and lecturing. I have been both part of its body and one of its children, as it has undergone profound changes. I have watched the ethnic mix of the administration, the faculty, the staff, and the student body transform. Having lectured for over a decade in three different departments at both graduate and undergraduate level, I have witnessed the evolution of the face, the mind, the goals, the attitude of the student body. Still, in recent years, in the wake of affirmative action, fluctuating admissions policy, tuition increases, and related debates, I cannot help but wonder about the future of this institution. Will it remain great? Will it grow greater than ever? At what stage of its life cycle is the University of California, Berkeley?

Shameful Admissions seeks to hold this university up to the world to serve as a mirror. How do great institutions move through time into the new world order? What will it take for higher education and other major social institutions to survive what may be the failure—or the fatal myopia—of the naive, or at least incomplete, dream of equality? What do modern university admissions policies tell us about both the changing world order and the long-established ideals our founding fathers set forth at the birth of this nation?

To begin to answer these questions; to provide information to concerned students, parents, and citizens; and to contribute to the current rethinking of free world ideals, I have woven selected references to the research and writings of others into my own research, thinking, and writing. Readers will note that I have placed key terms and phrases in quotes, except where I have coined them. In these instances, I take responsibility for the use of the particular term or concept by italicizing it. I assume this distinction will protect my interviewees and sources from any implied association with the conclusions I have drawn. Readers will also note that the labels for various ethnic groups have been selected with great care, and with the knowledge that even these labels are far from fair, complete, or satisfactory in this time of cultural confusion and competition.

Chapter One, The Admissions Furor: Battle Cries or Mere Confusion?, casts the personal side of college application and college matriculation in our tumultuous times against the backdrop of current political trends and double standards. Chapter Two, What's at Stake in the Drive for Access?, looks at your—our—stake in society's investment in higher education and the "human capital" of our young people: tomorrow's workforce. It reviews the unwieldy expansion of the higher education industry and examines the link between the historically defined dream of equality, also termed "equal opportunity" and "egalitarianism," and the difficulties encountered by modern higher education as it seeks to implement this dream.

Chapter Three, Who Gets In?, links the history of university admissions to traditional American ideals of unity and individual equality and then to modern ideals of diversity and multicultural parity. This chapter also examines the compromising, mixed admissions criteria which was employed by U.C. Berkeley at the direction of the State of California and replicated in various forms by numerous other colleges and universities. Students and parents may wish to study this section to understand the issues affecting college admissions processes, because Berkeley's drama is going to be played out and, in some cases, is already being played out at institutions throughout the nation.

Chapter Four, "The Nasty Problem" of Fairness on the Multicultural Campus, shifts focus, extracting a profile of U.C. Berkeley from responses to questionnaires I distributed to students, faculty, and administrators in the year preceding the first official efforts to repeal affirmative action policies. To explore the dimensions of this situation and to acquire a cross section of perceptions, I distributed this exploratory questionnaire to a sampling of 750 students, 200 faculty, and 150 administrators. Four hundred fifty-nine students,

99 faculty, and 95 administrators responded. I interviewed another 200 students, 35 faculty, and 20 administrators at U.C. Berkeley and about 50 faculty and administrators at other universities. Based on the questionnaire and interviews, Chapter Four looks at political correctness in its many conflicting forms—as a euphemism, an Orwellian soma for the masses, and also as a laudable vision and realizable ideal: as a motive for the design of the admissions policies that are examined in Chapter Three. Chapter Four also deals with the notion of political correction (a step beyond mere political correctness)—a societal remediation built into special admissions and affirmative action policies, and with the various problems of responding to racism.

Chapter Five, Frustrated Students and Teachers in the Diverse Classroom, moves into the matter of *academic stereotyping* and *color grading*, with an interview with U.C. Berkeley vice chancellor of admissions, Patrick Hayashi. It looks at diversity, disability, average ability, and high ability, and the effects of accommodation to diversity on classroom and university policies. This chapter also suggests that gender is the most basic form of diversity, a binary male-female diversity, and that the complexities of gender diversity precede and model other diversity issues.

Chapter Six, Shameful Admissions: Offering Less and Less to More and More, touches on evidence that higher education as we know it is in decline or at least in a troubled and most agitated state. It asks whether or not the university is still valuable—relevant to society—and outlines the key aspects of knowledge transmission in the modern world. On a more optimistic—but implicitly more contradiction-fraught—note, Chapter Seven, Can We Serve Them All?, juxtaposes and merges views regarding diversity, excellence, and opportunity.

Why are the almost-overused catchwords "diversity" and "multiculturalism" so relevant to this discussion? Because multicultural diversity is here to stay, and the way we respond to it today affects our future. It was the fall of 1993 when chancellor Chang-Lin Tien (who was interviewed for this book) announced that "excellence through diversity" would be the new motto of the University of California, Berkeley. Chancellor Tien formulated in that three-word phrase the central challenge: achieving excellence *through*, rather than *instead of* or *in spite of*, diversity. In Tien's formulation of this challenge, diversity policy is an ingenious orchestrating of what have frequently been seen as competing goals. By contrast, in the worried eyes of its detractors, ethnic diversity on campus, and in all social institutions, is viewed as a powerful threat to the standards of academic, and general, excellence long-maintained by the university and thus the encompassing society.

Chapter Eight, Rethinking Pathways to the American Dream, offers alternative visions for the future—new ways of seeing higher education or its replacements, new means of healing what I have come to describe as the *social psychosis of modern populism*, a state of social mind developing in the face of the massive institutional and social changes of our era.

All of the thoughts in this book are fueled by responses to the interviews, letters, and questionnaires discussing these and related issues with hundreds of members of the U.C. Berkeley community and many members of other colleges and universities as well. This look at what people have to say about higher education is certainly incomplete, in that there are millions of citizens with whom I did not have an opportunity to speak, and perhaps not statistically representative, in that this is an exploratory study: the opening of a dialogue rather than an in-depth and highly abstract statistical analysis, the genre of analysis which is all too available and considered all too valid. *Shameful Admissions* is a very human look, a sort of first-hand, experiential, political anthropology of higher education at this tenuous juncture in history. To engage readers in one of the greatest discussions of our times, I quote specific responses, comments, and dialogues in several chapters. I see some reports as fascinating, others as thrilling, hopeful, discouraging, or frightening.

But they are the various visions of higher education held by past and present students, faculty, and administrators.

Over two-thirds of the faculty and high-level administrators I interviewed at U.C. Berkeley and at other colleges and universities asked that I not use their names should I choose to refer to or quote what they were telling me. Some actually permitted me to use their names and then withdrew permission in the wake of heated events such as the renewal of the nature-nurture IQ debate inspired by the release of Richard Hernnstein and Charles Murray's book, *The Bell Curve*, in the fall of 1994; the flaring of the heated debate, brewing for years and eventually coming of age during the 1995–1996 political campaigns, regarding the repeal of affirmative action policies at university, state, and federal levels; and the numerous lawsuits against and investigations of institutions of higher education, which continued throughout the 1990s. Time and again, I was told, "Quote me, please quote me. I want you to quote me, but just don't use my name."

This directive, coupled with the content of what these individuals were saying anonymously, made me aware of an underlying discomfort, one becoming increasingly explicit as we move deeper into the modern multicultural era: an upwelling of concern regarding this country's utilization of mental ability, the changing definitions of excellence, the quality of teaching and learning in college classrooms, and the overall future of higher education in the United States. The upwelling of concern is like a rising wave, a slow motion tidal wave of doubt. Is this increasing lack of confidence in the growing American higher education industry going to be its demise? Or is this a form of critique that is part of the growing process that will give new life to colleges and universities everywhere?

Shameful Admissions seeks to distill the viewpoints of many people into a single stream of insights frozen in time: the precious and perilous time of the moment that looms just preceding the immense future of humanity on Earth. Lest this be heard as overly profound, let me suggest that there is something very big about the future of the human species lurking behind the issues addressed in this book. We have put ourselves on notice, and our universities are sounding the alarm. We are fighting a worldwide war of ideals, and our young people are the cannon fodder.

September 1995

Angela Browne-Miller
Tiburon, California

Acknowledgments

· ·

I wish to acknowledge the many superb teachers I have had, all along the way, in and out of school. Several of these teachers revealed to me the gates—the doors to knowledge, to insight, to kingdoms otherwise unseen. I want to thank specifically a few of these persons for showing me what is often omitted from formal education at even the "best" institutions. Professor Kenneth Norris, one of the most outstanding professors who has ever lived: he taught me to "see" nature, in magnificent detail and truth, while I was his biology student at the University of California, Santa Cruz (UCSC) in the 1970s; professor Gregory Bateson, who allowed me to participate in his graduate seminar on epistemology while I was an undergraduate at UCSC: he made systems thinking a given; printmaker and UCSC professor Kathryn Metz, one of the few female professors I had: she taught what was for me an undergraduate, elective art course in etching and printmaking and scolded me for almost settling for "housewives art, the way too many women do"; University of California, Berkeley (UCB) social welfare professor Neil Gilbert, a major contributor to the field of social policy, whom I was fortunate to meet in graduate school: he demanded clarity of thought in research design and vigilantly fought sloppy thinking; UCB professor emeritus C. West Churchman, who went from the Haas School of Business at UCB to found the Peace and Conflict Studies Division on that campus: his courses in ethics and systems theory made a lifelong impression upon me; director of the assessment forum at the American Association of Higher Education in Washington, D.C., Tom Angelo, who was a visiting professor at U.C. Berkeley when I met him: he was by far the best model of professionalism, efficiency, and responsibility in teaching that I encountered in all my years of higher education; UCB professor Bernard Gifford, a biophysicist, policy analyst, and educator, who also served as vice president of Education at Apple Inc.: he exemplified for me the possibility of a person achieving excellence in more than one discipline in one lifetime; UCB professor Aaron Wildavsky (now deceased), with whom I had the pleasure of writing about policy implementation: he taught me the "art and craft of policy analysis" from the high place where soul and intellect merge; Lee Browne, my father (now deceased): he fostered in me a deep respect for the workings and the Great Mysteries of the mind; Louisa de Angelis, my mother (now deceased): she told me that I must go to school every day and then come home and let my parents teach me whatever school had missed. I am, thanks to my parents, a product of years of dual schooling—public schooling and home schooling concurrently.

I also wish to thank Gale Erlandson, a senior editor at Jossey-Bass, who was able to hear my message regarding our era's critical conjunction of multiculturalism, egalitarianism, and demand for higher education, and to assist me in sharing it. Gale's intelligence permeates her work, her conversation, her being. I am forever grateful to Gale for her marvelous insights, her diligent fairness, and her remarkable patience.

And then there is Lynne Byrne, whose fine research, editorial, and computer assistance made this book possible; Alyssa Mudd, a student at Brown University at the time she worked with me, who is one of the best research assistants an author can hope to find; Greg Thompson at the Office of Student Research at UCB, whose data analysis proved invaluable in summarizing the findings of the questionnaire survey on which I report herein; and Kathryn Gant-Bradley, a wonderful woman and dedicated mother, whose comments on my first draft were an invaluable wave of support and encouragement.

The life of this book is a conglomeration, a mosaic, of so many people's perceptions regarding college admissions and the larger issues of multiculturalism, democracy, and equality. In writing *Shameful Admissions*, I found myself guided through the issues by some invisible hand, a hand that pointed me in directions I had not expected to go at the start. I thank the source of that guidance. I feel it brought me to all of those who granted me interviews for this book: some anonymously and some with their names attached. Among those who have allowed me to use their names are Debra Chermonté, director of admissions at Oberlin's College of Arts and Sciences in Ohio; Wayne Greene, who was a student at UCB in the late 1960s, a man who taught me more about the more unusual difficulties of special admissions privileges than I could have discerned from someone not so intensely affected; Tony Rey, assistant dean of students and director of the Admissions Committee at the University of California at San Diego in 1970 and 1971, now owner of Executive Consulting, a Dallas-based research and training company, who brought the truth about institutional racism home where it should be; UCB vice chancellor Patrick Hayashi, who was good enough to remind me that many of the cries from the broken gate are actually cheers; and, lastly, one of the most inspiring people I interviewed, the brilliant University of California, Berkeley chancellor, Chang-Lin Tien, who injected a powerful optimism and vision into the picture.

I also must thank a particular student I once had, who shall remain unnamed here, who told me that without a college degree she would probably go back to a life of prostitution, that the only way out of the streets for her was a college education, that most of the students she was meeting in college had absolutely no idea—no appreciation—of the immensity of opportunity they were being provided by higher education, that too many take the opportunity to learn for granted. This student's determination, appreciation, drive, belief in the value of education, and her sense that each of us is the master of her or his own destiny inspired me more than I can say in these few words.

The Author

Angela Browne-Miller holds two masters degrees (one in public health and one in social welfare) and two doctorates (one in social welfare and one in education) from the University of California, Berkeley, where she has served as a lecturer in the Schools of Business, Public Policy, and Social Welfare. She is an educator and a licensed clinical social worker in California, where she has worked with children, adolescents, and adults in schools and universities, and in residential, outpatient, and corporate settings.

Browne-Miller is author of numerous books on social and psychological issues. Her writing has been published nationally and internationally in the popular and the professional press. She has discussed her work on national and local television and radio, and at national and international conferences and institutes. She has served as a policy analyst for the White House Conference on Families, as a member of the U.S. Office of Juvenile Justice Task Force on Drug Abuse, and as a National Institute of Mental Health Postdoctoral Fellow. She is author of *Learning to Learn: Nurturing Your Child's Intelligence* (Insight Books), a book that lays the groundwork for her teachings in what she terms "consciousness technology," a method of ability and identity enhancement, which can be applied to people of all ages and can be used as a means to raise mental performance. Another of her recent books, *Intelligence Policy* (Plenum), proposes and models the analysis of the impact of assumptions and theories regarding intelligence on social and corporate policies.

Browne-Miller currently resides in Tiburon, California, with her husband and children. She can be reached through *Metatek* at 98 Main Street, #315, Tiburon, California, 94920.

The Admissions Furor:
Battle Cries or Mere Confusion?

Ben is an Asian-American high school student. For a month, Ben has been rushing home to check the mail. Every day he waits to hear whether or not he has been accepted to the universities to which he applied. His parents have invested everything and sacrificed a great deal to educate him. Acceptance or rejection can make or break him. Finally, three letters come. Ben, who has a straight-A average and top entrance exam—Scholastic Aptitude Test (SAT)—scores, is rejected from all three of his first-, second-, and third-choice universities. Fortunately, he has a few hours to figure out how he wants to tell his parents this news. However, he is devastated, almost suicidal.

Cathy is White, twenty years old, and a sophomore in college. She was raised by her single mother, who received no child support from Cathy's father. While Cathy never felt "poor," as she described it, she did grow up with a sense that money was always very tight and that she would have to do very well in school to get into a good college and qualify for a scholarship. Cathy felt that she had no choice but to excel in high school, which she managed to do while being employed nights and weekends. Now, as a sophomore in a top public university, she continues to excel; holds three part-time jobs; receives no family, scholarship, or financial aid support; and feels guilty for doing well. She explains that she does not understand these feelings, as she has earned her way all the way through, but somehow, in the multicultural university environment in which she finds herself, she is ashamed to be White and a good student.

Art, a Native-American student, feels that the White teaching assistant is discriminating against him in her unwillingness to explain carefully, during special extended office hours, the complex mathematical equations that are rapidly scribbled on the board by the African-American professor. The White teaching assistant contends that this student wants more time than she is paid to offer, that this is not a case of discrimination, but of the college's unwillingness to fund greater tutorial programming. The student's complaint is reviewed. The assistant's response is reviewed. Nothing is done. Art drops the course. The following semester, he drops out of college.

Anita, a high school senior of mixed ethnic heritage (her father is Hispanic and her mother, White) will graduate from a public high school in a low-income neighborhood with an A-minus average. Although she probably would have qualified for admission to several four-year colleges, she did not apply. Her parents urged her to continue living at home, take a part-time job, and complete her first two years at a local junior college. They said it would give her more time to think about her college choice and to save enough money to pay the tuition for her third and fourth years of college. Although she knows she will feel left behind the other A students, Anita also knows she will soon adapt to the plan and decide that this is not only good for economic reasons, but that it really does give her more time to think about her college choice. It also gives her time to decide whether or not she really wants four years of college. Her parents do not realize this last point. Their dream is finally to have a college graduate in the family.

Wayne, an African-American man in the latter half of his forties, is now completing his undergraduate education. He has waited years to undertake this effort again; it has been years since his first attempt, with all of its glowing promise, was aborted. It was 1967 when Wayne, a new graduate of Berkeley High School in Berkeley, California, was brought in via a special admissions process to the elite, then predominantly White, and highly competitive ranks of the University of California, Berkeley. In 1968, his academic career was interrupted and then virtually destroyed when he was falsely accused of and then arrested for the bombing attack on local police during an anti-war protest on the border of the campus. Although he was eventually acquitted, the university and its special admissions program, which had originally recruited Wayne for admission, had by then abandoned him. This promising student, who once aspired to major in political science and then, perhaps, law, never returned to the University of California, Berkeley.

Every year, hundreds of thousands of young people apply for admission to college. The majority of them never even consider applying for admission to the most competitive universities. Many of them do not even attempt to gain admission to more than their local community colleges. For many of these people, the gates of opportunity reached through a degree from a college or university of good standing may never open. And, each spring, thousands upon thousands of those who do apply to compete for admission to the more prestigious schools are rejected either on the basis of academic merit or on the basis of other personal characteristics. We have no foolproof way of knowing whether these students are truly any more- or less-qualified to attend such schools than those who are accepted. How can we really know what is contained within the obscure human material we call an "applicant"? How can we be fair to all who apply? The process of college admissions has become far too muddled, far too elaborate, and far too bureaucratically defined.

As colleges and universities have opened their doors to a broader range of citizens—from a broader range of life and with a broader range of cultural, academic, and intellectual characteristics and needs—American higher education has changed. There is something about our commitment to the democratic process and the related drive to bring citizens of all races and ethnicities into the "fold" of opportunity that has caused a shift not only in admissions policies but also in what takes place in the classroom, on the campus, and upon graduation. Despite the controversies about these shifts—about their importance, their effects, their extent, and their value—no one argues that nothing has changed, that higher education is just the way it was 100 or 150 years ago. Things just aren't the way they used to be. Let's step back and see how this is so. We have both a right and a responsibility to know.

The Expanding Access to Higher Education

It will be said that the final centuries of the second millennium A.D. witnessed a global trend toward what has been most optimistically described by some as "democratization." In the United States, this development has been based on the fundamental—although now seemingly naive—belief, expressed by the nation's founding fathers, that "all men are created equal." Despite the amorphous nature of equality, this egalitarian theme is still heralded as central to freedom. This basic tenet has been manifested via the broadening of access to a multitude of opportunities. Declaring freedom from enslavement, extending full rights of citizenship (including the right to vote), expanding protection against occupational discrimination, and, most importantly, universalizing education, have been some of the hallmarks of this trend.

Of all these, an equable distribution of educational opportunities is, perhaps, the greatest guarantor of freedom. Theoretically, an increasingly educated citizenry is increasingly alert to both overt and subtle threats to its freedom and to weakenings within the democratic process. Good citizens are trained to think well. But, alas, democracy is not formulated so easily!

Yet, we do have an increasingly educated citizenry. Prior to the late 1870s, a high school, or secondary, education was available only to those young people who were presumed "able to profit by an education prolonged to the eighteenth year" and whose parents could support them while they completed high school.[1] Then, in the late 1870s, a national system of free, public secondary education was initiated. Even so, as social theorist and *U.S. News and World Report* journalist Thomas Toch points out in his insightful book, *In the Name of Excellence*, at the end of the 1890s, only 9 percent of all high school–age Americans were enrolled in high school, and only 6 percent graduated high school.[2] However, with a major influx of immigration, the illegalization of child labor, and the legislating of compulsory school attendance, these data changed radically. By 1920, about 60 percent of the country's high school–age children were enrolled in high school. In the succinctly stated view of Toch, it was thus that "very rapidly, the American Secondary School was transformed from an exclusive enclave of the best and the brightest into an institution of the masses."[3]

Now, the better part of a century later, we see that this trend—the universalizing of access to schooling—with certain variations, has also affected higher education. What was once reserved for a narrow social elite is now available to a much broader range of citizens: college. The ultimate institution of the masses—the proverbial highest level of education: the college of the people—has arrived. And quite rightly. The people have demanded it.

In fact, all of the issues highlighted in this book have emerged within a climate of mounting demand for higher education. Today, higher education is no longer an ideal; it is an industry. As Chapter Two documents, there are increasing numbers of applicants, students, and schools. Even economic fluctuations such as recession do not generate a significant and lasting downturn in demand. Ernest L. Boyer, president of The Carnegie Foundation for the Advancement of Teaching, assures us, "There is now more higher education than ever. Predictions of decline are not supported by the trends."[4] Even if overall attendance fluctuates from year to year, overall enrollment remains high. Few will disagree that higher education has become a mainstay of American life.

But with all the expansion of higher education, there appears to continue to be proportionately little room at the top. Something strange is going on: many of our very top students are turned away from their first-, second-, and even third-choice universities, while they see many of their less academically qualified fellow students being accepted. What does this new phenomenon in college admissions say about our contemporary society?

The Cyclical Interest in Equality

It is easy to say that fair is fair, or at least that fair is as fair does. However, there is no single definition of fair upon which to base all admissions. When author Francis Fukuyama, in his fascinating book, *The End of History and the Last Man*, reminds us, "The class differences that exist in the contemporary United States . . . are primarily due to differences in education,"[5] he is speaking for many who believe that equal access to education can correct political inequalities. When child advocate Marian Wright Edelman, of the Children's Defense Fund in Washington, D.C., suggests we "remember and help America remember that the fellowship of human beings is more important than the fellowship of race and class and gender in a democratic society,"[6] we know we are forgetting something. But, why would we forget? What might drive us to fracture into competing subpopulations? Obviously, equality is not so easy to bring about. In fact, the concept itself seems to swing in and out of fashion.

So here we are again, examining human equality: now you see it; now you don't. I call this behavior of ours *cyclical egalitarianism*. When it is politically fashionable, we are egalitarians. When a critical mass of the citizenry has grown impatient with egalitarianism, equality is interrogated for its significance and its authenticity, and its biological validity or invalidity. The drive to reexamine egalitarian values cycles back predictably every few decades.

I actually call it *cyclical pseudo-egalitarianism*, because even when it is in full favor, egalitarianism is difficult to transform from a beautiful idea to a political reality. And, deep down inside, most everyone knows this. We pay a sort of two-faced lip service to the ideal of equality, knowing that no one knows exactly how to implement the reality mirroring that ideal.

To assert that all men, whatever their race, creed, (or gender!), are equal is to confront a dangerous semantic morass with the feeble weaponry of idealism. This is a futile contest. Words and ideals, although linked, are not calibrated for competition in the same battlefield. Equality is a good idea, a basic tenet for civilized man (according to many men—and women—who claim to be civilized). Yet, equality is an impossible thing to define at the basic level of first principles. The continual cycles of emphasis and de-emphasis on what is, in reality, a false egalitarianism is foolish, expensive, and hypocritical. Those who know this are part of the movement away from cyclical pseudo-egalitarianism. (I like to call their way of thinking *"dis"-cyclical–pseudo-egalitarianism.*)

Where we get confused is in the translation of egalitarianism. There is no reason that all people must be exactly equal to each other to have equal political and social rights. Is there? What a dull world this would be if we were all exactly the same. Nevertheless, for some reason, the argument keeps coming back to the absurd debate over whether we were born equal and were then subjected to a series of environmental exposures which rendered us unequal, or not.

Eventually, the argument ascends or descends (depending upon who is interpreting things) to the issue of "opportunity." Of course, no one argues that we are all exposed to equal opportunity. We are not. Instead, we argue about whether or not we *should* all be exposed to equal opportunity, and if we should, what this would look like.

We cannot help but come to the central matter of education, or more aptly stated, the education of human intelligence. How do we provide everyone with equal educational opportunity? Can we do this when each one of us is so very different? Ideally, we would each have at least twelve, precollege years of full-time, private tutoring, tailored to our individual learning characteristics and needs. Perhaps this one-to-one training would render us a society of persons more equally prepared to compete with each other. Perhaps it would speak to egalitarian ideals more than any of the present day alternatives. Perhaps it would be so useful that today's undergraduate college education would be unnecessary. But can any society pay for such a massive, labor-intensive, individualized education system— even if a large part of such individualized education were computerized? And would the computerization of education sap it of its human aspects? And would individualized education, whether with a human teacher or with a computer, deprive students of the socialization, the learning to live with and respecting of one another's differences, which all those years of group schooling presumably imparts?

It is in the education of human intelligence that all matters of political equality find their hub. No matter how hypocritical and unrealistic most egalitarianism is, no matter how fashionable this false egalitarianism may sometimes be, no matter how powerful the arguments against the semantic misalliances of human alikeness and political equality are, we do have the technology to bring about a far more educated and intelligent citizenry than exists today.[7] We have the technology, but we are not making it available. We are not distributing it. We are able to transform pseudo-egalitarianism into true egalitarianism through education, and we are not doing so. Why?

Consider the possibility that keeping people unintelligent is a powerful form of social control. I am not accusing anyone in particular of withholding knowledge; I am accusing all of society of not making number one on our priority list the development of the cognitive potential of our citizenry. It is as if we instinctively seek to preserve, are *driven to preserve*, some form of social pyramid, some old notion of the appropriate power structure, based on the old adage: knowledge is power.

Tiers of Change

The issue is not a simple one. The origins of the problems with higher education are difficult to determine in their entirety but are most certainly not entirely traced to college campuses. I am reminded of the comments of Mr. David Siggers, an African-American school teacher at the George A. Lewis Middle School in Roxbury, Massachusetts (in the Boston area). "The problem with the schools is in the homes. We have too many kids raising kids, their siblings and/or their teenage pregnancy babies. These kids come from broken homes, single parent families, full of drugs, alcohol. You can't blame K–12 teachers for not educating the kids well enough to do well in college."[8] Mr. Siggers, working on his doctorate at the time of this interview, was born and raised in the same neighborhood as his disadvantaged students. He says, "I went to college—I was recruited by a number of schools for my sports ability. I was a bad boy though, 'til I was thirteen. Then I got shot at. Then I went to college." College changed Mr. Siggers's life chances. It would, more than likely, change the life chances of many of the children from his neighborhood.

This sort of information demonstrates the great importance of expanding access to higher education. Yet, however valuable this access may be, it leaves higher education to do the work not completed by the K–12 schools and the broader social safety net—often through no fault of their own. Remediation and catch-up become part of the college curriculum. Instead of investing more effectively in the living conditions of school children, or even in precollege, preschool, and K–12 education, we are expecting higher education to make up for the mental deficit we either create or allow to continue being generated.

And so we have flung the gates of higher education wide open. We have created admissions groups and tiers: categories with different, competing, and sometimes even contradictory criteria for the admission of different students to the same university. We have expected higher education to correct the educational and thus the social inequalities it inherits from the K–12 schools. This is the trickling up of a fundamental problem, a problem that is far more difficult to treat in people of college age than it is in children: the inequitable distribution of mental training and knowledge. Because knowledge is so related to power, the responsibility for correcting the inequitable distribution of power has now fallen into the lap of higher education.

We are conducting a massive social experiment on our college campuses. It is there, on these sacred grounds, that the time bomb of egalitarian opportunity is exploding. The troubles reported to me as I wrote this book, and the accompanying predictions that they would worsen, are now appearing like clockwork, as if programmed to erupt together at this particular point in history. There are cries coming from all levels of our social system, from the broadest political forum right down to the smallest classroom. If we organize some of these cries by level within the social system, the list looks like this:

Classroom Level

- Overcompensating biases

- Stereotype-based classroom management

- Color grading

- Classroom clusters

- Professor frustration

- Neglect of the average

- Neglect of the able

Campus Level

- Racial tension

- Emergent (newly learned) discrimination

- Ongoing gender stress

- Demands for compensation and support for special groups

- Failures of compensation and support

- Perceived decline in academic quality

- Graduation rate problems

- Clandestine rise of the university within

Institutional Level

- Institutionalized (or systematic) racism

- Institutionalized (or forced) multiculturalism

- Conflicting policy goals

- Reverse discrimination

- Institutional irrelevance

- Institutional embarrassment

Societal Level

- Potential decline in the composite intellect

- Misuse and misappropriation of human capital

- Rising costs of higher education

Political Level

- Demise of the egalitarian ideal

- Old and new populisms in conflict

- Political hypocrisy

- Distraction from the real issues

The following chapters of *Shameful Admissions* examine these unsettling cries. These cries are the sounds of growing pains. We must hear amongst these cries what is actually being demanded: a new vision of higher education. Only radical change in what we now call "college" can turn today's angst into fuel for a much-needed transformation in the education of our citizens. This transformation is, I hope, a real part of our near tomorrow.

In the meantime, I see how colleges are failing, and I see how colleges prefer not to have this said about them. I see students graduating who cannot write a business letter, balance a ledger, or use a computer to do so. I see other students, graduating from the same colleges with the same degrees, who not only are able to perform these tasks but also are clearly very well prepared. Should both groups of students be receiving the same degree? By lumping all these students together, colleges have brought about a condition in which today's undergraduate degree stands for less and less, and is rapidly losing meaning. Wouldn't it be fairer to award classes or levels of undergraduate degrees? Wouldn't it be more reasonable to see what is happening to higher education and the society it feeds, to talk about what is happening honestly and objectively, to hear all sides, and then to take intelligent action?

Power has many faces and wears many masks. Our political system was designed to give citizens a great deal of say in what happens to them and to give them the power to be heard. However, in seeking to share, or as political scientists say, "distribute," power among the citizens of a free society, it is important to question not only the mechanisms of distribution but also the power that is being distributed. Anyone who believes that leading disempowered citizens to think they have been well-educated when they have not been is trading away the distribution of power for the distribution of the illusion of power.

Misleading any citizen this way, regardless of his or her socio-economic status, is dishonest. Misleading ourselves this way is denial. While fantasy games work well in some contexts, only the truth is going to work in this one. Let's set out to find it. We will have to look carefully. Even the truth wears many faces.

What's at Stake in the Drive for Access?

Most citizens of the United States have heard of the Statue of Liberty. Many know of its inscription: "Give me your tired, your poor, your huddled masses, yearning to breathe free, the wretched refuse of your teeming shore. Send these, the homeless, tempest-tost to me: I lift my lamp beside the golden door!"[1] What do these words mean? What do they promise the masses? It is the American dream! But is it only a dream? Today, many would say so.

We have let freedom ring—at least we have tried. We have advanced the egalitarian ideal, the belief that all persons should be free to be equal, through several centuries and into the modern era. We have made massive efforts to redistribute broadly the power of a once very small class of ruling elite. We have broken open many heretofore rigidly locked gates to opportunity.

Yet breathing free has proven easier idealized than accomplished. Now we hear a confusing cacophony of cries from the broken gate—this time, the gates of America's colleges and universities: cries of relief and of triumph, cries of dispute and of disillusionment, cries of injury and of anguish. It turns out that the implementation of equality through equal access to education—that vague, but marvelous, ideal—is far more complex than expected, especially in the realm of higher education.

Failing to Pave the Pathway to Prosperity

The reason for this emphasis on higher education is that it is viewed as the pathway to prosperity, or at least to economic security. After all, what is freedom without the education that enables one to earn an income that permits the exercise of this freedom? Higher education, income, and equality are linked as sequential steps in the American dream of life success. It is now education that separates us into social strata. Mickey Kaus, senior editor at the *New Republic*, wrote in his 1994 book, *The End of Equality*, "It's one thing, after all, to have an economy in which the distribution of income is unequal. It's another to have a distribution of income ever more rigorously based on schooling and ability, where the successful can claim not just that they have more money, but that they have something else—knowledge, talent, brains—that sets them apart."[2]

The conceptual links between freedom, equality, and education are subtle, elusive, but inherently powerful. As Bill Clinton explained so many times during his winning 1992 presidential campaign, in this "new world economy, what you earn depends upon what you can learn."[3] Based upon this contention, and the advice of the man who became his secretary of labor, Robert Reich, Clinton and his people proposed a massive training effort, which was to include school improvement, expansion of college loans, employers retraining employees, and apprenticeship programs for what was called the "forgotten half"—those who are not going to college.[4] However, not everyone sees such a plan as a good one. Kaus contends that such an effort, after but a few decades in operation, will have "increasingly nasty social implications," and that such "state-of-the-art neoliberalism" will render a new and tougher system, a "meritocratic stratification," which will be overwhelmingly counterproductive and "will undermine the traditional American sense of social equality"[5] by even further separating Americans based on training, education, occupation, and income. Kaus warns that, once training is universally available and all societal barriers to opportunity are broken, *the responsibility for an individual's degree of success or failure in the social system is even more the individual's*. What a heavy consequence, a backfire, to universal educational opportunity he depicts. Could he be on to something? Could such massive social intervention on behalf of the "forgotten half" be counterproductive?

Where exactly does higher education fit into this scenario? Right into the middle of it all. Higher education has become an integral and quite central component of American universalism. As a matter of policy, we already seek to provide education and training for all our adult citizens. Of course, not all adult training is officially considered higher education, even when it takes place after graduation from high school, but it should be if what goes on at colleges is deemed the measure. After all, colleges and universities teach sciences, humanities, research, abstract thinking, and other complex topics, but they also teach basic skills, some of which are at a vocational level. In this sense, community and state training and college systems across the nation have virtually universalized higher education.

The Admissions Business

Where does the process of college admissions fit into all this? The process itself is both the great and the breaking gate. The process of college admissions, the key point at which the gate to opportunity has been cracked open, has come under fire from all directions. Yet, while the admissions process is being torn apart by competing demands and attacked by critics of all kinds, including those who say the process is becoming virtually meaningless, college admissions is becoming a vigorous freestanding enterprise. Currently, it is an activity almost entirely separate from the education of college students. Isn't it amazing to discover that the main gate to the American dream is to be found in bureaucratic admissions offices around the nation?

College admissions is indeed bureaucratic. Points are given to applicants. The ones with the most points get admitted. Someone must award and record such points. The process of admission is becoming ever more intricately formulated. Many criteria besides academic merit come into play these days. Some of these criteria include details of family finances. For example, the admissions formula at Oberlin College of Arts and Sciences, Oberlin, Ohio, is a point system in which, out of a total of 52 points possible, some 4 points are used to indicate an applicant's ability to afford a college education. One of the admissions directors I interviewed for this book expressed what many of them told me: the world of college admissions is changing and "one of the biggest changes that we've experienced is the increase in emphasis on the financial picture as it relates to the decision-making process. Admissions professionals are being drawn much closer to the financial aid issues of applicants' families."[6]

We do not like to admit this, but the dollar value of a college applicant is frequently a serious admissions consideration. Let's consider the broader economic origins of this bizarre development. Economic pressures affect application, admission, and enrollment rates, with effects varying according to both the quality of the college and its public or private status. Generally speaking, tuition increases tend to limit application for admission to students who think they can afford this tuition. Although across the nation tuition is increasing, financial aid is not growing at a comparable rate. The average national tuition increase from the 1990–91 to the 1991–92 academic years stood at 13.6 percent, while the average financial aid increase in those same years was only 5.36 percent.[7]

Special scholarships are under increasing scrutiny. This is a particularly controversial matter when the scholarships are given to athletes. Despite the debate regarding the merit of athletic scholarships, it is difficult to deny the dollar value of outstanding athletes at least to some colleges. Economist Robert Brown, assistant professor at the University of North Texas, Denton, has conducted some of the first studies ever designed to weigh the "value" of revenue-generating top college athletes. Brown reports that when a college recruits a football player of such caliber that he later is drafted into the National Football League, that athlete may net that college over half a million dollars a year while in school.[8] Such financial incentive can translate into another form of pressure to lower admissions standards. In fact, Brown has shown that "the incentive to lower admissions standards is financially very compelling." Brown's findings demonstrate that for each decrease of 0.124 in the high school grade average required for admission, a college team is afforded the opportunity to recruit one more outstanding football player.[9] What an equation! The dictum is simple: lowering standards, at least for particular types of students at particular colleges, raises revenue.

It is not only athletes, however, for whom lowered standards are deemed profitable. Financial woes affect admissions standards in a multitude of other ways. There is an increasingly aggressive effort to recruit students who can pay full tuition, especially among the small, so-called "second-tier" private colleges. Many schools of this caliber are, therefore, targeting relatively mediocre students from relatively well-to-do families, even hiring businesses whose primary purpose is to assist in these targeting efforts. For example, in 1993, College Marketing Technologies in Crystal Lake, Illinois, was hired to conduct a study for some fifty second-tier colleges, analyzing the "paying ability" of potential students.[10] Many tuition-hungry colleges struggling for survival are employing techniques such as mass mailings, telephone campaigns, and home visits, often rather intrusively. At these hungry colleges, admissions standards are adapted downward to fill annual enrollment quotas with students who can actually afford the tuition. Quality of admit gives way to quality of admit's family finances. Sure enough, and all too often, the targeted students have little to recommend them other than that *their families can pay.* Furthermore, the payment demanded is increasing. Charges at private colleges rose more than 125 percent in the decade between 1982 and 1992, while the consumer price index rose only 47 percent in those same years.[11]

Public colleges and universities are not immune to such pressures. The decade of the 1990s began with growing economic pressure for states to cut their public higher education budgets. A 1992 study by the American Association of State Colleges and Universities (AASCU) noted that the immediate consequences of cuts in state higher education budgets are tuition increases, program cuts, and, for schools in great demand, enrollment caps.[12] Program cuts can affect admission rates by forcing the upper-level, public sector colleges and universities to narrow their admission selection processes and institute enrollment caps or limits. With at least 28 states already drastically cutting their higher education budgets by 1992,[13] the shifting and narrowing of admissions standards and the trickling down of would-be applicants to the community college level have become national issues requiring careful analysis. The growing sense that, no matter how qualified they are for admission, they may not be able to pay their way discourages more and more applicants. They know that their chosen colleges may offer little or no assistance with tuition.

The Demise of Need-Blinding

The overarching result of economic pressure on colleges is that the egalitarian-minded, *need-blind* admissions of the late 1960s and 1970s—admissions of students regardless of their ability to pay tuition—are becoming a thing of the past. At private institutions, this shift is increasingly explicit. At public institutions, this same shift is more hidden, sometimes most evident in students' simple awareness that if they cannot find a way to pay tuition, they just will not be able to enroll.

Some of the more well-endowed, private elite universities are, despite economic pressure, managing to make the continuance of need-blinding a priority. A director of admissions at one of the nation's top and oldest ivy league universities explains, "We're still able to admit need-blind, and we are doing it. It is now the highest priority of our endowment campaign. We want to preserve our capacity to do need-blind admissions through the next few decades."[14] Where need-blind admissions do linger, they tend to be backed by such endowment or other special funding or to be, in reality, only need-blind to a degree: rating students by balancing merit with relative ability to pay at least a percentage of the total cost. While this approach has always been part of the need-blind admissions process, it is now becoming the main part. When a college chooses to drop or even to reduce its need-blind perspective, the so-called "affordability" issue comes into its own. Affordability demands an answer: can a student, no matter how qualified, afford to attend this college if admitted? And can the college afford to admit this student? Today the business of admission involves the explicit asking of such once unseemly questions.

With colleges competing for students who can pay, the admissions profession must become ever more adept at marketing and recruiting. This requires more staff. The burgeoning admissions field is thus hiring throughout the nation. Richard Moll, who has served as director of admissions at three colleges, Bowdoin, Vassar, and the University of California, Santa Cruz, writes that "there are many parts of this package called 'college' to be defined, designed, marketed and sold." He depicts the competition for students in terms of "colleges' scramble to recruit the next freshman class," refers to what he calls "doom-and-gloom talk regarding filling the freshman class in both the public and the private college," and has been one of the first to discuss "'White flight' to neighboring states' institutions in reaction to the strong proportions of students of color in California's public institutions."[15] On its cover, *Change: The Magazine of Higher Learning* subtitles Moll's article on these matters, "The Admissions War Heats Up."[16] And it has certainly heated up. Now admissions officers are professional soldiers in a battle for applicants and enrollees.

Patricia McDonough, assistant professor of higher education at the University of California, Los Angeles, adds, "Skyrocketing competition for college places is caused, at least partially, by the discovery of marketing by moderately selective institutions. Fearing life-threatening enrollment declines, colleges increased marketing budgets 64 percent from 1980 to 1986, and on average spent $1,700 to bring in each new student."[17] The determination of how much should be spent on recruiting a student—in this case an average of $1,700—to produce an increase in revenue several times this amount is frequently determined by formula. So now the recruiting and marketing processes are mingled with the work of affordability analysis.

Are the consumers of education—the students and their families who foot the bill—getting lost in the shuffle of an expanding industry? Are they being protected from the potentially unsettling and intrusive effects of this unwieldy expansion? Debra Chermonte, admissions director at Oberlin, voices an important concern and warning regarding the privacy of these consumers: "There is a lot of sharing of financial documentation provided by families among colleges. . . . I am amazed at the level of intimacy that relates to personal lifestyle and financial background of families that people are willing to share."[18]

Apparently, many parents are so hungry to get their offspring college educations that they will meet requirements that they might normally consider highly intrusive or see as making themselves naked, just to get their children into certain colleges. The downplaying of need-blinding is thus a trend to be taken most seriously by any parent, student, administrator, and citizen-at-large who values privacy. Need-blinding has done more than ensure opportunity. Without intending to do so, it actually has protected the privacy of applicants' parents, especially parents of students who were not applying for financial aid and who would therefore never have been asked to reveal their family finances before this shift in emphasis on students' ability to pay. But now, the *need-aware* search for students who can pay requires the collection of ever more information from applicants' families.

Whether or not they can be highly concerned about the privacy of individual citizens, many private colleges do find the decline of need-blind admission to be painful. Their reputations are threatened as they lower their academic standards to raise their financial standards. Increasingly, a baccalaureate degree from these schools carries a certain stigma, a loud yet unspoken doubt regarding the quality of education represented by their baccalaureate degrees: rich kid but poor student goes to expensive school. Buy your child a degree. With this doubt about the quality of their baccalaureates comes a general undermining of undergraduate degrees everywhere.

It is inevitable that the downgrading of admissions standards at some institutions will reflect upon the bachelor of arts (B.A.) awarded by all institutions. Already we hear, "A college degree doesn't mean what it used to." "College graduates can't be counted on anymore." "College is what high school used to be." These are some of the current popular perceptions. The undermining of the college degree has so permeated our awareness that it is surfacing in conversations, hiring interviews, contemporary jokes, and even in the comics, as was poignantly exemplified in a segment of the comic strip series by Garry Trudeau, *Doonesbury*, which satirized the weakening of college education. Trudeau's character, Professor Deadman, asks the college president, President King, "Have you created the expectation on campus that all students are entitled to high grades?" When the president says he has not, that grades are linked to performance, the professor reads to the president from the college catalogue used to recruit applicants, "Have your sights set on graduate school?" The president then confesses that the college indeed "guarantees its students straight A's."[19] What a marketing tactic! (You will find a few of these comic strips in Chapter 5.)

Innovative Responses

The sort of affordability analysis referred to in the preceding pages is but one of many responses to economic pressure. Another response is to encourage enrollment by letting it be known that the college is raising the academic performance of students after their admission in an effort to shift popular perception of the college's quality from the quality of its admits to the quality of what its admits do after admission. As yet, and in the face of economic pressures, this shift has not been a significant one—many colleges must continue to deal with the old, and likely accurate, perceptions of their true quality.

There are many other responses to economic pressure. Some schools are demonstrating remarkable entrepreneurial spirit, a creative drive to survive, in their fascinating efforts to innovate. Note the case of Albert Magnus College in New Haven, Connecticut, a small (and relatively high in tuition) private college competing to stay open in the face of declining enrollment. Magnus College decided to attract students by offering a condensed three-year baccalaureate program. It compressed its standard two fifteen-week semesters into thirteen weeks and added a third semester, also thirteen weeks, to the school year. Students are given the choice of either attending two semesters a year and graduating in four years or attending three semesters a year and graduating in two and two-thirds years. The latter option can save the student over $11,500 in tuition and room and board[20] and is quite popular. This model is attractive, and a number of other colleges, such as Middlebury College, Upper Iowa University, and Valparaiso University, are either already implementing a similar system or planning to do so soon. Other "big name" universities, including Oberlin and Stanford University, already offer three-year degrees to students who arrive with many "advanced placement" college credits earned during high school.

There is a down side to this model. Students at Albert Magnus are under more pressure, having to do a semester's worth of work in two fewer weeks each semester and having three semesters (or trimesters) instead of two per year. Some students complain that this school has become a "degree factory." They report that, rather than having a sense of the "college experience," they are undergoing a community college sort of process, one with less adherence to the institution, fewer campus activities, and less social life. On the other hand, the trimester plan offers a variation on what is, by contrast, the "leisurely way to earn a liberal arts degree" (in four years).[21] Perhaps the four-, and five-, year B.A. is too much of a luxury, too leisurely in the face of economic pressure. Could it be true that most undergraduate students have no way to calibrate hard work? College is not a vacation. It is a job. Why take four years to do what can be done in three?

Regardless of their size or status, marketing techniques, or program design, institutions of higher education are staggering under the weight of economic pressure. "Most institutions can't afford to be what they've become," says Sean C. Rush, of Coopers and Lybrand, an accounting firm serving nonprofit organizations including colleges.[22] This sense of overexpansion and overcommitment permeates much of higher education, from the small, tuition-hungry private college to even the largest, most in-demand, well-listed, "first-tier" public university.

The New Monstrosity: Today's Higher Education Industry

By traditional indications, the value of a college education is undeniable. During the 1980s, the wages of college graduates rose by 11 percent, while those of high school graduates who did not have college degrees dropped from 20 to 28 percent.[23] Although the costs of college are rising, the costs of not attending college are growing at an unprecedented rate.

Supply and Demand

Americans understand this. Although the number of high school graduates in the United States was among the lowest in decades in the spring of 1994 (a mere 2.49 million),[24] many colleges experienced record or close-to-record numbers of applications. And a significant number of institutions of higher education at least held steady in numbers of applicants.[25] Generally, public colleges and universities experiencing an increase in applications report a 2 to 5 percent increase, while the private colleges and universities experiencing an increase report an increase of 5 to 20-plus percent.[26]

Not only has the application rate grown, but the actual number of students attending institutions of higher education continues to expand. This number approached fifteen million in 1994, with the greatest increase being in enrollment at two-year colleges.[27] Furthermore, the number of colleges and universities has climbed from 3,389 to 3,600 between 1987 and 1994.[28] The greatest growth has been in the number of junior colleges, 113 new ones opening between 1987 and 1994, yielding 1,480; however, the greatest percentage gain in numbers was among research universities, a gain of 25 percent, yielding 88 such institutions.[29]

Enrollment has expanded along several dimensions. While part-time enrollment at community colleges is dropping, full-time enrollment at these colleges is increasing.[30] Two-year colleges are reporting an increase in the number of students expecting to go on to four-year institutions.[31] At many predominantly White colleges and universities, minority enrollment is on the rise, while at the same time, there is a resurgence of African-American interest in African-American colleges.[32]

All of this increase in demand is occurring in the face of the spiraling costs of this higher education. This spiral began in the early 1980s, if not before, and suggests no end to itself. As of fall 1993, the average annual tuition at community colleges had risen to $1,229; at public, four-year colleges and universities to $2,527; at private, four-year colleges to $11,025.[33] Given the ominous trend—consisting of a 4 to 13 percent annual increase at two- and four-year, public and private universities each year from 1987 to the mid-1990s[34]—the payment of higher education expenses will be an ever-growing investment on the part of students, families, and taxpayers. Time and again, these cost increases outstrip the inflation rate. And there are no price controls in sight.

As of 1994, 126 public institutions were charging $3,000 or more annually for tuition; 39 of these were charging $4,000 or more.[35] Also as of 1994, 279 private institutions were charging $12,000 or more in annual tuition; 127 of these were charging

$15,000 or more.[36] Among the 68 schools in the United States that charge more than $17,000 in annual tuition, only 16 are ranked high enough in *Money Guide* to "justify their lofty prices." Among them are, in ranked order: Yale University, Princeton University, Swarthmore College, Johns Hopkins University, Harvard University, Columbia University, Williams College, Dartmouth, Stanford University, Bowdoin College, Wellesley College, MIT, University of Chicago, Washington University, Amherst College, and Duke University.[37] (This is not an endorsement of *Money Guide* as the arbiter of quality in education, but rather an indication, or dictation, of media and other public perceptions of rank.)

You Own a Share

Higher education is a major industry, with revenues of higher education institutions estimated at over $150 billion, with outlays at almost that same level.[38] Public higher education, as well as part of all private higher education, is a publicly subsidized industry, one that we all support. It costs us all money.

The business of providing higher education to individuals is an informal partnership shared by students, students' families, and various other components of society such as taxpayers who support municipal, state, and federal governments, and employers, foundations, and other organizations who may donate, provide scholarships, or furnish training and advisors. These partners are co-investors in the production of a highly (or at least assumed to be ever more highly) educated citizenry.

As one considers the state of higher education at this time in history, it is important to ask oneself whether this has been, is, and will continue to be a worthwhile investment. If the education of a student at a public college or university is costing taxpayers hundreds and even thousands of dollars per student per year, then taxpayers should demand a regular analysis of the results of their investments. A taxpayer might ask, What are the results of *x* percent of my tax dollars going, on a regular basis, to public education at the college level? What's in it for me? Will someone discover the cure for cancer more rapidly? Will someone find a way to end crime? Will the world be a better place, devoid of homelessness, war, pollution? Will I spend less (in tax dollars) on prisons?

Answering these taxpayer questions is tremendously difficult. How can we assess the effects of our society spending at least $150 billion a year on higher education?[39] So much of what must be assessed is both subtle and long-term. Historians of the future may be able to look back and have a long view of the outcome of trends affecting humanity at the time of the new millennium. Historians may be able to pinpoint which shifts in today's college admissions policies led to the restructuring of our political system, the redefining of our quality of life, the remolding of opportunity and freedom beyond any heretofore imagined boundaries. But we, the contemporary players, cannot see the forest for the trees.

What we can do is think the way financial investors do. This sort of thinking will enhance our understanding of our own personal investments in, as well as society's general investment in, higher education. For example, consider the matter of ascertaining the "time horizon," the time in the future at which present investments are expected to yield. An investment that looks poor today or in the short-term may prove its great value only after many years. Financial analysts know that most investors find it very hard to forecast radical change. We tend to be, as they say, "anchored" in the now, believing that whatever conditions exist today will continue on. Our expectations of investment outcome tend to be either unrealistic—as a result of such anchoring—or irrational—clouded by excessive optimism or pessimism. So we investors in higher education are caught between being unrealistic and irrational. What's a taxpayer to do?

If the thinking of the finance industry can help instruct society in its analysis of its investments, then perhaps the advice that an investing entity (an individual or organization) "diversify its portfolio" is especially relevant to the theme of *Shameful Admis-*

sions and the contemporary debate regarding diversity-promoting policies, such as affirmative action. It is only during the past 100 years that any real diversification of the college-level student body has taken place and only in the years since World War II that the most significant expansions of opportunity have occurred in higher education. It is only since the affirmative action era (with affirmative action efforts beginning in the 1960s and first being repealed by the University of California Board of Regents in July, 1995) that major policy efforts have been made to integrate colleges and universities. The trend toward diversification has been a movement from the education of a White, well-to-do male elite to the education of men and women of all races, creeds, and walks of life. Society has thus diversified its investment in higher education by expanding and diversifying its student body. Prompted by affirmative action policy, society (and its components: legislative bodies, various organizations, employers, families, and individuals) has invested in the higher education of far more than the traditionally restricted, very homogeneous group of citizens it once favored. As a result of this diversification, and expansion, of public investment, the higher education industry has been greatly changed. Only time will tell whether society will continue to choose to diversify its portfolio by force of policy (as it has done with affirmative action).

The Product

Economists emphasize the investment aspects of acquiring or passing on a skill or an education, describing this as an investment in "human capital." Human capital is specifically defined by economists as the "accumulated skill and knowledge of human beings."[40] From this perspective, economists can place a value on an individual's human capital, represented by the value (adjusted for the present value of future earnings) of extra earnings received by that individual as a result of that person's acquiring of education—skill and knowledge.[41]

We are back to the original issue. It costs money to acquire skills and knowledge. Someone must pay, must invest in the development of the individual. Economists are quite detailed in their analysis of such a cost, noting that it includes the costs of tuition, room and board, as well as the cost of missed opportunities and earnings lost (money not being made) while the individual is being educated or trained.

Some perceive the human capital perspective as being a far too technical and seriously inhumane view of what educational opportunities mean to individuals and disenfranchised subpopulations. Should a human being's skill and knowledge really be described as "capital"? In economic terminology, capital is defined as "all the goods and services that have been produced and can now be used in the production of other goods and services."[42] Although the knowledge and skill of a human being is not a building, a jet plane, a piece of factory equipment, a hydroelectric dam, or a computer, it is, in the end, a form of capital. This is especially the case if we consider the accumulated knowledge and skill of all members of society together. Human capital is the product, or at least the primary product, of the higher education industry.

Evaluating the Product You Help Produce

Students, parents, and other taxpayers have invested in the accumulated human capital of the citizen body. So, taxpayer, how is your investment doing? Has your portfolio diversified? Is it over-diversified or under-diversified? What is your time horizon? Are you too anchored in the present to place value on the long-range outcome of your current investment? Are you pleased with the present and/or potential yield? Can your product compete in the global market? How does your country compare? Do you want to continue to support production of this product?

The product: a citizenry educated beyond high school graduation. Human capital: increased knowledge and skills within the population, distributed to an ever-larger number and more diverse range of people. But, to what end?

One of the professors who discussed this question with me commented, "It is not so much the specific product of higher education that you should focus on. It's that, when we put young adults in college for four years after they finish high school, we keep them out of the labor force about half a decade longer, thereby helping to control unemployment." In his way of thinking, universal higher education would predictably stagger all young adults' entry into the full-time workforce until at least the age of twenty-three. "So why not just make four years or even five years of college a requirement, as is high school?" he suggested.

Universalism has been a useful policy response to a number of social issues. The most cogent example of universal education is in the universalizing of kindergarten through twelfth grade. Today, every youth not only has the right to attend public school but is required by law to do so for a certain number of years. Universalism is a fact in elementary and secondary schooling. The evolution of public education demonstrates that as the trio of demands—for its availability, for its product, and for recognition of its value to all society—increases to a critical mass, a social service, in this case K–12 education, becomes universal.

Early childhood education, or preschool, is slowly building to such a crescendo. Demands for its availability, its product, and its recognition as having social value are reverberating throughout all sectors of society. Still, we must admit that, to a great extent, the demand for universal preschool surfaced only after large number of mothers of preschool children began entering the workforce in the 1970s.[43] However, a national system of child care, whether or not educationally oriented, is a costly proposition. At minimum, it calls for the addition of at least two more years to the already universal K–12 system. In that preschool-age children require a higher adult-child ratio and other safety precautions in the physical environment, these additional years may cost society more than two additional years at the other end, the community college end, of the K–12 spectrum.

What if we focused on young adults instead of young children? Certainly, if all freshman and sophomore years now spent at four-year colleges were spent at community colleges, the dollar savings would be marked. But what if we were to universalize and *require by law* two years of community college for *everyone?* In the end, the taxpayer picks up the tab. The taxpayer must examine the utility of such an investment and compare it with other investments.

Diminishing Returns

The economists' law of "diminishing returns" is applicable here. Taxpayers already pay for a significant amount of higher education for their own, as well as most everyone else's, children. Are taxpayers willing to pay for more? Will the benefit to society be as great for each additional person provided with a higher education as it has been for those already receiving it? Or do the returns diminish after a critical mass of citizens have been provided the opportunity? Maybe taxpayers are already investing enough.

Maybe the limitations of egalitarianism can be found in this sort of "microeconomic theory." Equal opportunity may pay off, but only to a point. After that point, it may be too expensive, and the return may be too small to justify it. An instinctive awareness of the law of diminishing returns may explain the massive assault on affirmative action waged in the 1990s. The returns on equal opportunity policy may diminish as we approach its complete realization. In the case of higher education, the human capital produced by further expanding the system of higher education to the point at which it becomes a national requirement may be not great enough to justify the expense. How do we evaluate this proposition in advance?

From this generalization regarding any form of higher education, let us look to the higher education offered at a high-profile institution such as U.C. Berkeley, our pioneer institution. We are going far past the cost of community college here. At an estimated cost to the taxpayer of $11,000 per student per year, can we afford to provide a U.C. Berkeley sort of education to everyone? If there are some citizens for whom such a societal investment in their development would be of little value, how do we identify them? Admissions policy has been the means of selection thus far. Is it adequate? Are we satisfied? Thus far, affirmative action policy has been the vehicle for liberalizing selection to meet multicultural needs. Are we satisfied?

Central to the majority of admissions processes at four-year institutions is the Scholastic Aptitude Test, the SAT. Because of its dominance in selection, this test and its parallel tests warrant attention here. Despite controversy regarding its use and the fact that it has come under so much fire that some colleges are dropping it from listed entrance criteria, the SAT score is usually combined with a grade-average factor to rate applicants. Because the SAT has been accused of cultural bias, gender bias, age bias, and other tendencies to identify a narrowly defined type of student, a few colleges are experimenting with making the test optional. For example, Bates College made the SAT (as well as all standardized admissions and achievements tests) optional. Once it did, Bates found that applications for enrollment increased. Since it instituted its entrance-exam-optional policy, almost a third of its applicants have been "nonsubmitters," declining to submit to testing or to submit the results of their tests. Of these nonsubmitters, almost two-thirds are women and about two-thirds are African-American.[44] William Hiss, dean of admissions and financial aid at Bates, says that this data "speaks volumes to the real or perceived bias against women and minorities."[45]

There is, however, substantial support for the continued use of the SAT in admissions. First and foremost, the test has become an institution. Secondly, as Susan Murphy, dean of admissions and financial aid at Cornell University, claims, many believe that the SAT, when combined with high school rank, is almost twice as effective in predicting freshman performance as are high school grades alone.[46] Third, and perhaps most convincing, as the 1991 director of the College Board, Robert Cameron, states, "If all colleges stopped using admission tests, and students stopped taking them, there would soon be a return to a test requirement."[47]

There really is no way out of the problem of selection. Were a four-year higher education of quality made available to all citizens, the system would still have to identify those students best suited for particular types of training. It would be inefficient and even unfair to expect every student to be able to learn and apply advanced calculus. It would be foolish to train and then depend upon everyone to do emergency, open-heart surgery. As I suggest in Chapter Eight, the most reasonable approach would be to require of everyone, regardless of race, creed, color, gender, socioeconomic status, or other group membership, nationally defined basics of higher education to be learned at community college and in no other and no higher institutions of higher education. Only when and if these basics are measurably learned by a national measure, can anyone, regardless of race, creed, color, gender, socioeconomic status, or other group membership, move further on in the academic realm. There is no philosophical, political, or other reason to shift the economic burden of teaching the basics to any higher-level institutions.

Whether it be by the national and uniform measurements of basic academic achievement I propose in Chapter Eight, or by other means such as aptitude, ability, previous academic or on-the-job performance, self-selection, motivation, or personality type, some mode or mix of modes of selection will always be used. Again and again, especially in the absence of a basic bottom-line minimum standard required of students to move on to more advanced higher education, the problem of fairly allocating opportunity will surface. Fairness and efficiency have become mated as eternal sparring partners—a painful marriage, but one of necessity.

Students: Human Capital or Cannon Fodder?

We may be able to accept the ebb and flow of debate about fairness and efficiency in higher education. However, the real human lives of America's youth are caught in the crossfire of ideals.

Of course, the question of who gets the opportunity is with us forever. Certainly, there will always be a deselection of some of us. The intensity and ultimate essence of this issue was hinted at during the Vietnam War when student deferments were sought by many students and resented by those who could not get into or afford to go to college. The message was simple: go to college or go to war. (And risk dying on the battlefield.) For those ending up in the military, either willingly via enlistment or because they were drafted, the problem of opportunity allocation pursued them. In the military, those deemed least trainable, least bright, ended up as the lowest and most shot-at military personnel on the battlefield. Complaints of racism in the military arose around test-based opportunity allocation.[48]

So, deselection is actually a form of selection. The drive to become human capital of great value thus arises almost instinctively. The choice is, both metaphorically and, at particular times in history, quite literally, to be either top human capital or relatively expendable cannon fodder. Given this reality—and current indications that today's military has become more selective than most colleges—a top-quality, elite college, which should be graduating the least expendable, top-quality, human capital, sounds all the more desirable.

Caught in the Crossfire of Ideals

Being cannon fodder in today's war of ideals may be less physically injurious than actual military battle, but young people's life chances are most definitely at stake here. And the war is an extremely complicated one. We must encourage the young generation to see its place in this conflict of ideals. A strategy of political awareness of one's participation in the big picture is essential. It is one's defense against growing institutions and oscillating political trends. Today's college applicants must survive all the trends discussed in this chapter and somehow acquire the best possible college education. But these students must never lose sight of the vast political chess game in which they are just pawns. Any individual effort to ensure one's own life success cannot be made ignorant of these larger issues. Students, as the gates burst, will you be trampled, or will you run through victorious?

The bullets in this battlefield are concepts, often disguised as other concepts. Let's think about how this can come about. We deceive ourselves by overlooking the nuances of political change. Certainly, previously locked gates to opportunity have been opened. However, in many cases, these gates were not flung open in a gush of generosity or a sudden revision of deeply entrenched biases. Instead, these gates, the barriers to privilege and opportunity, were chiseled away slowly and deliberately by intense pressure from constituency groups and eventually, when political pressure accumulated to the point of critical mass, through the force of legislative and judicial mandate.

We confuse ourselves by assuming that the allocation of educational opportunity is straightforward and progressive. It is in the problem of allocating educational opportunity that lies the most tragic flaw inherent in the implementation of freedom. Such a noble idea, *opportunity allocation*, requires great feats of judiciousness and practicality to take the idea from the paper describing it and into the real world. The problem of democratic access to quality higher education is very much like the predicament of poor mythological King Sisyphus. When in Hades, Sisyphus was condemned to rolling a boulder up a steep hill only to have it roll all the way back down each time he approached the top. Similarly, progress, in the form of expanding educational freedom, may be only an illusion. But even if we are making progress, we must ask: progress to what end? Progress, but in which direction? Are there only two directions in this arena—forward and backward—or are there many ways to proceed uphill and just as many ways to slide back down or off to the side again? Perhaps what we are calling progress is actually an increasing of the muddle.

The evolution of our higher education policies is certainly Sisyphian and disturbingly counterproductive. It is not uncommon to find that shortly after a perceived breakthrough in some higher education policy has been achieved, a seeming backslide or reversal of policy takes place. Remember the December 1990 pronouncement by the Federal Department of Education that colleges would no longer be allowed to use money from their general operating budgets for what have been described as "racially based" or "race-exclusive" scholarships: special scholarships awarded based on ethnicity, aimed at helping disadvantaged ethnic groups. This pronouncement abruptly closed off what had been a relatively new and short-lived form of educational opportunity. College administrators complained, and civil rights activists were infuriated; a national firestorm was initiated.[49] This sort of about-face, this retrenchment from special efforts to expand opportunities to particular segments of society, may be more tension provoking than would have been the failure even to begin to address the issue in the first place. Expectations have already been raised.

Now consider a contrasting policy decision. An April 1994 vote in the U.S. Congress extended a special allowance, which had already been in place for four years (prior to the Clinton administration, since the time of the Bush administration), continuing a special institutional exemption—an institutional, student-loan-default exemption—for two groups of colleges: African-American and Tribal.[50] Because these special colleges have a significant number of students who depend upon student loans and because these colleges tend to have extremely tight finances, the loss of such an exemption could be catastrophic for them. How so? The explanation goes like this: the original requirement necessitated that colleges maintain loan default rates under 25 percent to maintain eligibility to participate in federal lending programs. This is a difficult requirement to meet when past students are having difficulty paying back their loans in a timely fashion. Without the exemption, African-American and Tribal colleges not meeting this requirement would lose the option of having their present students receive federal loans to pay college expenses. This would result in a drastic reduction in students, a reduction so great that these schools would have to shut down.

Although the U.S. Senate unanimously approved the April 1994 continuation of the default rate exemptions to African-American and Tribal colleges, the U.S. House of Representatives was split with 284 pro and 136 con.[51] In the House, among those voting con, there were members of both parties who felt that the exemption was inappropriate in that there were (and still are) other schools serving underprivileged populations who had not (and still have not) been awarded the exemption and that it was (and still is) more just to have all or none of the institutions of higher education abide by the rules passed by Congress. But proexemption House members responded that this specific and narrow exemption is indeed fair and essential because it is only African-American and Tribal colleges that have student bodies composed almost entirely of low-income students, who can only attend college if they borrow money.[52] The economic plight of Native-American students attending Tribal colleges is especially profound, with 80 percent of them living below poverty level.[53]

In the case of a default exemption continuation, a policy decision was made to extend, rather than to reverse, a seemingly egalitarian education policy. Yet, although the chief argument against this decision was that it was unfair, not egalitarian enough, it was also too egalitarian. It all depends on the unit of analysis. Should we strive to treat groups or to treat individuals equally? Should we distribute opportunity fairly—equally—among ethnic or other social subgroups or fairly—based on relative need—among members of those groups?

We must not overlook the fact that education policy is not only riddled with reversals and contradictions, but the questions it asks are quite complex. What type of policy is fairer: one that promotes access to educational opportunity for individual members of especially disenfranchised social groups or one that treats these and other social groups more equally? Clearly, the notion of "more equally" is so slippery and value-laden that it is impossible to standardize or to regulate with any degree of objectivity. Round and round we go, arguing valiantly for fair and equal treatment. The situation degenerates into confusion. No one is wrong. Everyone is right. But nothing turns up equal.

There are other, perhaps more controversial, areas of higher education policy, which add to the conceptual confusion. One arena of heightened confusion is academic freedom: the right of professors to say what they want in their own classrooms, even when they are heard as attacking university policies such as admissions criteria. Take, for example, an unprecedented announcement that, while not in any way connected to the above-noted 1990 reversal on race-exclusive scholarships, came but one month after this reversal. This announcement generated a major uproar at U.C. Berkeley surrounding physical anthropology professor Vincent Sarich (now professor emeritus). Sarich reportedly voiced opposition to the admissions policies that had brought about a very ethnically diverse student body. Apparently, Sarich's justification for his opposition was his assertion that all types of racial differences, including possible differences in the brain, could be expected as a result of evolution. Sarich was interpreted as saying that African Americans (and perhaps females) could be of inherently inferior mental ability. In one of his articles, Sarich wrote, "Unfortunately, the levels of qualification, preparation or motivation are not randomly distributed with respect to race and ethnicity."[54] Apparently, this implied inherent racial differences in academic ability and performance.

Shortly thereafter, exhibiting behavior generally unacceptable at a university, protesters disrupted Sarich's course, carrying posters reading, "No more racist bullshit in the name of academic freedom."[55] Outrage was expressed in several sectors of the university, resulting in heated debate.[56] According to protesters, Sarich not only professed belief in this theory, but also was teaching it in his classes, bringing about additional debate relating to the issue of academic freedom: the right of a professor to express whatever viewpoint he or she chooses in his or her own classroom. Professors grew concerned about the potential for loss of more academic freedom.

Even some who strongly opposed Sarich's views fiercely supported his right to state them.[57]

Admissions Policy and Earthly Opportunity

A still larger and very nationwide debate was highlighted, one which had as its centerpiece the admissions policies that had, indeed, as will be discussed later, created the increasingly ethnically diverse student body at U.C. Berkeley. It is in this fierce debate that is reflected the greatest question our society and the world must now answer: how do we share the space, the opportunity, which our earthly journey affords us, among an increasingly vocal and diverse array of peoples? This question of the hour—of the twenty-first century—is powerfully mirrored in the debate over the intrinsic worth of an admissions policy that explicitly includes more than academic merit in its criteria for selection as it seeks to diversify its student body. There are those, and Sarich was assumed to be one, who claim that at a great university such as U.C. Berkeley, one with a longstanding reputation for excellence, an admissions policy that seeks to generate an ethnically diverse student body has, under liberalized admissions, relaxed academic criteria and thus contributed to the dangerous decline in the intellectual strength of that institution. Yet, university officials point out that during the years of its liberalized, affirmative action–responsive admissions, admission to U.C. Berkeley was in no way a product of significantly relaxed academic criteria. In fact, as Patrick Hayashi, associate vice chancellor of admissions and enrollment at U.C. Berkeley, explains, "You have to be in the top 12.5 percent" of California's graduating high school seniors to be considered for admission at U.C. Berkeley. Hayashi continues, further emphasizing the selectivity of his institution, "We have been selecting from the cream of the crop. Half has had to be on academic criteria alone. The other has had to be on academic criteria plus other criteria that reflect the [make-up of the state's] population."[58]

Hayashi says, "We have been selecting from the cream of the crop." The cream of the crop—this sounds impressive. Are we all in agreement as to who should be designated the cream of the crop? And by what measures? Tests and records of academic ability? Many social policies respond to or draw upon various assumptions, and tensions among those assumptions, regarding the basis of human intelligence and the comparative value of different mental abilities.[59] Inasmuch as education treats, speaks to, and utilizes mental abilities, education is the key arbiter of the societal utilization of these abilities. Education is the captain choosing the team. Will everyone be selected? And if selected, who will actually be sent up to bat or even given the opportunity really to play the game? Reader, whatever your stage of life, were you designated cream of the crop and allowed to join the top team? Or were you not? Either way, what position have you been able to play? How were you selected for it, or did you self-select?

Are Selectivity and Opportunity Mutually Exclusive?

We have to wonder whether or not there is an entirely fair way to allocate the opportunity for admission to a great university. This is a question asked with increasing fervor at all levels of academia, at colleges and universities around the nation and, for that matter, among educators and policy makers around the world.[60] The struggles that great public universities now face are typified by those at U.C. Berkeley, where the cries emerging from the broken gates are so very loud that it is impossible to ignore them. Indeed, U.C. Berkeley is considered by other colleges and universities to be the metaphorical canary sent into the mines ahead of the miners to test the safety of the environment. If the canary cannot survive, it at least saves the lives of those humans who have been forewarned. Often described as the "university of tomorrow," U.C. Berkeley now finds itself either in the throes of death or of birth. One suspects that it is actually undergoing the labor of rebirth—rebirth as a major broker and arbiter of opportunity in the new age of multiculturalism.

The U.C. Berkeley Committee on Admissions and Enrollment, referring to what it describes as the "minutiae of debates about particular admissions policies," insists that the university must, nevertheless, "remain guided by a larger vision of its mission." As it examined admissions policies prior to the U.C. regents' 1995 elimination of affirmative action standards in admission, hiring, and contracting, the committee asserted that "in the 1990s, this mission must include taking a leadership role in the construction of a genuinely pluralistic environment in which the best students from all segments of California's diverse population can meet and debate in an atmosphere of enlightenment and commitment."[61] But what exactly is a *genuinely* pluralistic environment? No social institution can reflect precisely or even begin to recognize every aspect of diversity in the surrounding and ever-changing social environment.

Still, although most institutions have multiple motivations for their actions, for a university to set as its goal the maintaining of "highest academic standards" *and* the continuing of a "tradition of service to the public" is highly laudable. As the committee itself contended, "This is a vision that is well worth pursuing, and it is a particularly appropriate one for an institution which has long prided itself on maintaining the highest academic standards, while continuing its tradition of service to the public that has so generously supported it."[62] However, such a vision is quite ambitious in an era in which these goals emerge in apparent opposition. Highest but traditional academic standards and service to the increasingly vocal multicultural public are not necessarily ready mates. And any increase in emphasis on the needs of a multicultural society is tempered by economic limitations. Egalitarianism, if it can be at all defined amidst the new multiculturalism, is expensive. So much for earthly opportunity.

The California Case

Let's consider the cries heard at the home of the prototype, my case in point, the University of California system. As always, money matters. At the beginning of 1992, U.C. Regents voted to raise student fees 22 percent, which was the third fee increase in three years.

These raises were aimed at reducing the statewide budget gap. Also in 1992, the next line of defense—or of opportunity—the California State University system, not part of the University of California system, but also public, raised its fees 40 percent, following a 20 percent increase the year before.[63] Californians were actually hit hard on all three of their roads to higher education: the junior college system as well as both the aforementioned California State University and University of California systems. California Assemblyman Tom Hayden, chair of the Assembly Higher Education Committee, spoke to this matter: "California's historic guarantee of higher education for every qualified resident is coming to an end." Hayden did not feel that the effects would be positive when he stated, "Closing the doors of higher education will have calamitous consequences."[64] Hayden consequently proposed that students be charged a sliding tuition fee based on family income, rather than having the state continue to pay $11,000 of the after-tuition cost of education for each student attending a U.C. school. Hayden noted that this proposal would save the state at least $50 million a year. To save an additional $10 million, he proposed that higher fees be charged for students in professional programs such as law, which, he explained, "are not in undersupply and thus less appropriate for public subsidy."[65]

At the same time, California's third line of defense—or of opportunity—the community college system, traditionally the affordable option open to everyone, is also hurting. California's community colleges have been hit especially hard. Those colleges now spend $2,809 per student per year, which is $500 less than the national average.[66] Budget cuts have required community colleges to increase teaching loads, with faculty teaching at least one more course per semester and accepting an average of fifteen more students into each of their already full classes.[67] In the 1992–93 academic year, the San Francisco Community College (SFCC) took an 8 percent budget cut from $104.7 to $96.9 million dollars.[68]

Speaking to the problem of budgetary pressure (and indirectly hinting at the role of higher education in defending society from greater expenses), University of California, Santa Cruz chancellor Karl Pister claimed, "This state needs the University of California, the California State University and its community colleges more than it needs its prisons. We've got to fight for higher education. If we fail, we will need those prisons."[69]

Perhaps we can learn from the trials and tribulations of California. California leads the way, but the pressures are, or soon will be, tremendous in most states. Can the institution of higher education survive? Is it worth saving? What are the fundamental trade-offs?

As David Gardner, the past president of the nine-campus University of California system, which includes U.C. Berkeley, and who himself was under attack for the large dollar amount of his retirement package, stated in his November 1991 letter of resignation: "Indeed, I know of no public university in the world that has afforded its students, regardless of their race, gender, relation, or socioeconomic circumstances, as excellent an education for so modest a cost while simultaneously attaining to levels of intellectual accomplishment that are world-renowned and internationally respected." Gardner described the University of California as California's "crowning jewel, the principal point of access for people of talent and ambition, the quiet force from which much of California's economic power derives, one of the world's greatest treasure houses, the repository of much of our cultural heritage, a cauldron of discovery, a marketplace of ideas—in short, one of the greatest centers of learning the world has ever known." Recognizing the tremendous pressures now exerting themselves upon this system, he also warned, "It will require from all of us continued and vigorous effort to sustain this institution and to preserve it for succeeding generations."[70]

In speaking about California's budgetary pressures, Gardner noted that the state would be unable to fund fully the university's essential needs in the upcoming fiscal year. Highlighting the ultimate trade-off, he added that when state funding and increases in student fees prove inadequate, "We will have only one alternative left, and that is reducing enrollments to match available resources." The wrenching reality hit when Gardner told the public, "On a temporary basis, at least, this would mean abandoning the promise of a place at the University for all qualified California residents seeking undergraduate admission. . . . Clearly, the racial and ethnic dynamics of the situation are not inconsequential."[71] Could the dream, the promise, be over, or had it ever been anything more than an ideal?

Reducing enrollments to match available resources in the face of ever-growing multicultural pressures is much like shrinking the eye of a needle while switching from a thin thread to a thick, multi-fibered rope. Threading the needle becomes all the more difficult. Gardner must have known this as he spoke the above words. By 2010, California's colleges and universities will be asked by the state to accommodate at least 800,000 more undergraduates than the number enrolled in 1994. It is expected that at least one-tenth, or about 80,000, of these students will seek enrollment in the University of California system.[72]

With finances tight and admissions limited, a large public university can become tuition-hungry the way some of the small private schools referred to earlier have done. But a public institution cannot respond to the problem by lowering standards for wealthier students. Attempting, therefore, to maintain some significant degree of need-blind access, the University of California regents approved a new policy for the funding of financial aid, one which was euphemistically and rather ironically called the "affordability model."[73] This policy was designed to "offset fee increases for needy students by bolstering the amount of financial aid money available systemwide," adding $37 million in grant money in the 1994–95 academic year and increasing the percentage of the student fee increase, which was fed into financial aid coffers, from 31.8 percent in the 1993–94 academic year to approximately 38 percent in the following years.[74] This affordability model assumed that "students will work to earn an average of $2,800 annually and borrow an average of $23,600 a year" to pay their costs of living while in school, with parents, federal aid, and other state programs covering remaining costs for needy students.[75]

As long as there is someone to cover the remaining costs, this affordability model is helpful. This way, some preservation of egalitarianism through educational opportunity is maintained. But what happens when there is no one to cover the costs, when families, taxpayers, foundations, and governments are broke? Does fairness fade away? Or does its definition simply change?

The Cries of Change

While these questions were once posed as altruistic concerns for the plight of the impoverished and underprivileged minority groups, they are now recognized as important questions for middle-class America. And the future of middle-class, college-age citizens could be bleak. Young adults with a significant financial need who are not deemed top, top-cut but who desire higher education of at least some degree of what they think is quality may have little available to them as time goes on and need-blind admissions become less of an option for colleges.

Where need-blind admissions may linger longest is in serving the most needy. What this means, at least in the words of one admissions director, is that "those that are impoverished tend to fare very well in a need-based financial aid system, and those that are in the upper group economically have freedom of access to college education. It is obviously the middle-income squeeze that is of great concern."[76]

And so, readers of all ilks, wake up. The average citizen is rapidly becoming the underprivileged citizen. The once safe, comfortable, and thus highly desirable middle-class–average-American status appears to be transforming before our very eyes to a life sentence— the doom of the frightful new disability: permanent and disenfranchised mediocrity.

Yes, this is the future of the middle-class American—most Americans. The sense that true educational opportunity is guaranteed is slipping like sand from the hands of average Americans. And just when they were beginning to take it for granted!

After more than two centuries of its implementation in the United States, the egalitarian ideal of equality is being reexamined. For all the lip service we have given and heard about our American dream, now, as the middle class itself feels threatened, we are finally awakening en masse from this dream. As we continue—almost out of habit—to try to realize this dream, especially in the realm of higher education, we are suffering a rude awakening. It is not easy to make a good dream come true, to materialize it. Equality is not necessarily definable, possible, or realistic. Even fairness, a vague look-alike for equality, is expensive if at all achievable. On this troubling issue of fairness in access to the university, Gardner commented that he could not "think of any policy issue more sensitive, more politically complicated, more socially difficult to deal with and [any] issues of fairness harder to calculate, to calibrate, or more important in the long run to the University of California and, in fact, to relationships among and between citizens of our state, than this issue."[77]

So here we stand, on the threshold of a new, more complex, more diverse social order, at the gates of great universities, which have traditionally restricted the bulk of their admissions to those who fit the mold of the dominant culture. Today, entrance into the greatest of these universities represents a new degree of access to a new, and ever more coveted, degree of social, political, and economic power. And today, entrance qualifications are being defined, questioned, and redefined at an ever-increasing pace.

There is no way an old social order, or an old intellectual order, can remain unaltered in the face of these explicit reexaminations and reallocations of opportunity. The entire house of cards, the shelter of longstanding and otherwise rigid intellectual and social tradition, is teetering and threatening to collapse. The sounds of change are blowing in the wind. If we listen closely, we can hear the sounds to which we have for too long been deaf, the massive structures creaking and groaning in the storm under the strain—the howls, the gusts, the breezes—the winds of change. The gate is breaking. We the people, the masses, are charging in, trampling each other. The cries from the broken gate are heralding tremendous change—change with all of its attendant excitement, relief, fear, and pain. Listen. "This is the time, and this is the record of the time."[78]

Who Gets In?

The problem reaches beyond basic cultural conflicts into levels of social, economic, and political complexity for which we are truly unprepared. In the words of J. W. Peltason, past president of the University of California, "One of the greatest threats to higher education is not public hostility but public preoccupation with a variety of complex and difficult social and economic issues. Our greatest strength in facing this reality is the fact that higher education is essential to the solution of most of these issues."[1] Perhaps then, the almost feverish societal emphasis on the spreading of higher education is attributable to instinct: society senses that it needs an increasingly well-educated populace to cope with an increasingly complex society. Perhaps we are instinctively driven to answer the question, Who gets into college? with a resounding: everyone!

Simple cultural conflicts are a thing of the past. Modern multicultural pressures are riddled with powerful complications and contradictions. The notion of diversity is giving way to the reality of complexity. The evolution of college admissions standards is a response not only to changing but also to increasingly complicated societal views regarding fair education and utilization of our increasingly complex matrix of human resources. This is especially so in public colleges and universities, which must be, by the very nature of their funding sources, more responsive to the public than are private institutions. The problem is that, these days, being more

responsive means being more multiculturally sensitive while striving for more excellence in more culturally relevant areas of knowledge than ever before imagined. This isn't easy.

Hence, we ask who it actually is that gets into a good college
these days. I am reminded that, for much of 1994, there was a large
and colorful billboard posted on the side of a building, which could
be seen from University Avenue, the main road into the U.C.
Berkeley campus. Every time I drove into campus, I looked at the
billboard and many times saw young people, junior high and high
school age, "hanging out" in front of it. Most of these youths were
African-American. I could not help but wonder if they were
impressed by the message the billboard relayed. "You can get in with
a B average" was written in a comic strip–dialogue balloon, which
seemed to be coming from a young White woman who was standing on a college campus, possibly that of U.C. Berkeley. Although
I never saw anyone look directly at the sign, someone had thought
enough of the message to spray paint the word *weird*, misspelled as
werd, onto it. It certainly was a "weird" way to relay this message:
you too can get in, even with your lower academic qualifications.

We continue to wonder, who really gets in? I am also reminded
of what one of the first Special Admits of the 1960s, an admit to
the University of California, Berkeley, once told me: "I am Black
. . . the reason I got admitted in the first place was definitely for
racial reasons."[2] Although the university never told him this was
the reason, the sense that he was admitted for other than academic
reasons has stayed with him. He explains, "There must have been
some pressure coming down from the University of California onto
my school, Berkeley High—pressure to come up with a list of special admit names. The process of admitting me was already started
by the time I became aware of it." This man, forty-four years of age
in 1994, was a student in Berkeley High School's graduating class
of 1967. He reports that his high school counselor submitted his
name to U.C. Berkeley without first informing him that this would
happen. Of his qualifications, he says, "Academically, I was all over

the place. I didn't think I had the grades to get into U.C. Berkeley, that's for sure."

Yet, he had something which qualified him for admission. In the university's explanation, offered him by a counselor, it was "adequate enough" academic standing. In his own estimation, it was skin color. If this man's analysis of his situation is even partially correct, the question of who gets in is magnified by social agenda, political cause, and the temper of the times. It is, then, a logical conclusion that more than this thing we call academic merit has been determining admission, and that a new form of merit, something we can call a *merit nouveau*, has been emerging.

This conclusion, that more than academic merit determines admission, however obvious, is not a simple one. Consider its polar opposite: that academic merit and only academic merit determines all admission. Such merit brings with it a host of underlying assumptions about the merited ones: they are academically prepared. They are academically adept. They will continue to achieve academically after admission. They have the particular mental abilities required to do well in higher education and to earn an undergraduate degree.

It is in this thinking that our short-sightedness of definition is apparent. When closely examined, academic merit, which was meant to be an unbiased, purely objective measure of a student's qualifications and achievement, loses some of its supposed objectivity. Why? Because merit itself is a subjectively contrived concept. And because our views regarding the mental ability of certain social subsectors are expressed in terms of our willingness to provide them with what we deem as mentally demanding opportunities, such as high-quality higher education. For those persons whose mental ability is viewed as less adept, is doubted for any reason, or just maybe, is limited due to prejudice, higher levels of education are quite frequently considered inappropriate, with the justification that these supposedly less adept persons simply do not measure up academically. This is how access to education, to knowledge, to social and political power, is restricted on the basis of academic merit.

Historical Restriction: Consider Women

Keep in mind that restrictive practice on the part of society is nothing new. It has existed throughout the ages. When the ancient philosopher Plato wrote that "a free man has the right to knowledge," he was in no way including slaves, women, and those belonging to other than the elite in his group of free men.[3] The mechanism of restriction is rather obvious to us modern, post-Marx people. It goes something like this: knowledge is power. Education is the passing on of knowledge and power. Restricting access to education controls the distribution of power. The restricting of access to education not only has been a long-maintained tradition but also has been so prevalent through time that even now, when we purport to have opened the gates of the hallowed halls to all who seek entry, we continue to restrict access. Only now, it is done in more subtle ways.

History, like a talkative child, reveals all of our forebears' secrets. Consider the evolution of women's access to higher education. This bit of history reveals the powerful effects of access to educational opportunity. Tremendous, unprecedented gains in social and economic opportunity for women have been made in a relatively short time as a result of women gaining access to modern higher education. However, at its outset, not much more than a century ago, higher education for women took a different form, a form that reflected the prevailing view that women did not have the intellectual ability to perform in the academic and professional arenas traditionally reserved for and restricted to men. Women's higher education was, for the most part, a sort of pseudo-education, a training appropriate to women's feminine level of mental ability, a training designed to prepare them to assume the social roles expected of them, a training designed to keep them in their place.

The prevailing view was that there was no reason to educate women "to the level of men," and that such education could be dangerous. Speaking against this prevailing view and in favor of the potential gains to be made in educating women to the level of men, the 1853–1854 *Catalogue of the Tennessee and Alabama Female Institute* stated that "when woman is thus completely educated the axe will be laid at the root of all evil and a new era will begin to dawn on the human race."[4] But this new era was unwelcome even at most of the women's colleges that were in existence at that time. In the majority of instances, women's colleges were offering only token education. Token education would appease the females and remain nonthreatening to men. In his 1914 book, *Before Vassar Opened*, professor of ethics and president of Vassar College, James Monroe Taylor, pointedly differentiated between what he termed the "nominal" and the "actual" or "true" college: "between the institutions that really aimed to do college work and those which laid great emphasis on the name of college and a degree made possible by a charter, but had a small regard for standards." Taylor identified several culprit institutions that were offering nominal education to women and calling it college. For example, he named the Elizabeth Academy in Old Washington, Mississippi, noting that although it was the first in its state to provide what it called college training for women, and although it offered "a diploma of parchment" for the degree of "Domina Scientarium," in Taylor's view, it did not qualify as a true college.[5]

Nominal or Actual College?

The differentiation between nominal and actual colleges was—and, in truth, still is—usually implicit. Why would a nominal college admit it was one, and why would an actual college claim to be one if it might be debunked as nominal anyway? Even at actual colleges, what was explicitly described as higher education for women was not the same higher education offered to men. This was a given. That this differentiation was often left implicit reflects a reliance on an unspoken and prevalent agreement that women and men differed in ability and social purpose, and that they should, therefore, be educated differently.

During the 1800s, the evolution of higher education for women followed several different courses, with a marked contrast between schools in the northern and in the southern United States. Curricula and goals differed markedly by region, as did economic and social motivations for separating young women from men in school settings. In the South, college education for women was almost universally separated from that for men. In the North, both separate and coeducational facilities could be found. Most of women's higher education was nominal regardless of its format. Female access to actual higher education rarely occurred.

However, everywhere in the country, women's demand for better education was building. In 1819, Emma Willard, a professor's wife, made an appeal to the legislature of the State of New York, as well as to the general public, for funding to create a female seminary. Most higher education in the Northeast was either church-sponsored or church-affiliated. Willard pleaded for a consistent and continuous course of education for women and for an environment that would offer women the moral and spiritual conditions essential to a sound physical and intellectual education. The New York Senate granted Mrs. Willard's seminary at Waterford $2,000, but the New York State Assembly failed to pass the bill. Nevertheless, taxation and subscription efforts raised over $4,000, and Mrs. Willard's Seminary at Waterford opened in 1821. This women's seminary was able to continue its existence by means of donation, including support from former pupils and teachers such as Mrs. Russell Sage.[6]

Willard was one of a few great contributors to the early development of higher education for women, higher education that attempted, yet, unfortunately, did not actually manage to approach the quality of the higher education available to men in those same years. Another leader in the effort to provide high standard, rather than token, higher education to women was Mary Lyon, who opened her Seminary at Holyoke in 1837.[7] Mary Lyon's goal was to establish a real college. While she was unable to offer degrees to her students, she did develop a solid three-year course of study for them. Lyon added to the educational quality of her school by creating entrance requirements, the first of which were English grammar, modern geography, United States history, and arithmetic.[8] These were some of the first academic admissions criteria specified for women.

A third major contribution was made by Oberlin. The well-known Oberlin College in Ohio opened its doors in 1833. Oberlin offered some of the most academic and rigorous education available to women in its time. Oberlin was coeducational; however, its "Female Department" was considered separate. Oberlin promised, through this department, "instruction in the useful branches taught in the best female seminaries."[9] In 1835, 37 of the 100 Oberlin students were female.[10] Students of both sexes were required to work four hours a day, receiving in exchange tuition, room, board, and furniture rental. The female students did the school's domestic work, washing, ironing, and sewing. The responsibilities of the male students were nondomestic. This separation of responsibility closely paralleled their academic work.[11] Although this setting may be described as coeducational, access to knowledge was still limited for Oberlin women. They were required to have only one year of preparation as opposed to the males' requirement of three years. Female students received no degree upon completion, while male students did.

Female Institutes, Women's Seminaries, and Young Ladies Departments of that era simply did not offer the education made available to men. "Girls' colleges" were basically designed to, as it was stated, "complete the education of [their] inmates, . . . to fit [a girl] for her profession, as the legal school prepares the lawyer [for his]."[12] Again, this education aimed at training women to fill their predesignated social functions.

The University of Illinois was one of the first public institutions to begin to admit women after the Civil War, which it began doing in 1870.[13] During 1870 and 1871, women were actually allowed to select from among the courses ordinarily available to men. By 1872, the university had become more organized and announced its intention to provide instead what it proudly called "a full course of instruction in the arts of the household, and the sciences relating thereto."[14] The regent and president of the board of the university made clear his belief that the university should recognize what he called the "distinctive duties of women." He planned a four-year women's program in which the first two years would parallel those of the males' School of English, and then domestic economy courses would replace the men's mathematics in the second two years.[15] Other players in curriculum development added courses that were considered "especially appropriate for women," such as music and fine arts. However, the university ruled that the study of art for aesthetic rather than utilitarian reasons would have a special fee attached. It was made clear that men studied the fine arts for utilitarian purposes such as industrial design and would not be required to pay such fees.[16] The implication was that women's study of anything beyond domestic economy, or home economics, had no practical purpose. Women either would not have the opportunity to put their learning to use or did not have the mental ability to do so, and these reasons were interrelated. The mental ability of men was considered greater than that of women; no amount of education would change this. Thus, the university pledged to educate women for their "distinctive duties."

Women's presence in the halls of actual rather than nominal higher learning was slow to take hold. Even in 1912, Harvard, which was not yet a coeducational campus, refused the use of one of its halls for a lecture by a representative of the League for Woman Suffrage. This was not a general attempt to avoid political debate on campus. Other political groups including the Socialists and Anarchists had been able to speak on campus during the same years.[17] At Harvard, women, independently of men, were not yet invited to join the American intelligentsia or even to participate in an adjunct manner in its forum. Access to the university environment and the inner circles of American intelligentsia was, here again, still closed to women.

Systematic Tracking

Although conditions have changed dramatically since then, and women now have access to the campuses and major halls of learning in all fields, the 1992 Report of the American Association of University Women (AAUW), *How Schools Shortchange Girls*, indicates that females continue to be affected by explicit and implicit assumptions regarding their propensities and abilities and their future utilization of those abilities. The foreword to this report refers to an increasing number of women and children living in poverty, pointing to the failure of education policy to address this condition.[18] According to the report, messages are sent both explicitly—via school curriculum—and implicitly—via classroom interaction, "systematically discouraging" women and girls. Girls are still "systematically tracked toward traditional, sex-segregated jobs, and away from areas of study that lead to high-paying jobs in science, technology, and engineering."[19] The AAUW Report adds that gender bias is also found in standardized tests such as the SAT, the most widely used college admissions test. Although by the 1970s, test company efforts were initiated to balance references to men and women and to eliminate test items offensive to women, these characteristics have not been completely eliminated from the SAT, which even at the time of this writing, has twice as many references to men as women. According to the AAUW, the SAT is a poor indicator of women's abilities.[20] Even when women are admitted in large and equal numbers, they may be admitted according to criteria preferential to a masculine intellectual perspective. Perhaps different women would be admitted were the admissions exam to be entirely redesigned. Here again is indication that although we purport to have opened the gates of the hallowed halls to all who would seek entry, we continue to restrict access in more subtle, implicit ways, including testing, admission

preferences, post-admission tracking, and even classroom interaction. Restriction is subtle and implicit, yet it is pervasive and
institutionalized.

The New Improved Brand of Political Inequality

The gender issue, even with all of its complexities and its long history, is one of the more basic issues. There are only two genders.
People of all ethnic backgrounds, socioeconomic groups, and levels
of ability are all either male or female. There are many other sub-
groupings of humanity that are susceptible to far more complex
stratification.

I have explained that the implicit barriers to admission and to
education are pervasive. Such barriers and obstacles to participation in higher education, even when highly implicit, almost invisible, reflect the standards of the encompassing social environment.[21]
Assumptions regarding mental abilities, the measurement of mental abilities, and the value of mental abilities continue to influence
admissions policies in higher education, *affecting differentially* the
various minorities and subsectors of society. Social policies, including admissions policies that, by their very nature, even without
explicit intention to do so, affect social subgroups differently, can
be described as policies having "differential impact."

Such differential impact may be virtually unavoidable in higher
education policy. One reason for this is that higher education
descends from its traditional or classicist origins. Past president of
Michigan State University, Walter Adams, speaking of the "classicist viewpoint," described the traditional obligations of a university
in his 1971 book, *The Test,* as being committed to three essential
purposes: one, "to transmit high culture—to shape students' mind
and character, to cultivate their aesthetic sensibility, to develop
their capacity for critical and independent judgment"; two, "to create new knowledge through pure scholarship and basic scientific
research"; and, three, "to select, train and certify elite groups: the

learned professions, the higher civil service, the political leadership and the top management in commerce and industry."[22]

By contrast, the "populist" view of higher education maintains that a university has direct obligations to a broader range of society, a range far beyond the parameters of the elite groups. To paraphrase Walter Adams's explanation of the populist view regarding the purpose of the university, it must: one, provide the opportunity to attend college to citizens, regardless of their social class, rather than perpetuate a class structure in our culture; two, provide ordinary citizens a chance to share in high culture for both its own sake and the sake of entrance into the elite occupations; and three, generate "fluidity in the class structure," in particular integration of America's racial and ethnic minorities into the melting pot.[23]

Fluidity in class structure: higher education is hard pressed to guarantee this result. Populism, though a laudable political tenet, is not readily brought into being. How hot must the burner be to bring about the once-idealized melting in the melting pot? Such a melting may no longer be possible—or desired.

Populism Nouveau and Merit Nouveau

A marvelously energetic but still young and naive attitude, something we can describe as a *populism nouveau*, has emerged. This new attitude calls for open opportunity without the once-dreamed-of melting. And here the greatest of political ironies is born. Differences are valued today; however, differential impact causes conflict. We appreciate differences in ability, aptitude, culture, and so on, and demand that each of these many differences be specially recognized; however, we do not like the outcome of this increasingly complex sort of recognition. In this and the chapters to come, we will see that even populist admissions policies, seeking to incorporate the emerging merit nouveau, have unavoidable and intractable differential impacts—between genders, among age groups, across ethnic groups, and across many other subdivisions of humanity. In higher education, it is clear that the drive for equality results in a multiplicity of differential impacts—or, more succinctly, in a new improved brand of political inequality.

Differential impact seems to come with the territory: no matter how we deal with diversity, the effects of our efforts are unequal. Since standards of excellence are inherently difficult-to-hold-to standards, standards must be reset to reflect realities of multicultural environments.

So, let's look closely at the case of U.C. Berkeley, where the growing pains of such virtually inherent differential impact are felt daily. No one concerned about the future of education, of opportunity, of equality, of this nation, can ignore the great experiment being conducted there. U.C. Berkeley is the oldest and most famous campus in the world-renowned University of California system. U.C. Berkeley is one of nine campuses in the public U.C. system, administratively linked under the jurisdiction of the very large and very culturally diverse State of California.

It is extremely instructive to study the particularities of and the challenges to the admissions policy of U.C. Berkeley in the examination of the differential impact of social policies in a heterogeneous society. As the U.C. Berkeley Committee on Admissions and Enrollment has maintained, U.C. Berkeley must take a leadership role in the construction of a "genuinely pluralistic environment."[24] However, no one has been able to create a "genuinely pluralistic environment" in the eyes of all segments of the plurality. As discussed in the following section, we may have allowed something far less than genuine: a double standard, a hypocrisy and a disingenuousness, which we may have preferred to overlook because we envision no alternatives.

U.C. Berkeley Admissions as a Prototype

The construction of this pluralistic social environment is highly dependent on the selection of students to be admitted into the university environment. Higher education admissions policy, especially the policy modeled by U.C. Berkeley, can therefore be a powerful tool in the construction of a truly pluralistic and egalitarian society (if we can ever genuinely agree on what that society would look like). So it is that the University of California has embarked on the adventure of helping to construct what is perceived by some as Utopia.

California's state government and all other state governments struggle to direct the policies of state colleges and universities in a politically satisfactory direction. Yet, this direction shifts continually. These shifts are quite tumultuous in states that are already experiencing marked increases in size and political power of once-small or quiet ethnic subpopulations.

Admissions Policy Evolves

Some admissions history is helpful here. Back in 1960, the initial *Master Plan for Higher Education in California* (fully adopted by the state legislature in 1964) set the stage for the tormented evolution of modern admissions policy when it moved in a more selective, more restrictive direction. The *Plan* sought officially to "raise materially standards for admission to the lower division."[25] In order to raise these standards, the *Master Plan* changed eligibility for all nine University of California campuses from 15 percent (a little under one-seventh) of the top California public high school graduates to the top 12.5 percent (one-eighth) of these graduates.[26] The policy was clearly moving in a more restrictive direction by raising the admissions ceiling up to 12.5 percent.

This "top 12.5 percent policy" of the 1960s was renewed by the California Commission for Review of the *Master Plan for Higher Education* in 1987, and remains in place as of this writing.[27] On paper, the policy appears to have held steady; however, it has not. The truth is that there has been a subtle change over time. What is most unusual is not the difference between the policy on paper and its reality; it is the many different interpretations of that reality. Some have found this change to be *more restrictive* and others have found it to be *less restrictive*. How can this be? It is quite simple: some college applicants now experience *increased* emphasis on academic merit, while others experience *decreased* emphasis on academic merit.

The official 12.5 percent just is not an accurate reflection of prevailing admissions outcome. How can the qualifying percentage become more restrictive when it remains the same? U.C. Berkeley demonstrates this unusual phenomenon quite well. Competition for admission to the nine U.C. campuses has been, and continues to be, most intense at U.C. Berkeley, the most prestigious of all the U.C. campuses. Therefore, the top 12.5 percent no longer have guaranteed admission there.[28] The percentage ceiling has evolved to a far higher level for those being admitted to U.C. Berkeley, at least when they are admitted based only on academic merit. Only the top of the top 12.5 percent get in.

Note that the top 3 or 4 percent of all applicants to Berkeley are overwhelmingly Asian-American and White, which signifies an ethnic imbalance of great extreme within the applicant pool. Speaking on this situation, the *Karabel Report* on admissions policy at U.C. Berkeley, released by the Berkeley Academic Senate in 1989, claimed, "The growing number of qualified applicants should make it possible for the campus to maintain and, indeed, to raise its academic standards *at the same time* that it broadens and deepens the process of diversification of its student body."[29] I highlight "at the same time" to underscore the reality of dual and counter-directional elements of policy at work—the split mind of modern social policy: restriction through higher standards and any derestriction necessary to bring about diversification.

The data on Berkeley indicate both an increasing number of applicants and an increasing number of turn-aways. Over the years, a generally decreasing proportion of all applicants have been admitted to U.C. Berkeley. In 1975, 3,896 of the 5,035 applicants were admitted; in 1980, 4,885 of the 9,115 applicants were admitted; in 1985, 6,329 of the 11,913 applicants were admitted; and in 1988, only 7,731 of the 22,439 applicants were admitted.[30]

The marked increase in applications and in turn-aways seen during the 1980s continued into the 1990s. In this trend, a major question arises for all of us who live in an ever more diverse and ever more competitive society. How can U.C. Berkeley or any institution maintain an admissions policy that is equally fair to each of California's or society's ethnic groups, that allows U.C. Berkeley or any university to maintain its high academic standards and prestigious reputation, and that garners the support of its ever more multicultural constituents—California's or any state's taxpayers? Although as the *Karabel Report* claimed, "This will not be an easy process, and it is sure to arouse controversy along the way," the report was optimistic that the university admissions policy could achieve its dual goals, even in the face of what the report officially recognized as the "tension" between them.[31] Now, why would the university acknowledge this tension between the dual goals of excellence and diversity were these goals not at odds? Excellence through diversity could be difficult to achieve without shifting out of traditional definitions of excellence. Have we forced diversity onto excellence so hard that we have smothered excellence? Or have we diversified excellence so well that we have guaranteed its survival in a new world order?

The question of who gets in is neither easily asked nor answered. There is no completely objective or fair way to make such a decision. Although the pressures of the older egalitarian populism garnered increased access to higher education and the social power it confers for members of more than just the social elite, the populism nouveau may now be running an ironic interference. Here again is the unit of analysis issue: populism nouveau, which focuses on the rights of social subgroups, is running an effective and perhaps even necessary crosscurrent to the original populism, which focuses on individual rights. In what group or individual unit do you find yourself? Where will your children fit in?

Crosscurrent Populisms

The history of U.C. admissions policy verifies that this troubled intersection of the old and new populisms is taking place. In fact, the construction of the state-mandated admissions formula has blatantly organized itself around these two populisms. By 1971, the California Council of Chancellors had established a "fifty-fifty criterion" for U.C. admissions policy.[32] This policy reserved the first half of the admission slots for applicants selected on an *entirely academic basis*—based on *the individual type of merit* of the old populism—and the latter half of the slots for those selected *for other reasons*—based on individual merit plus the relative merit of the *group need* per the new populism. The latter half constituted a "de"-restriction. This fifty-fifty split between the two admissions formats can be interpreted as an attempt by policy to balance academic standards against efforts to represent fairly less-privileged students: to strike a balance between not only political pressures but also opposing views regarding mental fitness for university education.

Let's get this balance issue straight, because the primary dilemma is surfacing around the nation and the globe. The *pro academic merit stand* calls for rigorous maintenance of top academic performance standards and, therefore, of the university's reputation via a rigorous admissions process. By contrast, the *pro fair representation stand* maintains that students overlooked by rigorous admissions standards can also perform well at the university and after graduation. Sounds very fair: fifty-fifty. But what exactly is it that constitutes *fair?* On the definition of fair, we remain painfully undecided.

History shows us how difficult balance is to formulate and to achieve. The official fifty-fifty balance of 1971 did not remain static. More derestriction was mandated. After 1986, this criterion was shifted to forty-sixty, decreasing by 10 percent the percentage of students who qualified solely on the basis of academic scores. Then restriction was increased again when, in 1991, the balance was set back to fifty-fifty, based upon *Karabel Report* recommendations.[33]

Swings in this balance reflect shifting views of the value of the two different roles of college admissions. Nevertheless, in California, from 1971 until the controversial 1997 implementation of the U.C. regents' decision to eliminate affirmative action standards, at least half of all admits to its greatest public university were not admitted via competition based solely on academic criteria.

But the best laid plans can fail. Fair as fifty-fifty and the short-lived forty-sixty and the returning fifty-fifty may have sounded, U.C.'s efforts to compromise these roles and mix admissions criteria did not make a significant difference in actual minority enrollment! Nine years after the criterion was initiated, only 3.9 percent of the 1979 freshman class was African-American and only 4 percent of it was Hispanic.[34] At the end of the 1970s, the official goal to diversify the student body fairly, even with affirmative action, equal opportunity programs, and special action efforts, was not realized—and this was after more than a decade of trying. In fact, after several decades, the goal of fair diversification has yet to be realized. Explanations for this shortfall, the likes of which have occurred in many public college systems across the country, are still being constructed. Although there is a great deal of finger pointing, no one can say with absolute certainty exactly why affirmative action and equal opportunity policies have not fully realized their goals.

In California, the result of the university's inability to represent the state's subpopulations fairly on campus was a further increase in governmental involvement in university admissions. This is a typical response to the challenge of fair integration: grow more government. Over the years, the slowness with which the U.C. system student population fairly represented that of graduating high school seniors prompted the California State Legislature to become, in the words of the *Karabel Report*, "increasingly explicit about what it considers to be the public service responsibility of the University of California, emphasizing the need for it to serve *all* of the state's citizens."[35] Here, the emphasis on "all" underscored the state's growing emphasis on the "egalitarianization" of higher education.

However, as the state became more explicit, it was clear that the broader opportunity called for by the older populism was not enough for policy makers. The state's increase in specification and emphasis on what it must do to ensure multicultural representation evidenced the intensified emergence of the new populism.

Broad Representativeness

A new surge of what had been dubbed "broad representativeness" took center stage in the 1980s. This term, although expressing a noble ideal, was one of the seeds of the affirmative action debates of the mid-1990s that exploded like a time bomb some thirty years after affirmative action was incorporated into policy. As the U.C. Committee on Admissions was rendering admissions policy to be what the *Karabel Report* called "increasingly explicit" in its serving of, representing of, and incorporating of the "all," this principle of broad representativeness was brought to the forefront of admissions policy with new force. Because it characterizes the nation's drive and therefore that of major institutions to adapt to the growing demands placed upon it by various ethnic groups, California's policy of broad representativeness, which was in place for many years, warrants attention.

This principle was originally ratified by the California State Assembly in 1974. Clearly, the 1974 call for broad representativeness to be in place by the year 1980 did not succeed. With the naivete that legislators occasionally exhibit, they reratified broad representativeness in 1983 and again in 1988 (as if reratification brings about change). The more explicit 1988 version of this mandate reads, "Each segment of California public higher education shall strive to approximate by the year 2000 the general ethnic, gender, economic and regional composition of recent high school graduates, both in first-year classes and subsequent college and university graduating classes."[36] Broad representativeness thus was as fundamental to the intent of admissions policy as the basic top 12.5 percent requirement. Still, while mounting competition for admission easily led to an exceeding of the top 12.5 percent standard at U.C. Berkeley, this competition did not really result in a speedier achievement of the goal of broad representation.

Who Actually Gets In?

Most Berkeley freshmen, regardless of the 50 percent to which they belong, by virtue of the fact that they are supposed to be among California's top 12.5 percent, really were admitted based upon this basic academic cut-off criterion. This is because U.C. Berkeley, in its own official words of policy, has believed that "it has a responsibility to dedicate a major proportion of its available freshman places to those young people particularly throughout California who have worked hard to prepare themselves for university studies, and have demonstrated a commitment to further accomplishment through their academic attainments."[37] Faithful to this articulated belief, U.C. Berkeley therefore assigned "a high percentage of its freshman admissions to those applicants who have obtained the highest high school grades and test scores."[38]

At U.C. Berkeley as well as most other colleges and universities, the selection of freshmen who have obtained the highest test scores and high school grade averages has been purported to be quite objective, accomplished by means of what is called a "blind" process that rank orders all applicants on an "academic index." This is a computer-generated ranking, which guarantees that it is a blind process. Of course, the computer is only as blind, as objective, as its programmer. In this case, the computer automatically grants enrollment to students from the top of the list on down until 50 percent of all slots have been filled. This designated percent can be changed and has been changed over time from 50 percent to 40 percent and back to 50 percent, as noted earlier, by admissions policy makers.

Academic Index Scoring

The Academic Index Score (AIS) is still, at least superficially, the most important criterion applied in freshman admissions. This score combines the applicant's high school grade-point average with the results of five standardized tests: the verbal sections of the SAT, the mathematics sections of the SAT, and three College Entrance Examination Board Achievement Tests (CEEBs). Before the recalibration (and score inflation) of the SAT in the mid-1990s, each of these five tests had a maximum possible score of 800 points. Therefore, the maximum test score total was 4,000. The high school grade-point average (GPA) was multiplied by 1,000 points. Because the basic upper recognizable limit on the GPA was 4.0, the maximum GPA score was 4,000. The test score total and the GPA total were thus equally weighted. Together, these totals render a maximum AIS of 8,000.[39] At the time of this writing, due to a recalibration of the SAT, these points will change somewhat, although their ratios will remain about the same.

However objective sounding the AIS system, we must again see that its very structure has resulted in differential policy. A policy admitting students based only on grades and test scores would yield a freshman class at U.C. Berkeley derived from the top 3 or 4 percent (along this AIS gradient) of California's graduating high school seniors, which, as noted earlier, would be a class overwhelmingly White and Asian-American.[40] This would, most likely, according to traditional expectations, produce an institution of high achievers, predominantly White and Asian-American. Yet, given its commitment to cultural diversity, U.C. Berkeley has "consciously rejected a policy of admitting students purely on the basis of grades and test scores."[41] Instead, under liberalized admissions, only that first portion, that first half of its freshman slots, were filled this way. Members of this first 50 percent were described as *Tier-1 admits*.

Why Tiers?

Basically, tiering is an easy answer to a complex policy problem. The necessity of imposing tiers or separate tracks onto the admissions process has been found at many colleges and universities. Create two or more sets of admissions criteria, each set speaking to the needs or demands of a different set of constituents: something for everybody, or almost everybody. One tier, that is Tier 1 at U.C. Berkeley, was admitted "purely on the basis of grades and test scores," known as "academic merit." The quest for Tier-1 acceptance has been fiercely competitive. The other tiers are variations on this theme of academic merit or deviations from it. A close look at what goes into tiering reveals how policy molds itself to social issues and contemporary politics.

At U.C. Berkeley, the remainder (other 50 percent) of the admits have been based on academic plus other criteria. Prior to the implementation of the *Karabel Report*, this remainder was broken into the following groups: Tier-2 admits, Tier-3 admits, and special action admits. A brief look at these tiers tells us how policy has found fancy terms for its need to please as many social subgroups as it can.

Tier-2 admits were students whose Academic Index Scores were not quite high enough to meet Tier-1 criteria. These admits were reviewed based on their AIS plus "supplementary criteria," such as California residency, economic background, an application essay, and high school course work.[42] Points were awarded based upon both the supplementary criteria and the academic index ratings. Students in this group with the highest point totals became the Tier-2 admits.

Complemental Admissions

However valiantly Tier 2 tried to balance out—"to heterogenize"— the relatively homogeneous student body, it was not enough of a deviation from Tier-1 standards to do so. So another admissions category was designed. This was called Tier 3. The size of Tier 2 was then set based upon the annual size of Tier 3. The percentage of total Tier-2 admits thus fluctuated from year to year (with 18 percent of the total admits being Tier 2 in 1986, 21 percent in 1987, and 16 percent in 1988),[43] because it has been dependent on the number of Tier-3 admits.

What was this mysterious new adaptation, this third tier added on to admissions policy? Tier-3 admits comprised what were officially described as the "complemental admissions category." This politically important category included students who had overcome physical or social disadvantages or who showed unusual excellence in a nonacademic area such as athletics, music, or drama. Tier 3 added the much-desired, highly demanded diversity to the student population.[44] Tier-3 admits were still all "U.C. eligible" but did not have academic scores meeting the level of Tier-1 or Tier-2 admits. Tier-3 admits, without the complementality policy, would not have won admission in the face of Tier-1 and Tier-2 competition. The contribution of Tier 3 to the total admits varied over time.[45] It is important to remember that Tier-2 admit contributions to the total were smaller than Tier-3 and were determined on the basis of the size of the Tier-3 contribution.

The goal of Tier 3 was to find a reasonable way to extend further the opportunity for a "good" college education. And so was born *complementality* or complemental admissions, yet another species of opportunity. Clearly, complementality has been a higher policy priority than recognizing the nearly top-cut academic standards achieved by Tier-2 applicants. Yet, this bit of truth has been neatly swept under the layered rugs of tier and other admissions terminology.

Even Tier 3 was not enough to satisfy the hunger for diversity. And so was included another species of opportunity, the special admit or "special action" category. This category was composed primarily of students whose racial or economic backgrounds placed them at a disadvantage or who had special (usually athletic) talents.[46] While well over 90 percent of the total U.C. admits, regardless of their tier qualification, were still U.C. eligible, a small percentage of admits were not. Instead, they were special action students, who were not officially U.C. eligible but who appeared to someone or ones in the administration to have a "reasonable chance"—a term not clearly defined—of graduating.

Admissions policy is always in the process of "becoming," reflecting its inability to bring about all that is desired and reflecting also the ever-changing world. Structural changes in the elaborate U.C. Berkeley admissions hierarchy were made in 1991, when the *Karabel Report* recommendations were implemented. Tier 3 was officially eliminated, but many old Tier-3 complemental categories were incorporated into Tier 2. The *Karabel Report* also added several new so-called "secondary-review" categories. Many of the elements of the former Tier 2 still remained in place, with its examination of student essays, extracurricular activities and extra course work as supplements to the AIS.

Tier 3 may have been eliminated but its purpose was expanded. The new secondary-review categories proposed in *Karabel* aimed to broaden the student body beyond what even Tier 3 had intended. In what we can call a small swing away from pure populism nouveau back toward the older populism, one new category was established to diversify socioeconomically the entering class. It was finally being argued (and it still is) that ethnic diversity was not the only form of diversity. Although significant progress had been made in the area of racial and ethnic diversification, *fewer than one-fifth of the entering class was coming from families with an annual income below the national median.* Also, students with highly educated parents continued to be overrepresented.[47] The new nonethnic criterion of socioeconomic status was to be the solution.

A second new category reflected a new tug on diversity. This category provided a secondary review to mature or "reentry" students. Although it was claimed that many of the reentry applicants "have extensive work experience and are highly motivated" and would add to the "intellectual and cultural richness of campus life,"[48] the majority of them were women who found it difficult to qualify for admission to U.C. Berkeley. The report attributed this difficulty to two basic sources: one, there are "gaps in their now-distant high school records" and two, these older female applicants have "relatively low standardized test scores," which, the report explained, are "often the product of having been out of school for some years."[49] Thus, for a special group of applicants, a formal forgiveness of low SAT scores was made.

A third new *Karabel* secondary-review category was composed of students "whose academic index scores narrowly missed gaining them admission in Tier 1 . . . these students are virtually indistinguishable from one another academically." Nonacademic criteria were, therefore, explicitly made the primary selection criteria within this group.[50]

The *Karabel* changes in admissions tracking avoided major departures from the pre-1992, Tier-3 complemental admission policies. However, specific terms were changed. Tier-3 targets—or quotas, as some unofficially dared to call them—were translated into what were now to be termed "flexible targets." These flexible targets were, in fact, acceptable *ranges* of admissions from among various applicant subpopulations. There were also a few more amendments to the list of complemental groupings: the expansion of the rural high school category to increase scanty admissions in this area, the combining of the former special talent and administrative review categories in order to promote the admission of a larger number of students with special talents, and the reduction of the Filipino target in response to an increase in the number of Filipino students qualifying for Tier 1.[51]

Was populism, old and new, retreating just a little? In what was viewed by some as a turn away from the egalitarian orientation of previous tracking, the *Karabel Report* recommended that the special action admission category be reduced in size. The new limitation stated that no more than one place in twenty in the fall freshman class be special action admits. But there were new diversity sensitive demands placed on special action. Now, at least two-thirds of these students were to be from socially or racially disadvantaged backgrounds. With this stipulation came the additional stipulation that all special action admit students be given "adequate support services," noting that only one-third of the special action students who entered U.C. Berkeley between 1978 and 1982 graduated in five years, a significantly smaller proportion than the sixty-some percent of regular admits who graduated in that same time span.[52]

Who Gets Out?

With this new (or renewed) emphasis placed on supportive services, the question changed. It was no longer just, Who gets in? It also became, Who gets out? The system had finally really learned that broader admissions policies necessitate the support of students who may have a more difficult time at the university than those admitted based upon purely academic criteria.

Yet another question reared its complex head after U.C. Berkeley made a commitment to diversify its student body, Who actually enrolls after getting in? It turned out that admission did not guarantee enrollment. The university came face to face with the reluctance of minority groups, especially African Americans and Hispanics, actually to register once admitted.[53] This glitch in the admissions system created a new layer of selectivity: *post-admission self-selection*.

I emphasize post-admission here, as it is already common knowledge that *pre-admission self-selection* determines, to a great extent, whether or not a student will apply in the first place. Whether it be motivation, confidence, financial standing, parental and teacher encouragement, the student's view of the university, or some mix of these and other factors, students tend to select themselves for application—to choose whether or not to submit themselves to the admissions process long before the institutionalized opportunity allocation of admissions begins.[54] This aspect of self-selection was considered a given long before its post-admission aspect became apparent, which is why recruitment efforts were built right into the budget.

However, once the mechanism for admitting an ethnically diverse student body was in place, it became disturbingly clear that the ethnic balance of the admitted class was not necessarily that of the attending class. In the early 1990s, the Office of Student Research conducted an extensive analysis to shed some light on this problem. Among its findings (reported in 1993) were some particularly fascinating odds pertaining to enrollment after admission: "The odds that a Chicano will register are .9 times as great as the odds that an African American will register. The odds that a White will register are .6 times as great as the odds that an Asian American will register. The odds that an Asian American or White will register are 7.3 times as great as the odds that an African American or Chicano will register."[55]

The last odds listed, that Asian Americans and Whites are seven times more likely than African Americans and Chicanos to enroll once admitted, can cast a veil of insecurity over any admissions process that seeks to ensure a particular balance of subpopulations within its student body. Again, we find that admission of a particularly composed student body in no way ensures that the actual enrolling student body will be composed as planned by admissions officers.

This Office of Student Research study revealed that ethnicity—as explained above—and home location—local students are more apt to enroll—exert significant influences on the decisions of admits to actually enroll. Athletic status, gender, and parental income are additional influences upon admits' decisions to enroll (listed in diminishing order), although less powerful than ethnicity and home location.[56] The data were analyzed in terms of "yield ratio," which is the term used to describe number of registrants divided by number of admits. It is perhaps a sign of the times that the very human experience of deciding whether or not to go to college once admitted must be reduced to a mass yield ratio in order to understand it.

These findings underscored the awesome realization that even if admissions policy could perfectly satisfy the competing goals of traditional excellence and contemporary diversity, the entering freshman class might not. There is no way to guarantee enrollment after admission. Such diversity cannot be ensured. It is important not to overlook this fact. The best laid plans of mice and men can fail.

Diversity Reexamined

What percolates to the surface after diversity is examined and reexamined almost ad nauseam is a lingering last word sort of question. What really is a fair representation of the population? As U.C. Berkeley associate vice chancellor Hayashi pointed out in 1995, it is more than a mirroring or attempted mirroring of racial proportions: "We make special efforts to include disabled students, rural students, inner-city students, older students, poor students, and students with special athletic, musical, or other talents." Hayashi stressed the notion that diversity is not only ethnic. Ethnic diversity is a big piece of social diversity, but it is only a piece.[57] The U.C. Berkeley admissions plan thus became known by a series of approved buzz words: "this commitment to admit a socially diverse and educationally rich student body."[58]

If we dissect U.C. admissions policy of the 1980s and 1990s into its thematic components, it separates into four elements. First, "this commitment," which was, to a great extent, actually mandated by the state, left U.C. Berkeley only some degree of freedom in choosing to make or not to make this so-called commitment. Second, "to admit," which made no reference to graduation. Although graduation rates are very important at Berkeley, it has been far more difficult for the institution to commit to graduation rates because, once admitted, students have a say in their graduation rate and thus determine the longer-range outcome of the university's plan. Third, admission of a "socially diverse" mix of students has been implemented, but who is the ultimate arbiter of diversity? What on earth is social diversity? How diverse should we get? Are efforts made to fairly—proportionately—represent ex-cons, alcohol addicts, people of fringe political parties, people with IQs under 85, people with IQs over 180? And fourth, an "educationally rich" student body? What, pray tell, is that? Official platitudes may appease the taxpaying public for a while, but eventually we all want more precise definitions.

. . . .

The "Nasty Problem" of Fairness on the Multicultural Campus

One day, a White undergraduate female student overheard me interviewing people on the U.C. Berkeley campus. She asked me if I wanted her comments. I told her I did. She sat right down and said, "Some days I think what I'm really learning here at this university is how to handle the world of the future. This place is crowded, competitive, full of conflict, noisy, chaotic, bureaucratic, economically stressed, risky (especially for a woman to cross campus alone at night), dirty, things in a state of decline, very interethnic, and also very international. And I don't mind because I think what's going on at this school today is a taste of the future of the planet. I might as well learn to deal with it now."[1]

It is difficult to predict exactly what the university of the year 2100 will be like or if there will be a university anymore. Perhaps higher education will redefine itself as continuing education, going on through life, in the form of continual training and retraining, ever responsive to rapidly changing technology. Or, perhaps society will have reverted to an intensely hierarchical structure with only the very elite or the high priests being educated past high school level.

Clues from the Flagship

In the meantime, we look to institutions that have been pushed to the brink of the future. U.C. Berkeley is one. It has been labeled "the university of tomorrow"[2] because the mix of its increasingly culturally diverse student body—along with the mounting social, political, intellectual, structural, and economic pressures it faces— is a manifestation of trends that many other institutions of higher education are now experiencing or will be encountering in the coming years. In fact, many colleges and universities in the United States and in other nations have already begun to experience the democratic tug to represent fairly the cultural diversity of the global population and the curricular and policy questions this representation raises, while concurrently struggling with growing financial restrictions. It is as if some of these institutions of higher education are swallowing powerful growth hormones while wearing ever-shrinking iron jackets. Everyone on such campuses feels these pressures.

This chapter examines the admission of and response to such pressures as exemplified on the U.C. Berkeley campus. Let's first examine the multicultural makeup of this campus at the peak of the affirmative action era and compare it with that of other schools. U.C. Berkeley, one of the flagship universities of the United States, long considered one of the leading universities in the world, was founded in 1868 in the city of Berkeley, California, a city that itself has become a densely populated and racially mixed urban environment. On the U.C. Berkeley campus as of 1993, the ethnic mix of the more than 20,000 full-time undergraduate students was, for U.S. citizens, 31 percent Asian American, 7 percent African American, 39 percent Caucasian, 15 percent Hispanic, 1 percent American Indian, and 7 percent Other, with 3 percent of the students at U.C. Berkeley being foreign nationals.[3] Ninety-three percent of all undergraduates attending U.C. Berkeley are California residents (as of 1993).

At first glance, many visitors to the U.C. Berkeley of the mid-nineties commented that the degree of cultural diversity that evolved there was highly unlikely to evolve on other middle-American campuses. The ethnic composition of the student body at U.C. Berkeley was, by the mid-nineties, indeed, distinct among major American universities. Yet, the diversity found at Berkeley rendered it one of the college campuses most representative of the surrounding global diversity, which is now, like a great wave, washing toward every one of our schools and institutions. No shift in emphasis on affirmative action and other diversity policies can ward off this global trend.

The forward-looking composition of U.C. Berkeley in the mid-1990s becomes apparent when the ethnic composition of its student body is compared with that of contemporary student bodies at other public institutions such as those listed in Table 4.1. Lowest on the list in Table 4.1 in terms of Caucasian admissions is U.C. Berkeley. However, note how the racial balance at Berkeley measures out distinctly differently from that of the statewide population of California, which, in the same year as the data listed above, was 9.56 percent Asian American, 7.42 percent African American, 68.97 percent Caucasian, 25.83 percent Hispanic, 0.81 percent American Indian, and 13.24 percent Other during that same period.[4] Clearly, in terms of proportion of state population, White students were, as of the mid-1990s, profoundly underrepresented there. The contrast between the ethnic mix at U.C. Berkeley and at private U.S. universities is also distinct. Consider the breakdowns of student body data for the private universities listed in Table 4.2.

University admissions policies, both when attending to the matter of cultural diversity and when ignoring it, are the primary determinant of ethnic diversity and racial balance on campuses. However much cultural diversity is directly determined by admissions policies, it is also indirectly determined through the competition these policies generate. As discussed in Chapter Three, competition for entrance into U.C. Berkeley is fierce. Of the 20,281 applicants for admission to the 1992–93 freshman class, only 8,700 were accepted. That entering class averaged 563 on the verbal portion and 654 on the math portion of the SAT (these are the old SAT calibrations).[5] Ninety-five percent of this class ranked in the top tenth of their high school class, and 100 percent ranked in the top quarter.[6] Consider the same data for the 1992–93 academic year at the institutions listed in Tables 4.1 and 4.2.

Table 4.1. 1992–93 Student Body Breakdowns by Ethnicity: Public Colleges.[7]

	Asian Americans	African Americans	Caucasians	Hispanics	American Indians	Other	Foreign Nationals
U. of California Berkeley	31 percent	7 percent	39 percent	15 percent	1 percent	7 percent	3 percent
Georgia Tech.	12	8	76	3	—	—	9
Louisiana State U. Baton Rouge	3	8	85	2	—	2	2
Michigan State U. East Lansing	3	8	84	2	1	2	1
Ohio State U. Columbus	3	6	85	1	—	4	3
U. of Colorado Boulder	6	2	82	6	1	4	2
U. of Florida Gainesville	5	6	78	7	—	4	2
U. of N. Carolina Chapel Hill	4	10	83	1	2	1	1
U. of Texas Austin	9	4	69	14	—	4	4
U. of Washington Seattle	19	4	65	3	1	8	2
U. of Wisconsin Madison	3	2	85	2	—	8	4

Table 4.2. 1992–93 Student Body Breakdowns by Ethnicity: Private Colleges.[8]

	Asian Americans	African-Americans	Caucasians	Hispanics	American Indians	Other	Foreign Nationals
U. of California Berkeley	31 percent	7 percent	39 percent	15 percent	1 percent	7 percent	3 percent
Brandeis	8	4	82	3	—	3	5
Brigham Young	2	1	88	2	1	7	6
Brown	15	7	72	6	—	—	7
Columbia	19	10	64	9	—	—	3
Dartmouth	9	7	63	5	3	13	7
Duke	8	8	79	4	1	—	4
Georgetown	6	7	68	5	1	13	11
Harvard/Radcliffe	18	7	61	8	1	5	7
Johns Hopkins	20	5	67	2	1	5	5
Oberlin	10	8	73	3	—	6	6
Princeton	10	7	77	5	1	—	6
Stanford	20	8	57	10	1	3	3
Yale	15	8	71	6	—	—	5

As is evident in the data in Table 4.3, U.C. Berkeley has a large number of applicants for admission, the largest applicant body among all the institutions listed. Although Berkeley is a large public university and carried an undergraduate student body of 21,841 during the 1992–93 academic year, it was only able to admit 43 percent of the 20,281 applicants that year. (See Table 4.3.) This places the admissions policy of U.C. Berkeley among the more restrictive in the nation in terms of applicant-to-admission ratio and among the most restrictive of the public institutions. Therefore, when combined with the unusual balance of ethnic groups actually admitted during most of the 1990s, the sheer turn-away rate at U.C. Berkeley renders an important example of what the most desirable institutions of higher education, especially public institutions, may be confronting now or in the coming years.

Utopian Illusions

This returns us to the nasty problem of fairness. Grappling with pressure to meet the needs of an increasingly ethnically diverse society and being a public institution, the University of California, Berkeley diligently implemented what have been euphemistically dubbed "fair representation" measures. These measures were designed to serve fairly the population of the state they serve.

The effects of these fair representation admissions policies did not go unnoticed by undergraduates. Students were quite mixed in their views of these effects, as were most of the players in the university. Of the students I polled at this critical juncture in modern history, the overwhelming majority, almost two-thirds, expressed an awareness that shifting admissions policies created more diversity on campus and the opinion that such diversity is better representative of society. Some noted proudly that "the current student population at U.C. Berkeley is the most diverse of any college or university in the country," that there was "more interracial interaction here than on a predominantly White campus," and that "the different races interact quite well here at Berkeley." One student

Table 4.3. 1992 College Admission Rates as Compared with U.C. Berkeley.[9]

	Total Applicants	Total Admits	Admits Verbal S.A.T. [ave]	Admits Math S.A.T. [ave]	Percent in Top Tenth [High School]	Percent in Top Quarter
U.C. Berkeley	20,281	8,700	563	654	95	100
Private Universities:						
Brandeis	3,827	2,752	—	—	36	74
Brigham Young	7,365	5,402	—	—	48	82
Brown	12,194	2,953	620	670	87	95
Columbia	8,014	2,546	—	—	75	—
Dartmouth	8,076	2,107	622	681	85	98
Duke	14,528	3,859	—	—	88	97
Georgetown	10,116	2,973	—	—	68	90
Georgia Tech.	6,970	4,321	541	655	68	92
Harvard/Radcliffe	13,029	2,135	—	—	90	100
Johns Hopkins	7,820	3,390	610	685	72	93
Oberlin	4,185	2,617	596	628	52	86
Princeton	12,716	2,026	640	700	90	100
Stanford	13,530	2,715	—	—	91	98
Yale	11,054	2,455	—	—	95	99

Table 4.3. con't.

	Total Applicants	Total Admits	Admits Verbal S.A.T. [ave]	Admits Math S.A.T. [ave]	Percent in Top Tenth [High School]	Percent in Top Quarter
U.C. Berkeley	20,281	8,700	563	654	95	100
Public Universities:*						
Georgia Tech	6,970	4,321	541	655	68	92
Louisiana State U.	6,707	5,266	—	—	26	54
Michigan State U.	18,407	14,871	461	525	26	69
Ohio State U.	16,158	12,759	—	—	26	56
U. of Colorado	13,761	10,473	—	—	28	66
U. of Florida	12,444	8,273	—	—	50	85
U. of N. Carolina	16,580	5,735	530	592	76	94
U. of Texas	14,235	9,319	521	60	48	84
U. of Washington	12,516	6,969	—	—	54	91
U. of Wisconsin	14,002	10,237	—	—	35	76

*Same specific campuses as referred to in Table 4.1.

noted that, because of this diversity, "Students, administrators, and faculty are forced to interact with one another in a variety of new areas, which is very necessary in our changing world."

Many students pointed out that liberalized admissions policies make a significant contribution to the well-being of society. "I think that admissions quotas are often misinterpreted by people according to how they have been impacted. Social benefits are for the benefit of society (the masses). In that case, admissions policies are fair—for they are meant to bring up the standard of living benefits for society, for all, and all ethnicities are included. Isn't that what education is about? To gain benefits for society?"

Another student contended similarly: "Diversity is good. There is increased interaction between ethnic, economic, religious groups, et cetera. More diversity allows for more possibilities, be it knowledge, friends, understanding between people. Someone who only listens to a particular type of music (for example, pop) is missing out on a whole variety of good music. This works the same with people and cultures." Of his comment, the same student observed, "Wow, what an analogy."

An additional benefit to the world beyond the campus was noted by this Hispanic student: "By graduating students who may not have otherwise come to college, U.C. Berkeley is doing the communities these students are from a favor. These students do graduate successfully and they do retain something from their years at U.C. Berkeley which can be of help to them and their people once they graduate."

Another student went into greater detail to explain the advantages of fair representation admissions:

> The admission policy acknowledges that there are individuals talented and intelligent enough to compete with other students at U.C. Berkeley, even though their SAT scores and grades may not be in the 90th percentile of high school seniors. U.C. Berkeley realizes that there are

social and economic factors involved that place Economic Opportunity Program (EOP) and affirmative action students at a disadvantage in the system that is standardized according to middle-class, White students. The effect of diversity is a positive one. Some say that the university has a diversified student body but that the separate ethnic groups segregate themselves anyway. However, there is enough interaction that groups can, and often do, understand each other. This small percentage is much better than not having the possibility to interact at all, such as in a 90 percent White student body.

Utopian Disillusions

But the picture is not entirely positive. The rose-colored glasses of many a myopic idealist were shattered as the implementation of affirmative action was experienced. At least a third of the students I polled, while expressing an awareness that shifting admissions policies had created more diversity on campus, were of the opinion that this was not a positive event. Some of these students' comments were that "with more diversity, there is now a much wider gap between the best and the worst students"; that this gap had led to an overall decline in the "academic quality of the university"; that "students are less interested in learning"; and that there was an "overcompensation to help those among the minority students who, under normal circumstances, would never have qualified for admission." Several students insisted that "blame and guilt is being cast in all directions."

One day, a student in one of my classes, upon hearing about my study of admissions policies, stood up in class and politely requested permission to state her views. I, quite readily, granted permission, only to find this young White woman literally pointing her finger at me and stridently reprimanding me:

It's people like you, your age group, that wanted affirmative action policies. You demanded them. Now people like me must pay. I'm White. I come from a family with a single parent. My mom worked hard to support me when I was growing up. She told me I had to do well in school so that I would have more choices in life than she did. I did. I worked hard. I was a top student. I deserved to be admitted to U.C. Berkeley. Now, I get here and I'm practically made to feel guilty that I'm White and I got admitted. But I'm not even rich enough to live on campus. I live at home with my mother, I commute to school, and I work practically full-time to pay my tuition. I'm still a top student. Why should people who haven't worked as hard as I have be here? And why is it suddenly bad to be White? Tell me that!

I opened my mouth to speak. However, at least half of my very ethnically diverse and much-too-large class of some seventy students spoke out at the same time. Over-shouted, I sat down and listened to them argue and agree with each other for a while. Sitting there in silence, I could see the marvelous effects of the changes that had emerged in the makeup of the student body— how much of the ethnic variation of the globe was represented here. A wave of pride and exhilaration washed over me. I was pleased to see the students organize themselves into a fair discussion in which all viewpoints could be heard. Yet, at the same time, I could still see the young White female student pointing her finger at me. I could still feel the accusation slung from her generation to mine. We were not even twenty years apart in age; we were the same race, yet our perspectives may have differed as much as any two persons in my classroom that day. For a moment, I recalled being her age, a student of the early 1970s in attendance at the University of California, Santa Cruz, and accusing my professors of being part of a system that denied access to other than members of the dominant culture.

Emergent Discrimination

Some of the comments from the students who spoke up loudly that day were that "there may now be more diversity on campus, but fewer students are interested in really learning," that the "overall esprit de corps is diminishing," and that there was "a new kind of dishonesty about achievement here." In various versions, these same viewpoints were expressed by at least a third of the students who participated in my study. So, according to a significant proportion of students, the results of diversity are mixed and are painful.

Some students claimed that, as a result of efforts to diversify admissions, "there is a rising arrogance and pride in certain minority groups," that "some groups are developing a new racist attitude," and that "there is actually an increase in prejudice." When pressed for further detail, some of their responses were that "there is rising hate against Asian women," and "it's a lousy time to be White and walking across the campus alone at night," and "just keep your gun close." I found this last answer unnerving but to the point.

It appears that a new racism is emerging, this *emergent racism* being perhaps the by-product of diversity policy. A male Asian-American student insisted: "When students are not admitted for purely scholastic reasons but, instead, are special admits for athletics, affirmative action, et cetera, extra effort and patience is demanded from both the professors and the academically admitted students while the special admits catch up."

Looking for more on this perspective, I discussed this with students. I was told several times that, in fact, special admissions policies have actually backfired: "I think that issues like affirmative action are used against Chicanos/Latinos and African Americans— especially against we Latinos—as another form of racism, as a way to say that we are not good enough to get in without affirmative action, not good enough to be here. And it appears that most people who talk about affirmative action don't really know the facts involved."

A young African-American student was certain that "The faculty's perception of a student's academic ability is very much affected by the student's ethnic group. So being here, where there are so many special admissions, works against some of us."

One of the best evidences of emergent racism and one of the saddest reports came from a White student who claimed

> The tension has most definitely increased because of affirmative action and related complications. I know that, on my end, the tension has increased because I was mugged by African Americans and had a few other unpleasant racially based experiences. I came to this school without any prejudice, and in my four years here, I've gained it. I know my feelings aren't "politically correct" and I'm rather ashamed to admit this prejudice. It's not prejudice against African Americans as a whole, but aimed toward a particular type. Right or wrong, I've created it to protect myself from further unpleasant situations.

This sort of comment, quite common these days, suggests the emergence of hitherto nonexistent prejudices. We wonder, can this be possible? Can special admissions actually generate new prejudices? Some 10 percent of the students I polled by questionnaire took the opportunity to write out answers to my questions about prejudice and racism, which they may have felt less free to answer had they not been able to do so anonymously. One student confessed anonymously in writing: "When I see academically inferior minority students in my classes, it becomes more likely that I assume all members of that group are charity cases and not academically prepared."

Another wrote that, if he could change current admissions policies, he would try to build in fairness: "If I could change anything about current admissions policies, I would make them more fair. I've known people with higher qualifications than others applying for the same program being rejected by admissions while those others were accepted. This doesn't make any sense."

Fragmenting Fairnesses

Some students indicated that we have been popping the beautiful bubble of fairness with the outcome of what seem to many to have been unfair judgments of admissions policies. The dream is over. Utopia is never coming. Fair is just another four-letter word.

The student body cannot help but be affected by admissions policy, as such policy determines its very composition. Ninety percent of the U.C. Berkeley students who participated in my study reported that they find admissions policy controversial. Nevertheless, this same sampling of students was divided in its views regarding the fairness of affirmative-action-based admissions policy, with only 2.2 percent finding it "fair to all," 31.4 percent finding it "mostly fair to all," 34.5 percent finding it only "somewhat fair to all," 23.9 percent finding it "not very fair to all," and 8 percent finding it "not at all fair to all." I was intrigued to find the ethnic variations in the perceived fairness of this admissions policy. Eighty percent of the African-American students I polled found admissions policy "mostly" (70 percent), or "entirely" (10 percent) fair to all. Close to the same proportion (76.5 percent) of the Asian-American students polled found the policy only "somewhat" (41.2 percent), or "not very" (31.4 percent), or "not at all" (3.9 percent) fair to all. Close to the same proportion (68.7 percent) of Caucasian students polled found the policy only "somewhat" (32.2 percent), "not very" (24.3 percent), or "not at all" (12.2 percent) fair to all. Hispanic students were most evenly distributed in their perceptions of fairness, with only 58.6 percent reporting that the policy was only "somewhat" (37.9 percent) or "not very" (20.7 percent) fair to all.

Of course, most students are not enrolled in a university long enough to have personal experience with the changes in admission policy over the decades. Their evaluations of fairness are, presumably, time-limited. Still, almost all (48.9 percent) of the students I polled reported that policies had either "totally" changed (2.6 percent), or "substantially" changed (43 percent), over the last decade, and another 45 percent reported that policy has changed "somewhat" over the last decade. This indicated that most (93.9 percent) students were aware that policies have changed.

Did these students have a sense of the intensity and nature of the liberalized admissions policies? Yes: 22.1 percent reported that changing admissions policies have had a "profound effect" on the makeup of the student body, another 46.5 percent reported a "distinct" effect on that makeup, and 26.2 percent reported at least "some effect" on that makeup. Moreover, 76.4 percent of the students polled felt that changing policies affected the classroom. Students were very split on the matter of whether or not it had become more difficult to receive a B in a class at their university, with 40.9 percent claiming it was "about the same," 27 percent claiming it was "less difficult," and 32.2 percent claiming it was "more difficult."

Students were quite split regarding whether the level of race-related tension at the university had changed. Forty percent of the students polled claimed racial tension had "increased," 42 percent claimed it had "fluctuated," and 18 percent claimed it had "not increased." Similarly, 46.4 percent of the tenured faculty polled claimed that racial tension had "increased," 33.9 percent claimed it had "fluctuated," and 19.6 percent claimed it "had not increased." All but one ethnic subgroup of these tenured professors bore a similar reading, the exception being the Asian-American professors, with the majority of them (71.5 percent) reporting that racial tension "had increased," 14.3 percent reporting that it had "fluctuated," and another 14.3 percent reporting that it had "not increased."

I noted with interest that the students were split on the matter of whether or not admits "arrive prepared" for the demands of academic life, with 51.1 percent answering "yes" here, and 48.9 percent answering "no." Whatever the perceived level of preparedness at admission, students perceived preparedness at graduation more positively, with

25 percent reporting that students graduate "very much prepared," and another 43.9 percent reporting that students graduate "prepared." This means that 68.9 percent of my sample perceived students to graduate prepared. Another 25.5 percent claimed students graduate at least "somewhat" prepared. Although the majority (83.2 percent) of students polled felt that employers were satisfied with graduates of their university, most (63.8 percent) of these same students did not feel that the university provided "adequate support" to the students it admits.

An Asian-American female wrote

> I don't feel we can call it racial tension, but with such a large non-White population, we are very aware of ethnic groups. We are a part of society as a whole and students and faculty staff bring with them their stereotypes and prejudices learned in their homes and communities. Many, for the first time, are living with or in contact with people from other racial, cultural or religious groups. Quite often, incidents that are not racially motivated at all may be taken as racial if students do not know how to deal with the bureaucracy and are already feeling alienated. In the classroom, professors teach using developmental theories geared to White middle-class males, overlooking the fact that this may not be the most effective theory with non-White students and women. This may also cause feelings of isolation, and some students may see this as a form of racism.

Moreover, as another student noted: "EOP and affirmative action students are sometimes made to feel as if they didn't 'earn' their way into Berkeley. This can demean an individual and, thus, affect his or her performance."

A significant proportion of the students were apparently quite torn, seeing both sides of diversity policies. This split percolated into the confusion experienced by this student:

I think that in order to keep the campus up to legal standards as far as multiethnic diversity of student body, the
campus may have had to cut off the number of students
of a certain ethnic background to allow other ethnic
backgrounds to enroll. Although "others" have argued
that they still must compete among those "others" for the
slot, the person with the background of the majority cannot even compete for that slot after a certain number of
slots have been filled. Although on this campus majority means a high number of students of that background,
is this fair? I also realize that lower socioeconomic conditions and historical oppression are impacting this issue
which is a balancing act between the fairness to the individual versus the fairness of making amends to races of
people done wrong over time. At the same time, if we
don't bring up the standards of living of everyone then
we, as Americans, suffer together.

Again and again, students I interviewed insisted that, although
it officially claimed not to, the University of California, Berkeley
had maintained a quota system as part of its admissions process. Students made comments such as, the university had been "overcompensating to help minority groups," that it had been "admitting
fewer qualified Whites while admitting more students who are not
as academically qualified as the Whites that are rejected," and that
race quotas had been "bringing less-qualified students into the university and lowering academic standards."

Classrooms as the Front Line on the Battlefield of Change

Given that the university administration claims that, during the years
of its fifty-fifty diversity-incorporating admissions policy, the academic level of entering students was raised, this must be the case.[10] Why
would administrators report that the academic level of entering students had been raised if it had not been?

Personally and privately, on a one-to-one basis, I discussed specifically this matter with some 200 students and 35 professors. Some students and professors (each of whom specifically asked to remain anonymous on this) suggested that claims regarding the raising of academic standards were "merely public relations hype"; were "aimed at the taxpayers"; were "supposed to help a once great, now crumbling, university save face"; and were, "no matter what the test scores and grade averages say, not borne out in the classroom."

There are, however, other explanations. Perhaps the academic quality of the entering class had remained constant or, as the administration reported, even had been raised. Yet, the administrations' measures of students' academic quality upon admission may have been too narrow or arbitrary to indicate the true intellectual capacity of the student body. Is it difficult to assess the effects of admissions criteria upon what can be described as the *composite intellect* of the university?

It may be that the demands placed upon the institution and the professors have changed so significantly that, regardless of a student's academic merit upon arrival, the university cannot serve successfully as a melting pot and, at the same time, as a purveyor of the intellectual tradition that has come down through the ages and that many hope will survive the social and political pressures arising at the time of the new millennium.

University faculty and administration overwhelmingly reported that the fifty-fifty admissions policy was controversial (82.7 percent, or 144 of the 174 respondents). Nevertheless, over half of them (55.9 percent) responded that diversity-incorporating admissions policies were "mostly" (53.5 percent), "or entirely" (2.4 percent) "fair to all." The breakdown of this set of responses was especially interesting: 68.8 percent of the high-level administrators responded that the admissions policies were "mostly or entirely fair to all"; 62.5 percent of the tenure track faculty responded that the admissions policies were "mostly or entirely fair to all." Somewhat fewer, 50.8 percent of tenured faculty, responded that these policies were "mostly or entirely fair to all." Whether or not they viewed them as being controversial or fair, 63.7 percent of all faculty and administrators agreed that admissions standards became "broader" in the years up to 1995.

Did the liberalized admissions policies affect the classroom? Fifty-seven point six percent of tenured faculty answered "yes, somewhat" (25.8 percent), "yes" (27.3 percent), or "yes, profoundly" (4.5 percent). Of tenured faculty, 59.6 percent responded that receiving a B was "less difficult" now, while 71.4 percent of tenure track faculty responded that receiving a B was "less difficult" now.

Inasmuch as the general tension level on a campus affects the classroom, we can surmise a distinct effect when the makeup of the student body changes. When asked if there was racial tension on campus, those indicating "yes" included 81.8 percent of tenured faculty, 50 percent of tenure track faculty, 86.7 percent of high-level administrators, 91.9 percent of midlevel administrators, and 95.5 percent of the administrative support staff.

So the university of tomorrow is with us today, resplendent in its transition from an institution of the past to one of the future. Can it hold together as it gives birth to its new form?

Trapped Between Political Correctness and Political Embarrassment

"That's a good question," an Hispanic U.C. Berkeley graduate student replied when I asked him whether or not the university can hold together as it gives birth to its new form. "A lot of things are tearing that place apart. And the problems we see now have been developing for decades. Take affirmative action for example. It's been around a while. But now people are really fighting about it."

From Special Admit to Abrupt Neglect

This awareness triggered my line of inquiry regarding the long view of racially sensitive college policies. I was quite surprised when an African-American U.C. Berkeley dropout, Wayne Greene, revealed his view that, "As a single group, I think Berkeley's EOP students caused more political embarrassment to the university than any other single group there."

A little more history is useful here. In 1964, the federal EOP was started to assist students from economically disadvantaged backgrounds. These were primarily students who would otherwise have been unable to afford to attend colleges and universities. This program, along with policies and programs around the nation, sought to open the narrow gates of opportunity to a broader range of citizens. As explained in the previous chapter, it was to this end that academic standards for admission were altered. In California, the U.C. regents established, in the California *Master Plan*, a special requirement that 2 percent of all admissions be offered to those students who *did not* meet the top 12.5 percent standard. In 1968, the regents increased the size of this special non-top 12.5 percent group from 2 percent to 4 percent of all admissions. This special action category allowed the university to admit minority students and to bring in athletes who might not otherwise qualify.[11] From 1964 to 1974, U.C. Berkeley began, via more than the basic official tier mechanisms described in Chapter Three, to diversify its predominantly White student body, which, as of the early 1960s, was 90 percent White, middle- and upper-class.

It was during this phase that Wayne Greene graduated from Berkeley High School. This was in 1967. Late in his senior year of high school, and fairly close to the time of graduation, Greene was told by his school counselor that his name had been submitted for participation in U.C. Berkeley's EOP program. This is how Greene became one of the very first EOP students at U.C. Berkeley. As he explains, "There must have been some pressure on Berkeley High School to come up with a list of names because the process was partly started by the time I was even aware."[12] Although he was in the top tracks in English and history, Greene describes himself as having been a "barely B" student. "I didn't think I had the grades to get into U.C. Berkeley, that's for sure." He is quite certain he was "admitted for racial reasons." He recalls being told that, although his "grades were marginal," " . . . there were some special slots for 'promising' minority kids." Greene was told that this meant that tuition would be paid, that there would be a book stipend available, and that it would not cost his parents any money to send him there.

There was one hurdle. In Greene's words, "The one caveat was that I score high enough on the SAT tests. So I had to, at the last minute, scramble to get signed up for the SAT's, which a lot of my other friends, middle-class doctors' and professors' kids had already set up long in advance." He did quite well on the verbal portion of the SAT, but not well in the mathematics section. This reflected his academic performance in high school. "One of the things in high school that was always really frustrating to me was that I couldn't understand how I could be so smart in English and history and barely scrape by with C's in physics, chemistry, and biology. I think I decided fairly early on that I was just not smart in those subjects and gave up."

For whatever combination of reasons, Greene does not remember the day he found out he was accepted to U.C. Berkeley as being a big day in his life. His explanation is that, although he expected to be admitted, "The process was initiated and guided by somebody else. . . . In a lot of ways, I was sort of going along with a tide that had already been set up. Nobody made me feel this was an especially valuable opportunity, so my attitude about the opportunity took on the spirit in which it was offered."

The apparent ambivalence and relative detachment toward him, which Greene experienced during the admission process, did not contrast sharply with his experiences upon entry into the university. Although there was an EOP office on campus and there was a counselor, an "EOP guidance person," there, Greene was not actively sought out by that or by any other office. He says, "I think among the acceptance forms I got was a form stating where the office was, who the contact person was, and that he or she was available to discuss academic planning with me. I might have gone in— I went once. I don't think I went more than once." He explains that he did not get help with academic planning: "If I'd been more aware, if I'd initiated or been active [through the original application process] myself, maybe I would have been better prepared to take advantage of the little EOP office." Greene was not prepared to take the initiative when confronted with the largeness and complexity of his new school, and no one came to draw him in. No counselors sought him out; no one brought him to meetings; no one applied pressure such as, we brought you in here; now you are required to do this or that. Greene negotiated the university system as if it were high school: "It didn't seem that different from high school. And I knew how to do high school. You sign up for the classes you want and you go."

He now wonders, "Where, in the whole EOP admission process, was the recognition of or concern for my family or the community I came from?" He says that being made a special admit was "like a kidnapping—no special day for parents of EOP students—nor any effort to involve them in my education."

The freshman experience of Wayne Green was not unlike that of other EOP students, or of many other students (whether or not admitted via a special admissions program) in the late 1960s and even thereafter. Where his path diverged, and where he exemplifies the extreme of the political reality of special admissions, is in what happened next. In 1968, Greene became involved with an off-campus draft resistance group. This was not unusual, as such activities, especially in Berkeley, were in keeping with the climate of the times. Young people were actively expressing their disenchantment with the system. In Greene's case, the group with which he affiliated contained few university students. Only one other member was African American, and none of the others was adolescent—18 or younger. The other members were in their twenties. This was one of the many off-campus groups that operated on or near the university during the 1960s.

Greene describes the process of his engagement in the group as his having been "swept up. I didn't know what the consequences of getting involved would be. I would have probably gone to the first meeting—when they invited me to come back to their house and learn more about anti-war organizing," but, he says he "would definitely have drawn the line at dropping out of school." As a student, he had respectable goals. He would major in political science and then, probably, head to law school.

But this student's academic fate was sealed early on. In participating with the anti-war group, he was caught up in one of the infamous "People's Park" demonstrations concerning the University's appropriation of a popular park near campus. Things happened quickly. The demonstration flowed onto the campus. Someone, a White man, threw a Molotov cocktail from the campus into the street at some policemen. It exploded. A couple of California highway patrolmen were severely burned. Two days later, Wayne Greene was arrested on the street for this crime. As he describes the arrest, "Four police pulled up. Screeching brakes. . . . About a dozen University of California police in full riot gear jumped out of the car and said, 'Wayne Greene, you are under arrest,' and they threw me into the back of the police car and took me to the U.C. police station." He had absolutely no idea why it was that he was being arrested.

As I discussed this event with Greene, I was surprised to hear that these were university police. He explained that "the whole case was generated from within the University of California Police Department. The two main witnesses who claimed to have seen me throw the bomb were campus cops." Greene was held for two days and then released on bail. Two days after that, when he was arraigned, he found out what the actual charges were. Although the arresting officers were campus police and the case against Greene was originally brought by the University of California, it was turned over to the District Attorney's Office of Alameda county (where U.C. Berkeley is located) for prosecution.

As soon as he was arraigned, Greene quit going to classes. No one from the EOP office came to see him. Wayne received

Incompletes and F's for the entire semester. Looking back, older and wiser, he sees that he might have handled this differently to facilitate his later readmission. But he did not have the foresight or the maturity, amidst the chaos and anguish of the events following the unjust arrest, to understand this.

It is unlikely that Greene's professors and the EOP office were unaware of what was happening to him, as the story was all over the press. Greene's case—including the lack of official support from the university community—became a political issue. The person who did throw the bomb was not African American, but the student arrested for the crime was African American—and he was an EOP student. As Greene assesses the politics of the situation:

> The EOP students on Berkeley's campus certainly did cause more political embarrassment to the university than any other single group there. The university people got their hands on a bunch of kids who had social consciousness, who had some kind of political savvy and a sense of responsibility and who were really eager to use that knowledge right away. We were not going to wait until after we graduated or after we had our degrees or after we were making lots of money to go back into the community. . . . One of the grass-roots messages coming to Black kids in colleges was: "don't forget where you came from. Don't get up there and get your nose in the air and think that you're better than everybody else or forget that you came from poor communities." So there was a split that was going on—trying to be in the university community, get an education, aspire to that way of life, those ideals, and be academic and, at the same time, be active in your community. It was a tough split . . . a lot of kids dropped out because they couldn't deal with trying to be in two places at the same time. . . . Very few of the EOP students I knew personally graduated.

When Greene was finally acquitted, his attorney, Vincent Hallinan, demanded the resignation of Alameda County District Attorney Frank Vukota, claiming that Vukota was fully aware that Greene did not throw the bomb but prosecuted him anyway. Hallinan also charged Vukota with attempting to suppress police records identifying another person as the one who had thrown the bomb.[13]

Being acquitted, while a great relief for Greene and his family, did not automatically lead to the restoration of Greene's student status at U.C. Berkeley. This is not surprising. Acquittal came from the county court system. Reinstatement would have to come from the state-run university, an entirely separate organizational body. Greene's attorney advised him to petition the student body senate to advocate for his readmission. He did so and was readmitted on probationary status. But, in his words, "I didn't make it though. Too much pressure, too little (if any) administrative support, too much of an outside life in the intervening eighteen months, too much water under the bridge."

Greene, once a special admit invited into the U.C. system by the EOP, was now left alone by all portions of the bureaucracy that had once sought his presence as a part of a massive effort to adjust the ratio of Whites to minorities in higher education. But why should this be surprising? The EOP, unaware or unprepared to coach its early intakes, had never really sought Greene out to help him while he was a student who had not been in any trouble.

Retention and Graduation

The story of Wayne Greene is an extreme case. Yet, many of the special admits I interviewed commented that they have felt and still feel rather unsupported in the university setting. Nevertheless, a great deal has been learned since those early years of special admissions. Above all, it is now well understood that admission into and enrollment in a university does not ensure graduation from it. As during the affirmative action years, admissions policies shifted to take in students who, for whatever reasons, may be less-prepared for the academic, social, and financial pressures of the university, two very basic measures became and now will remain increasingly critical: retention rates and graduation rates. The first of these measures is often defined as the *one-year retention rate*. This measure simply determines how many students actually make it through the first year. The retention rate is formally defined by the Office of Student Research at U.C. Berkeley as "the percent of an entering class either graduated or still enrolled at a given point in time . . . calculated on a beginning-of-fall-to-beginning-of-fall term basis."[14] In admitting students who may be less likely to thrive in the university environment (again for an array of reasons including cultural conflicts, prejudice, lack of preparation, economic stress, and so forth), the risk is that these special students may exhibit a higher drop-out rate than the norm for the student body. Over the years, their retention rates have been significantly lower than the norm; however, with increased attention from the university, these are improving. At U.C. Berkeley, the one-year retention rate has varied markedly by ethnic group. In 1991, this rate was 93 percent for regularly admitted students (based entirely on academic merit) and was an all-time high (to that date) of 83 percent for special action admits (based on academic merit plus other, nonacademic criteria).[15] This latter statistic was boosted to 89 percent by a marked increase in the Hispanic one-year retention rate.[16]

The other measure that took on increased significance is the "graduation rate" itself. This measure simply determines how many students actually make it all the way through college and through graduation. Graduation rates, according to the U.C. Berkeley Office of Student Research, are calculated in terms of "elapsed time since initial enrollment and not the amount of time students actually have been enrolled." We thus speak in terms of four-year, five-year, and six-year graduation rates.

Graduation exceeds retention in value.[17] It is a quite important accomplishment for a student to survive the first year at a university. It is more significant actually to complete the program and graduate with a baccalaureate degree.

Across the board, there has been a general increase in the overall graduation rate of all students, regardless of ethnicity. The U.C. Berkeley 1984, 1985, and 1986 freshman classes had, respectively, 69 percent, 71 percent, and 73 percent five-year graduation rates (within five years). National studies reveal that this is quite high, with the average six-year (within six years) graduation rate at similar universities being 52 percent.[18] The most marked improvement has been among the special action admits,[19] up 3 percent for all ethnic groups from 1982–1991, and up from 22 percent to 33 percent for African Americans, 28 percent to 35 percent for Hispanics, and 38 percent to 51 percent for Whites. However, special admission to the university often necessitates special efforts by the admitting university to retain and graduate these special students. Is it possible to provide adequate assistance? How far should a university go in order to do so? Is anything short of total commitment to the success of special students neglect of them?

As policies broadened to increase diversity, educational institutions learned something very important. It became apparent that even when a student is not admitted as a special admit, a student may have special characteristics that must be addressed by a university if this university desires high retention and graduation rates. Whose needs should be the highest priority?

Admissions of Guilt, but Whose?

But wait. Everybody is wrong and everyone has been wronged. No one is blameless. Regardless of the role one has played in the subordination of one ethnic or social group to another, one is a participant in, or at least an heir to, the process. In the spirit of social activism, unless one is part of the solution, one is part of the problem. So move over. Make room for others like you. And unlike you. We all have a right to be here, don't we?

Liberalized admissions policies became instruments of social remediation—devices designed to right perceived wrongs, to redress recognized grievances, to correct uncomfortable imbalances. That admissions policies have not fully succeeded in remediating social problems is not news. That these policies have and still are actually generating new wrongs, fresh grievances, and further imbalances—and that these policies are therefore sometimes counterproductive interventions or, worse yet, iatrogenic interventions (in themselves problem-causing)—comes as a stunning blow. Now what do we do? Do we repeal affirmative action and liberalized admissions? What do we do with the huddled masses still yearning to breathe free?

With all that has transpired in recent decades, it is difficult to dispute the notion that admissions policies can actually result in, rather than only relieve, disparities in educational opportunity. Admissions policies *select* by different criteria—or different mixes of criteria—at different colleges and universities. This fact alone is enough to demonstrate that opportunities for higher education vary, are not everywhere the same for everyone, and are thus unequal. The selectivity of admissions varies tremendously among colleges, and this selectivity becomes the brutal and uneven arbiter of life chances.

Selectivity and the Promotion of Excellence

Selectivity may be brutal, but for those who are selected, it is most beneficent. The most selective, most elite universities provide a rich academic environment for applicants who are perceived to have great promise. Why shouldn't at least some of our institutions seek to identify, recruit, admit, and educate those they deem best and brightest?

Selectivity manifests itself differently at various universities. At some, especially the most elite private universities, recruitment plays a powerful role in the selection. A director of admissions at one of the top private universities in the United States tells us, "At this university, we have some relatively simple objectives. We're trying to recruit a pool from which we can then choose to admit individual people, students, who will provide the most promising set of talents and enterprise to contribute to society later."[20]

Elite universities find that the active recruiting of ideal applicants facilitates a very highly selective and very specialized case-by-case admissions process. In each admissions decision, such a university works hard to balance not just academic ability but also other capacities to take the best advantage that the university has to offer. An admissions officer at one of these elite schools explains, "Our calculation of making that decision is not, and has never been, based on any formula. Each case is presented and discussed often, many times, by various groups of committee members. Folders are read many times, cases are presented, and people get in by a vote, and then by a repeated vote, because cases are compared again and again against each other." This person described this sort of admissions procedure as "a very individually centered process."[21]

When I interviewed administrators at elite private universities, I asked whether or not their schools, as private institutions, have more latitude in admissions processes and policies than do public institutions.[22] They all said yes: "Totally," one responds. "This is an institution supported by private American money, and we make whatever decisions we choose to make." Another official, this one at a major Ivy League institution, adds, "We have a great sense of social obligation. We are different from some of our other American educational institutions in that we have always intended to produce people who will be participants in society. We are not, and have never been, primarily in the business of producing college teachers or scholars. . . . We have produced more than our share of very fine scholars, but most of our students are not interested in scholarly careers."

Selectivity at such elite private universities is a specialized identification process, one that looks at individuals in terms of not only their academic abilities and their near futures but also their potential for marked contributions throughout adulthood. An admissions official explaining the long view talks about half a century of potential:

> We're looking for that thing that's going to make a difference later when you meet the graduate fifty years down the road. We're not so concerned, because our applicant pool is very strong, and we've taken pains to be sure that it is, with figuring out whether someone will have an A average as opposed to an A-minus average. We're really not admitting someone for four years. We're admitting someone to be here for four years and then go on to develop throughout adulthood. We hope to give them a good academic advantage, and then have them go do something constructive for fifty years.

The task of spotting this long-term potential is a tremendous undertaking for an admissions officer. "Our job in America has always been, at least for this century, to try to produce captains of industry and contributors to the professions. And that's what we've been successful doing. That's a fifty-year test run that's not a four-year GPA kind of thing." So the demand for higher education at these schools increases with their reputation for having successful graduates. "Almost 90 percent of our applicants this year were well qualified to do the work academically, according to the external measures [test scores and curriculum in high school, and how well they did in that], and we were able to admit 14 percent of our applicants this year."

Selectivity and Inequality

Selectivity is therefore a restriction process. The degree to which a particular admissions policy restricts access to a particular college or university is, in the professional texts, described as its "selectivity."[23] Although selectivity assumes a variety of faces, in college admissions, its traditional elements are the selecting of students for their academic merits, academic aptitudes, family backgrounds, and financial wherewithal. But selection has a hidden face. Although selectivity determines the opportunity for admission to higher education, it also has a strong impact on what researchers call "educational outcome." This is logical. Selectivity actually restricts the possibility of the desired outcome—graduation—by narrowing the opportunity to only those who have been admitted. Moreover, highly selective admissions policies actively seek to enhance this same desired outcome, aiming to bring in students who are certain to graduate and perform well after graduation. This way the school looks good. Why admit students who will make the school look as if it does not educate its students well?

The matter is not so very cut and dried, however. To say that traditional selectivity is entirely responsible for what are described as educational inequalities is a gross oversimplification. Although educational opportunity is indeed unequally allocated by admissions policies, variations in the academic preparedness of applicants as well as the educational outcomes of students once they are admitted are also the product of a multitude of other factors including the quality of high school preparation, the student's motivation, the college campus environment, the peer associations formed, and the economic pressures faced by students. Our understanding and application of selectivity is especially hindered in the overlap between selectivity for academic merit and for motivation. The picture is further muddled if selectivity also, in some way, selects for resilience in the face of economic and other environmental and peer pressures.

In this manner, selectivity is a form of insurance: the selection or admissions process serves the ultimate purpose of ensuring society a return on its investment in each particular student's education. As professors Ernest Pascarella (University of Chicago) and Patrick Terenzini (Pennsylvania State University) point out, although it is relatively apparent that a bachelor's degree "provides a sound return on one's investment," why this is so is not as clear.[24] Two independent explanations have emerged, both well-supported by evidence.

The first explanation, which I call the *development explanation*, is the "human capital or socialization hypothesis," which says that "college graduates earn more than high school graduates because college provides the former with cognitive skills and/or personal traits that make them more productive employees."[25] The second explanation, which I call the *identification explanation*, is the "screening or certification" hypothesis, which says that "college does not so much influence the cognitive and personal traits related to productivity as simply certify . . . those who are most likely to have those traits to begin with."[26] It is in this second explanation that is buried the argument against a broadening of admissions policy: a loosening of selectivity to the level of social remediation. If college merely screens or certifies, then the B.A. is only as valuable as the admissions policy—or as the admissions policy plus the dropout rate.

It is not entirely clear whether selectivity is primarily a selection of students with development potential or if it is an identification of students already most likely to succeed. There is considerable evidence supporting both the development and the identification explanations, and it is most probable that both not only are reasonably plausible but also are relatively valid explanations.

It is important to ask just what kind of success can a highly selective admissions process actually ensure? The relationship between admissions selectivity and college outcome is, no matter how statistically correlated, ambiguous. We just do not know exactly why some things happen. Not even a scientific statistical analysis can really pinpoint truth. Any honest examination of the causes of inequality must begin with this fundamental admission. Furthermore, inequality itself is one of those general terms used as a "garbage pail diagnosis" for a whole host of social problems.

Let us take a look at college quality. After all, competition for places at the most selective colleges and universities is occurring because the general opinion is that these are the best schools—that they are of high quality. Students, parents, and employers all consider the "quality" of institutions granting the B.A. degree they require. Yet, quality itself is as slippery as any other definition discussed here. Mainstream, traditional analyses determine college quality in terms of selectivity, resources, and cost.[27] A school that is difficult to get into, has a lot of money, and charges high tuition must be a good one!

Recent studies show that the magnification of earnings achieved by graduating from college is potentiated significantly by college quality. While going to college will increase the graduate's income, going to a good college increases it more. Indeed, the overall impact of the quality of the college attended, when measured in terms of earnings, shows earnings increasing 15 to 30 percent by having attended a "quality" school.[28] Simply stated, from the identification perspective, earning a B.A. at a highly selective college with an excellent reputation, one that typically charges high tuition, really pays off. Why? A degree from an elite college may simply screen for the talent and ambition required to earn more money later in life. Also, a graduate of an elite institution may receive preferential treatment from employers. Whether employers believe the quality of the graduate has been developed by the college or that it merely has been identified by the college may not be relevant to employers. However, Pascarella and Terenzini suggest that, from the standpoint of the identification arguments, a degree from an elite institution, which enrolls and then certifies "high level talent" acts as an "inexpensive selection or screening device."[29] You don't send your kids to Harvard for a better education; you send them there to improve their prospects after graduation.

Do the elite universities do anything special beyond screening and certifying? Do they educate in a way that actually enhances human potential better than less elite schools? This is a key question. It hits home. It interrogates for truth the nature of an educational opportunity at an elite university, an opportunity that is scarce and restricted to an elite group of students who pass admissions and financial hurdles.

Although the research findings are mixed, the predominant finding is that college selectivity and related college prestige have little or no impact on either the job productivity or the job performance of students in the first few years following their graduations.[30] Although analysts are debating whether or not immediate postgraduation job performance is enhanced by a more selective college, something more important to many students—earnings—may be. Inasmuch as college reputation and college selectivity, both used by researchers as determinants of college quality, cannot be unraveled, there may be some weight to findings which show that college reputation positively influences starting salary.[31]

Either way, the picture becomes clearer later in adulthood. Much of the research demonstrates that salaries of students from elite universities are increasingly affected as the years past graduation add up. While their starting salaries may not be significantly increased by the fact that they graduated from highly selective colleges, the rate of salary increase they experience over time is markedly impacted by the selectivity of the college from which they graduated.[32] What a young person does in the now will, in the long run, affect his or her future.

When comparing public and private schools, the data on the effects of college selectivity and college reputation are now somewhat inconclusive. It is no longer certain that it is better to attend a big name private university than it is a public one. The issue is more one of the reputation, size, and selectivity of the school, as opposed to its public or private status. In their thorough review of the research, Pascarella and Terenzini conclude "that a significant net earnings advantage accrues to individuals who attend major research universities . . . and that a correspondingly small disadvantage accrues to those who attend unselective liberal arts colleges."[33] Again, it is the degree of selectivity that has a great effect. Admission to an unselective liberal arts college says very little about one's identity. The identification effect of an unselective college or university is negligible. Furthermore, from the development perspective, the public tends to presume that greater development takes place at a big name research institution, whether or not this is true, and increasingly these days, whether or not it is a private Ivy League school.

Although no one—not students or parents or employers or researchers or educators—can prove what it is that makes a college education contribute to the quality of one's life, everyone seems to know that being admitted to whatever is most widely known as a good school can make a big difference. Although the generalities upon which our opinions are based are astoundingly irrational, we tend to believe that in the end, admissions processes can make or break a life. As we move into an even more competitive meritocracy, those with the highest merits—degrees from what are perceived to be the best universities—are best equipped to compete. Without merit, one is doomed to mediocrity, a life of irreversible "averageness."

Recruiting for Selection

By comparison with public universities, private universities experience little government involvement in their admissions policies. Instead of being ever responsive to state mandates such as the fair representation legislation that was enacted in California, private universities are relatively autonomous. Contrast the admissions processes at a private university to see the differences and similarities with public schools. We have looked at length at U.C. Berkeley, a very large public university. Now, consider Brown, a medium-sized private university. Brown University, located in Providence, Rhode Island, had an undergraduate student body of 5,905 in 1993. Brown receives annually about 13,000 applications for freshman admission and admits about 2,800, or some 22 percent of all these applicants.[34] The majority (probably 85 percent) of all applicants to Brown are in the top 10 percent of their high school class.[35] This percentage is in no way state mandated; it simply comes about. This suggests that there is a powerful self-selection process taking place prior to Brown's own admissions process. This also means that Brown has a relatively top-of-the-line applicant pool from which to select.

At Brown, every applicant file is brought to committee; each receives the personal attention of admissions officers. Michael Goldberger, director of admissions at Brown, describes selection at Brown as "a very subjective process."[36] There is no specific academic index used as a criterion for admission. In fact, the academic index is not calculated until after admissions are completed each year. It is done at this point in the process to ensure that athletic recruits are "representative of the student body" and not outside the academic range of other students who have been admitted. On shifting the emphasis away from selection, Goldberger says, "The message seems to be: the more selective you are, the better you are. But I don't know what this means. It is, perhaps, better to look at applicant pools, with the goal of pursuing applicants. Creating the right applicant pool is critical. Recruiting is at least as important as selection."[37]

Can recruiting and selection make or break a life? These days, the thought of being average, living at the midpoint of the bell curve is no longer pleasant. Not being picked to play in the big leagues looks like losing the game. Even if we were willing to allow ourselves mediocrity or to accept not being selected, we certainly would not want to accept this for our children. Nowadays, being average is a plight deemed unfair. In the pluralistic mind, college recruitment and selectivity have emerged as a counterpoint to fairness, a threat to our children, a predator consuming or denying our human rights. Our futures are at stake. We, the huddled masses continue to yearn. But for what exactly?

Matching as a New Form of Selection

Recruitment, by nature, takes place before selection. Another form of fitting the student to the institution is called "matching," which can take place either before or after admission. Those who would question the fairness of admissions policy must carefully examine the issue of matching and the ensuing problem of "mismatching." Students who are inappropriately admitted are actually hurt by these so-called special opportunities. Controversial author and educator Thomas Sowell, senior fellow at the Stanford University Hoover Institute contends that "mismatching" turns "prospects of success" into "failures."[38]

Recall fair representation. This profile of the population must not only be apparent at admission, it must also be there at graduation. Critics of the U.C. Berkeley admissions policy to accept half of all freshmen on a mix of criteria, rather than on the purely academic criteria to which the other half are subjected, point to the gaps in graduation rates among racial groups. They note that the graduation rate for Hispanic and African-American students, the majority of whom entered Berkeley during the affirmative action era by way of Tier 2, which involves more than merely academic merit, has been little over half that of the graduation rate for Whites and Asian-American students,[39] many more of whom entered the university based purely on academic criteria.

Critics of affirmative action–type admissions argue that it is unreasonable to admit students in the name of fair representation who cannot perform at the level of U.C. Berkeley and that these students may not be well matched to this university. Let's dissect this argument. First, it is improbable that policy encourages admissions without the institutional and individual goal of graduation. What is more likely is that one or both of the following assumptions drive Tier-2 and special action admissions: either these students are properly matched in the first place, and/or they can be made to match University of California subsequent to admission. In the latter case, post-admission matching is expected. Matching can be ad hoc, by means of a general acculturation to the academic environment of the university,[40] or matching can be more directed, with post-admission matching being a specific goal of officially designated supportive services on campus.[41] Such directed post-admission matching is designed to help ensure the graduation of admits.

The debate over matching is clear. To assert that matching can be accomplished after admission assumes that the university environment can indeed develop the abilities that influence academic performance.[42] To assert that matching cannot be accomplished after admission to a demanding educational environment, such as that at U.C. Berkeley, assumes that the mismatching generated at admission cannot be corrected. Several related assumptions may support the latter side of this debate. One assumption is that young adulthood is too late in life for a university or any environment to have such an effect, that elementary through high school years are the times when the real matching must take place. The other is that the educational technology necessary for the university environment to have such influence is nascent or lacking.[43] Someday, we will know how to match, but we are still learning.

Although it has been argued that adequate pre-admission matching did not occur at U.C. Berkeley, the facts appear to contradict this argument. During the 1980s and well into the 1990s, while affirmative action admissions were at work, the overall academic merit of the student body *increased* rather than decreased. The average SAT score of all entering students climbed. Although GPA for Asian-American and White admits is currently 4.0 and their average SAT is 1,260, the high school GPA for underrepresented minorities is also very high, 3.5, and their average SAT is 1,040.[44] While there is a gap between the two GPA and SAT averages, the lower of the two is certainly not a poor academic presentation. Any way one looks at a high school GPA of 3.5 and an SAT of 1,040, it is undeniable that this is a relatively high-quality applicant. So what is it that so many parents, students, professors, and administrators have complained about?

Reverse Discrimination

For one thing, the gap between a high school GPA of 3.5 and one of 4.0 may sound small, but in terms of numbers of turn-aways, it is quite large. Critics of liberalized admissions calculate that, in the liberalized admissions process of the nineties, an African American with a high school GPA of 3.5 and an SAT score of 1,200 (out of 1,600) was 2,000 percent more likely to be admitted to U.C. Berkeley than an Asian American with the same GPA and SAT score.[45] This means that a large number of Asian Americans and Whites with high academic criteria were being turned away, while persons of other races were being admitted with lower GPA's and SAT's. Fair begins to look highly subjective. Several investigations are still underway at the time of this writing, being conducted by the Office of Civil Rights of the U.S. Department of Education, into what has been called the "aggressive" affirmative action policy in admissions at U.C. Berkeley.[46] Many in the press suggest that the studies will find the policy amounts to a form of reverse discrimination against White and Asian-American applicants.[47] This is the way the concept of reverse discrimination—its very possibility—has filtered into American consciousness, as is piercingly obvious in the heated debates over affirmative action in college admissions and hiring.

A related, but different, investigation of Harvard's admissions practices was closed by the U.S. Department of Education in 1993.[48] This case involved the giving of preference in admissions to alumni or "legacy children" and its allegedly negative effects on the admission rates of highly qualified Asian Americans to Harvard. Harvard's contention was that it was important—essential—to maintain good relations with its alumni. Although Harvard conceded that this preference did indeed result in a lower acceptance rate for Asian Americans than for students of other ethnic backgrounds, the Education Department chose not to challenge Harvard regarding this practice.[49]

The U.S. Office of Civil Rights found that, while they were "similarly qualified," only 13.2 percent of Harvard's Asian-American applicants as compared with 17.4 percent of its White applicants had been admitted over the past decade.[50] Presented with the findings of the investigation of Harvard's admissions practices, then Deputy Assistant Secretary of Education for Civil Rights Policy,

Richard D. Komer, claimed that Harvard had provided "reasonable, defensible justification." Nevertheless, several leading members of the Asian-American community protested, with claims such as, "No link was shown between admissions policy and alumni giving," and the investigation itself showed a "lack of diligence."[51]

These events overshadow the activities of admissions offices everywhere across the country. With the potential for federal investigation and legal action looming, admissions officers cannot help but be wary, secretive, and closed about their practices.[52] I certainly found this to be true in my interviews with these people.

So much has been done in the name of ethnic diversity that many who were once members of the dominant culture feel as if they are sinking. Yet, liberalized admissions policy recognizes that diversity is more than ethnic variation. No single attribute can earn a student the highest score on the social diversity rating used in the admissions process. Even geographical diversity plays a significant role in the admissions decision these days.[53]

Racism Versus Multiculturalism: Masks on the Same Face?

Even the "Pledge of Allegiance," which many baby boomers remember saying daily in grade school, has come to sound like a dead platitude: "I pledge allegiance to the flag of the United States of America . . . and to the republic for which it stands, one nation under God, indivisible."[54] Are we indivisible? Has liberty and justice for all been achieved? Will it ever be achieved? Is it possible to provide liberty and justice to all social groups at once? What would this look like if we were able to achieve it?

Perhaps we have achieved liberty and justice for all and this is how it looks: a continual balancing and rebalancing of opportunity; a continual monitoring of ourselves and our institutions, especially by those who perceive the presence of injustice—the restriction of access to opportunity.

If the university of tomorrow is a stage, a theater in which we act out the growing pains of a nation in transition, then the ongoing drama of justice is an endless play with no conclusion. Such a university becomes a mirror of our society living on the edge of the future. Ever present, immense issues are highlighted by the university. We must all become students of this process of transition from the twentieth century into the twenty-first. We must all enroll in the courses that our national and our global citizenship provide—lessons in freedom, liberty, justice, and opportunity, and lessons in sharing the planet with a diverse array of people.

Lessons in Racism

Books can be great teachers, especially to their own authors. I have found this to be very much the case in writing *Shameful Admissions*. I heard some unexpected cries from the broken gate during my interviews for this book: I was indeed startled to find that some of these were mine—mine and those of some of my closest associates! *Could we, even those of us who fancy ourselves proponents of justice and disseminators of opportunity, be racists?*

An elementary school child who was present for a public reading of this chapter interrupted at this point and demanded to know, "What is a racist?"

I began immediately to answer and then stopped myself short. "Well," she demanded again, "what is a racist? Don't you know?"

"I, I, uh." I grinned foolishly. "I know, at least I think I know, but let's see what the dictionary says it is."

"Racism" but not racist appeared as an entry in the *American Heritage Dictionary of the English Language*. Racism was defined as "the notion that one's own ethnic stock is superior." I read this definition to my listeners.

"Then a racist is one who believes in racism, at least the racism which holds his ethnic stock superior," one of my audience added.

I had raised the question, "Could we be racists?" and I returned to it, suggesting that, even if we did not as individuals appear to meet the dictionary definition of racist, we might be participants in belief systems that had racist components.

These days, our understanding of racism goes well beyond its traditional dictionary definitions. This is because, more than ever, we are enlarging our unit of analysis from self to social system. Now we begin to say that crime is the product of more than one individual's illegal behavior. Child abuse is the result of something much larger than one parent's poor handling of a child. School failure is not only the failure of a student to perform. In analyzing problems such as crime, abuse, school failure, and poverty, the enlarged unit of analysis places greater emphasis on the social system than on the individual. The benefit of this shift in analysis is a wider focus on social problems, a focus likely to capture more of the whole picture. The downside of this shift in analysis from focus on self to focus on system is that the temptation to blame the system for all difficulties dilutes personal and even institutional responsibility down to a thin, ever-evaporating stream of vapor. We can say I haven't discriminated against you; the system has. I haven't denied you opportunity; the system has. This university hasn't discriminated against you; the system has. This university hasn't denied you opportunity; the larger social system in which this university exists has generated a situation in which you are not prepared to compete for admission to this university.

So where, if anywhere, is the racism? I asked several of the people I interviewed for this book. Tony Rey, director of the admissions committee at the University of California, San Diego (UCSD), in the early 1970s,[55] adeptly related this question to the matter of admissions policy. The discussion we had captures such an important part of the college admissions story that I have included several portions of it.

The adjustment of college admissions as a means of correcting social injustices was a new idea at the time Dr. Rey took his position in that admissions office. According to Rey, we were all quite naive about racism back then. In the fall of 1970, Rey was hired by

UCSD to serve as an assistant dean of students and was given the title of admissions committee director. As the story goes, this admissions committee was charged by the regents of the University of California to come up with what were being called "variance criteria" for the admission of students to the university.

Variance criteria. These words contain an entire chapter of admissions policy history. I asked Rey about these criteria. He explained that "variance criteria was a deviation from the standard admissions parameters such as a grade B or better on a core curriculum of classes taken in high school. There were some classes that students had to get a B or better on to get into the University of California. In predominantly minority neighborhoods, schools did not offer some of those classes, so it was institutionally impossible for minority students to qualify for U.C."

"When you say 'did not offer the classes,'" I asked, "do you mean that the teachers did not teach these courses or that the students did not take them?"

"The school was not providing the course," he responded and then explained further, "Let's say second-year mathematics. I think you had to have three years of mathematics and in some inner-city schools there was no third year. There was first-year algebra, first-year geometry, no trig. That's just a hypothetical example of an institutional barrier."

An "institutional barrier." This is a kind of organizational wall, a wall that blocks entry into the kingdom of opportunity. The blocking may not be explicit or planned; it may just evolve and continue over time long enough to become part of the woodwork. In this case, the kingdom of opportunity was a "good" university. I asked Rey how his admissions committee chose to tackle the problem.

He had an interesting story. He explained that once he filled the position of assistant dean of admissions, he was enmeshed in a major effort to remediate social wrongs—to bring down social barriers to admission. Rey claimed that the strategy was simple: "We found White and frequently White Jewish kids, many of whom were likely to be young feminists and high school Marxists, likely to be quite politically liberal, who were ceiling the SAT and had top grades. We wanted to create a community out of the campus, one where people would interact—where the White kids and the kids coming out of the barrios and ghettos would interact."

Create a community where people of various ethnic cultures interact. Do this on campus. This sounds, even today, to be a marvelous plan. Yet, now we know so much more about racism and its stubbornness and its resistance to its own demise. As Rey told me, "We thought these groups—liberal Whites, together with Blacks and Hispanics of lower socioeconomic status (SES)—would be predisposed to not be racist." Rey sighed. "That was before we understood the nature of racism. Back then we thought racism was bigotry and prejudice and discrimination."

"What is racism perceived to be now?" I pursued this discussion.

"Now we know it to be a cultural phenomenon, an institutionalized belief system," Rey replied.

Institutionalized Racism

"Dr. Rey, when you talk about an institutionalized racism in terms of admissions policy, would you use the term, 'institutionalized exclusion'?"

"Right, or 'systematic exclusion,'" he responded.

"So, you are saying that racially biased admissions policies are part of the social process: of systematic exclusion."

"Yes, as Professor Mario Barrera showed, there are three basic ways of explaining underachievement by minority people. There are those who claim that there is a genetic biological component. There is the sociological explanation that economic and certain other environmental factors inhibit people from performing up to snuff. But the explanation that has won out—Barrera laid it out— is that there are systematic patterns of institutionalized policy that account best for low performance."

"Might we call this 'differential policy'?"

"Well, actually, it is differential impact of policy. Differential impact is a euphemism for racism. Institutionalized differential impact is palatable to the majority. Anybody can see that. But when you confront White people with the ideas that institutionalized patterns of exclusion are reflections of their own ideology and that we can call their subconscious ideology racism, most of them freak out, because to them, racists are like the Ku Klux Klan, the skinheads; they think those are the racists."

Institutional Irrelevance

Rey told me that seeing higher education as the solution to the problems of the poor is a romantic notion and that "there are still a lot of romantic minority people who see higher education as the solution." He also said that he was once "also fully committed to that view: in other words, we increase the number of engineers, architects, physicians, school teachers, chemists, et cetera and then we send them back into their own ethnic communities."

"Well?" I asked him, "Were you wrong?"

I saw him shrug and shake his head. "We didn't take into account that so many of them would choose not to come back to their communities—that they would choose to go out of their own communities to work, in other words, to climb out."

"So, broadened access to higher education had some negative side effects?"

"Right. Two things happened." He went on, "First, most people from poor communities wanted to escape and saw education as a way out. That was something that we should have been more concerned about when we opened up college admissions. After all, all of us who were already there at the university were escapees. . . . And, second, something we never imagined and no one ever talked about . . . the minority birth rate was just too high. And the Chicano and Latino immigration rate was too high. . . . Well, we kind of foresaw this, but refused to believe this would happen . . . that everything would become totally unmanageable."

I heard a new sort of absolutism in his voice now. "So what are you saying with all this?" I inquired.

"We're at the point today where the discussion about college admissions and equal opportunity, which you wanted to have with me, is irrelevant to the well-being of the minority community."

"This discussion is irrelevant?" I wondered.

Rey became more assertive. He told me that he did not think that the broken gate of college admissions had a positive effect. "Now, at the turn of this century, with existing information technology, the university is irrelevant."

Frustrated Students and Teachers in the Diverse Classroom

Higher education trudges on through thick and thin, similar to the U.S. Postal Service ideal, to serve the people through rain, sleet, and snow. Higher education insists that it delivers what it calls an education. This is hard work. One professor, clearly frustrated by the changes in his classroom, practically cried on my shoulder:

A few years back, when student reviews rated me low because of my lack of attention to ethnic issues, I worked hard to build sensitivity to ethnic issues into the content of my lectures. But I continued to receive low ratings in the area of attention to ethnic issues. I subsequently increased my attention to ethnicity and diversity several times, each time with negligible effect on my ratings. Eventually, I realized that I had shifted the focus of my class from its actual content to more of how its content was relevant to and varying by race. One day an irate student raised her hand and advised me to shift my emphasis away from relevance to ethnicity and toward relevance to social class. She sounded as if she felt this would be an advancement on my part. She was too young to remember that that's where we were before the rising emphasis on ethnic diversity: concern regarding social class. I found myself discouraged, surprised and quite frustrated. I felt defensive. I muttered something about how professors were supposed to take ethnic diversity into their curricula, and this was what I had been trying to do.

This professor was kind enough to introduce me to the student who had made these remarks. I was fascinated to hear her explanation. The young Hispanic woman, named Anna Maria, began apologetically, "Maybe I was too harsh with the professor. He really is a very good teacher. He cares a lot and tries to do the right thing. It's just that all this diversity stuff is getting to me. I feel so stereotyped." She went on, "I'm Mexican, and I am not necessarily more like some other Mexican than I am like some other person who is not Mexican."

I commented to Anna Maria that she sounded upset about this stereotyping. I asked her if this was something she experienced frequently. "Yes, professors seem to assume that I need special help just because I am Mexican. People think I was admitted so that there will be enough of my type on campus. But what's worse is that socially I am treated a certain way here because I am Mexican. I was at an event last weekend and I met a guy. He seemed to like me a lot. Then he asked, 'What country in the Middle East are you from?' When I told him I was Mexican, he wasn't interested in me anymore. He just said, 'See you later.'"

I asked Anna Maria what this stereotyping was about. She said, "It's a control thing. If people can say, 'I know what you are,' 'You're this' or 'You're that,' then they can control you. They can put you in an ethnic category and leave you there. So all Mexicans should be the same. This is the weird side of all this diversity stuff."

Color Grading: Academic Stereotyping for Convenience and Control

The stereotyping experienced by Anna Maria is not unusual, not socially and not in the university classroom. It is as if this sort of stereotyping comes along with the mixing of peoples who might not otherwise come in close contact. That hasty assumptions regarding academic ability are made according to skin color should not be a surprise. Hasty assumptions regarding everything from honesty to criminality to diligence to intentions have been made according to race.

Implicit but Pervasive Stereotyping

Ethnic and cultural diversification of campuses may be inevitable; it may be necessary; it may be desirable; yet it has its complications. One of these is pervasive and often implicit stereotyping.

Let's back away to gain a wide-angle view and look at the context in which Anna Maria's experience occurred. In California, as in several other parts of the country, the cultural diversity of the general public is increasing more rapidly than the cultural diversity of the pool of high academic achievers, at least as measured by traditional standards. Confronted with different rates in the progress of these trends and with ongoing political conflict over what to do about them, authors of higher education admissions policies enter a territory where trade-offs, compromises, and the ongoing redefining of priorities are increasingly deemed not only valuable but essential.

We know that admissions policies of the 1990s and the new millennium are, whether or not they do it fairly, serving, and will continue to serve, an increasingly diverse public. This means that, more than ever, these policies answer to competing constituencies. With classrooms and campuses becoming more crowded, stereotyping is almost a survival—or at least a coping—skill. Why? The shorthand of relying on prejudice occurs as the time available for knowing individuals well diminishes. Stereotyping on campus is a natural consequence of mounting and myriad multicultural pressure.

There is no unified public from which to select students. Especially for public colleges and universities, the official goal of "public service" through admissions policy translates, once in action, to a patchwork kind of service delivered to a heterogeneous, fragmented mix of cultural *subpublics*. Things can become chaotic. Policy can fragment. In such a fragile atmosphere, we discover the power and the problems of the argument that says it is in the best interest of public service to call for across-the-board loosening rather than maintaining of those "highest academic standards," for a modification of standards on the grounds that traditionally defined standards were defined by the dominant culture, once largely White, along its rather narrow continuum of grades and test scores.

Such *standard shifting* is interpreted as a public service, a service to those socioeconomic groups, or subpublics, who may not be served by maintaining the traditional academic standards. In this line of thought, traditional standards are no longer viewed as standards. Instead, they are viewed as barriers by those who are denied educational opportunities at the most selective universities. Consistent with this view is the argument that barriers to higher educational opportunities result in later barriers to higher occupational opportunities, which, in turn, result in barriers to socioeconomic parity among the many subcultures within a society. Admissions policy can thus be seen as one of the most brutal barriers, and barriers are not readily broken. Even when standards are shifted somewhat, old perceptions can linger. Perhaps a more forceful shift is required. Yet, entire revolutions have been fought without people's minds changing, either for better or for worse.

Differential Access to Opportunity

It all boils down to the old nature-nurture debate. And here the oversimplification of stereotyping is as much a part of the thinking on one side as it is on the other.

The nurture side: Proponents of nurture say remove the barriers and inequality will fade. Everyone can learn. Nurture says mental ability is the product of the sociopolitical environment—the result of opportunities for, stimulation toward, and access to knowledge and mental development within the environment. The problem of access to opportunity is one that self-perpetuates in the absence of profound intervention on the level of social policy.

The nurture argument also says that higher education admissions policy can play a major role in redressing disparities of opportunity, that education is the currency of empowerment for individuals and social subgroups. On this side of the argument, barriers are all about withholding power from the masses or some subgroups of the masses. The old adage that "knowledge is power" is central to this view of a sociopolitical reality. Education is the source of the knowledge that is power. If the powerless are educated, they will become powerful. Higher education is considered an intervention on a citizen's environment; it is a powerful form of nurturing, one that counts on the ability of the mind to absorb information and to structure itself in response to the environment.

The nature side: Proponents of nature do not place much stock in barrier removal as a remediation of inequality. They see disparity as natural, part of human nature and difficult to alter. Proponents of nature note that although minority groups have experienced significant advances in access to all levels and components of education, this access has not resulted in equivalent changes in measured levels of intelligence. Along these lines, research scientist and professor Linda Gottfredson contends that although African-American–White differences in educational levels have been on a steady decline, the African-American–White difference in measured IQ, or general intelligence, "is not only very real but also very stubborn."[1] Proponents of nature say that what is borne out of the effort to use education as the solution to social problems may actually be a complication of these problems. Nurture—environmental interventions, that is, social remediation— may not be as powerful as is expected by adherents to the nurture side of the debate, according to adherents to the nature side. Therefore, the efforts of educators to alter people's fates fall far short of expectations and thus cost far too much. Nurture, according to nature advocates, is not the solution.

Regardless of which side of the debate, if any, one assumes, we see that many education policies not only fall short, they fall sloppily short. By the end of the 1980s, differential treatment of Asian Americans and non-Asian Americans in the admissions selection process at U.C. Berkeley had become the focus of public controversy. For most of the 1980s, from 1981 to 1987, Whites were gaining admission at a higher rate than Asian Americans[2] despite the fact that Asian-American applicants were scoring higher on academic criteria. At the same time, African-American and Hispanic applicants were gaining in their *relative likelihoods of admission*. What this relative likelihood signifies is that policy preferences are manifested in a sort of social cause calculus. For example, some critics of liberalized admissions policy claim that, as a result of affirmative action inspired efforts to balance opportunity, African-American and Hispanic applicants approached 2,000 percent greater likelihood of admission than Asian-American applicants with the same qualifications.[3] This is not just a minor relative difference. This is a huge gap in likelihood.

In his sweeping, hotly debated, and relatively one-sided critique, *Illiberal Education*, former White House–domestic policy analyst Dinesh D'Souza tells a now quite common sort of story, one of an Asian-American applicant for admission, who, in 1987, was turned down despite his straight-A average, his SAT's in the 98th percentile, and his long list of prestigious academic honors. Shortly thereafter, he and his family discovered that they knew several students with lower grade averages, lower SAT scores and fewer academic qualifications who had been accepted. This is how parents come face to face with what feels to them like a new form of systematized discrimination. These parents, and other members of the Asian-American community, realized that U.C. Berkeley did not impose the same admissions criteria on applicants of different races, and that Berkeley applied merit criteria *within* rather than across groups.[4] The parents contended that different levels of particular criteria were deemed acceptable for those of different races. This is a subtle, but nevertheless quota-oriented system of admissions: *the selective application of merit criteria.*

Inclusion Requires Exclusion

This effort to apply merit criteria selectively was made in the interest of fairness, with the unit under consideration being the group defined by race as opposed to the group defined by level of academic performance. D'Souza reports that during the latter part of the 1970s and the decade of the 1980s, the affirmative action program at U.C. Berkeley "went from one of recruiting Black and Hispanic applicants to lowering admissions standards in order to raise their representation in each freshman class."[5] He adds, "Since Berkeley's faculty could be expected to protest the dilution of the intellectual quality of the student body, the then chancellor Ira Michael Heyman called for rapid implementation of preferential treatment so that, by the time the faculty committees took up the issue, he would have achieved proportional representation or something close to it."[6]

Chancellor Heyman was successful enough that, by 1988, White students were actually underrepresented in proportion to California's population of high school seniors, and, by 1989, White admissions had dropped to one-third of the freshman class. Asian Americans and Whites began experiencing what appeared to be *policies of exclusion.*[7] Although the emphasis on "exclusion" was implicit, appearing more as a by-product than as a basic tenet of policy, the emphasis on "inclusion"—of more fairly representing underrepresented minority groups such as African Americans and Hispanics—was explicit. This is how exclusion becomes the tool of inclusion.

The U.C. Berkeley Committee on Admissions Enrollment *Karabel Report* itself stated that the Berkeley campus faces the "obdurate reality of large-scale differences in patterns of academic performance among California's racial and ethnic groups—differences that are reflected in a high-school drop-out rate among African Americans and Hispanics at least 50 percent higher than Whites."[8] The report insisted that "racial and ethnic differences in rates of eligibility for the University of California reveal an even more dramatic pattern," with 5 percent of African-American–high school graduates meeting the eligibility requirements, 4.5 percent of Hispanic, 15.8 percent of White, and 32.8 percent of Asian-American–high school graduates doing so.[9] The report stated with emphasis that these differences are "deeply rooted in larger patterns of racial and ethnic inequality" and that these differences "constitute a formidable problem . . . in trying to construct an admissions policy that is responsive to all of the major social groups that comprise California's population." The report emphasized, "How well Berkeley can respond to these challenges will be a crucial measure of its success as California struggles to adjust to the reality of multiculturalism."[10]

Here we have it. The reality of multiculturalism is what we are struggling to adjust to as we write and juggle admissions criteria. Who gets in is all about who will be included in the most precious of opportunities by means of ever more intricate allowances for ever more variations of and deviations from merit. Someone must be excluded to make room. One day it's them; one day it's you.

Inclusion or exclusion—or some mix of both—these are the options. We citizens must understand what this means. A *policy of inclusion* is likely to be based on the assumption that inclusion will have a positive effect on the individuals or on the public or subpublic it serves. Inclusion in educational opportunity assumes that those included can benefit from and utilize that opportunity to gain occupational and cultural opportunity. A *policy of exclusion*, even if relatively implicit, does not directly affect its recipients in a positive manner but does seek to achieve some form of broader social good. Simply stated, the exclusion of some leaves room for the inclusion of others. The inclusion of others is a public service to specific subpublics and, according to the laws of externality, to society-at-large. Exclusion assumes that a trade-off between academic merit and fair representation is acceptable and that society can afford to exclude some of its higher academic achievers in order to create a satisfied and fairly represented public. The consequent assumption is that the public will gain as much or greater satisfaction from fairness than from academic excellence if these two functions are at odds. This is the way exclusion policy can be seen as being good for those excluded.

Color Grading

All of this exclusion and inclusion at the policy level shows its most poignant face in the college classroom. When asked, students are especially vocal about how fair representation admissions policies affect what goes on in the classroom. Over half the students I polled indicated that mixed admission policy brings with it diversity on campus. They describe changes of this sort: broadened "interest," "opinions," "awareness," "needs." Many of the students claim that with this broadening, the campus environment, while more stimulating, represents "a distraction from classroom material," a sense of "disorientation," a sense that "the academic material is being diluted" in order to speak to a broader array of students.

Students report that they see specific effects in class, such as "the classes are less demanding as the focus is steered away from pure academics," and "class discussions are hemmed in by pressure to be politically correct," which often "renders open discussions about society hard."

The phrase "political correctness" is by now common parlance and, in some areas, already old and worn out. However, the pressure to be politically correct is still felt by both professors and students and is observed by professors in students and by students in professors.

Increased political correctness may be desirable on an increasingly diversified campus, bringing with it a new multicultural etiquette, a code of behavior in hitherto-unexplored territory. Yet, as with every bit of progress, there are certain drawbacks. Students comment that "everyone is more afraid of offending people these days," and that everything is slowed down and filtered by this. As one humanities professor explained, "There is a subtle, almost institutionalized fear here—a fear of offending someone with the wrong choice of words, a hesitation to express oneself freely. Something is suffocating the spirit of collegiality now."

To what could this professor be referring? What are the implications in the classroom? I asked professors about this and received a variety of responses. It took quite a bit of prying to hone in on some of the details. "No one is really talking about it, but it's as if we are carrying on business as usual here at this university while we are actually teaching at a second-level school, something more like a college or junior college, if you must know."

Another professor moaned, "I don't know what's right anymore. If I grade the way I have for years, I find that, with a few exceptions, there is clumping along the grading curve . . . an embarrassing clumping."

"What do you mean by this?" I asked the professor, hoping that I would hear more about this unspoken phenomenon.

"I am assured of anonymity?"

"Of course," I replied.

"The ethnic groups are clumped along the curve: Asian Americans, then Whites, with Asian Americans and Whites overlapping at the low end of Asian-American averages and the high end of the White averages. Then Hispanics and then African Americans, although there is a significantly greater overlap between these groups."

"Are you saying that you are actually grading by race, by color?" I asked, astonished, and then I allowed for a more reasonable possibility, "Or does it just work out this way?"

"Thanks for allowing another possibility. I'm not a racist. It just works out this way, without my intervention. I've made certain of that."

"How?"

"By setting up objective multiple-choice and fill-in-the-blanks tests with predetermined points for the questions and by having a number of other people, who do not know the students, score the tests and total the scores for the term."

"So the color grading that you find yourself doing is definitely unintentional?"

"Yes. In fact, now I go out of my way to add in-class means of achieving credit. I find myself remedying what I expect to be large racial clumping in scores by subjectively awarding the students least likely to do well a bit of extra credit here and there."

It sounded to me as if this professor had to stereotype in advance to predict and then compensate for those he saw as least likely to do well.

I asked Patrick Hayashi, associate vice chancellor of admissions and enrollment at U.C. Berkeley,[11] about this situation. He told me about a professor friend of his: "A really good friend of mine said something that greatly disturbed me. He said, 'I could grade my class by color. I know that the Asian Americans are going to be the A-students and that some of the Whites are going to be the B-students and some of the Chicanos and Blacks are going to be below them.'"

"Are you aware that it is not just your friend who is talking this way?" I inquired of Hayashi and added, "Let me read you what a professor I interviewed said":

> I find myself coming much more to grips with things that might be influencing me that I haven't been paying any attention to as I do this work—of making sure I don't let my grades separate out by race. Even if they do some-times, I add ways of grading that let me make it much more subjective to avoid that. I've noticed a few times in various classes that were sort of test-based [graded on tests], my plan wasn't working. I was so unhappy with what I saw myself doing, my curve, the way it looked. So I was going to great extremes to do anything other than let the grades clump by race. I hate grades and I happen to believe in subjective grading and teaching anyway, so

that was nice for me. But this avoidance behavior, behavior like mine, is going on here. There's a kind of dance to avoid the problem that some of the professors are talking about.

Hayashi nodded and replied: "Yes, I've heard similar stories. And I'm thinking, how can this be? Because I can't grade my class by color. Then I think about another friend of mine in anthropology. When he sees a multiethnic class, he says, 'Boy, this is an opportunity that I've never had before.' So he organizes his Chicano students to go out and see how the Day of the Dead is celebrated in the Mission District in San Francisco. They get involved in original research. They have to learn how to do interviews, how to schedule interviews, how to organize massive reams of qualitative data and start to pull out themes and hypotheses, how to pay attention to negative evidence, how to write field reports, and how to present their findings. He could possibly grade by color, too, but the grading would be reversed."

He shook his head and shrugged, "I just don't know what to do with so many very strong, starkly held positions."

I wanted to hear more from Hayashi. "Do you have any advice for professors struggling with this problem?" He certainly did, and his comments shed new light on the issues of multiculturalism. I have included some of the further dialogue he and I had to share his interesting professional and personal perspectives.

Problems of Scale

During my interview with him, Hayashi made reference to the problem of time. Professors do not have enough time to know fully their students' capabilities. Time? It takes time to avoid color grading? I wondered. There are many questions that must be considered. Are fair representation admissions policies placing new demands on already fiscally stressed institutions? Are professors struggling with larger classes and greater course loads while being confronted with ever more mixed groups of students who require ever more personal attention? When the variations among students—in ability, experience, preparation, and motivation—increase, professors have to work harder.

Hayashi must have heard me thinking. He continued, "I think that one of the things that we're experiencing is some of the problems of scale. If you're in a large class and you're predisposed to see the class in terms of distinct racial groups and maybe that initial bias is reinforced by the way people sit, and you don't have the resources or the inclination to make a personal contact and to get to know the students as individuals, it might be that the initial perception doesn't change and, in fact, is reinforced. But I know people who broke that pattern."

So what it is that goes on in the professor's mind affects his or her work with a more diverse class of students. I wanted to know more: "It seems as if, as we redesign—which we have done and are doing—admissions policy, we need to train professors to deal with the changing student body. Are professors getting some help with this? I am especially concerned about the older professors who have been here long enough to remember the old, less diverse student body."

"Yes, I think we should work with the professors on this," Hayashi responded, "and we do. But I think we should do more."

"Tell me how this is being done," I asked.

Who Is Smart?

"There's been a lot of conversation about how to respond to a very different student body. And it's not just different in terms of race. It's unfortunate that we focus only on that. First, it's a quite a lot smarter student body. The bottom edge of our class is higher now than it's ever been in terms of the empirical data that we have. Yes, we have diversified, but by all objective and quantitative measures, their standard test scores, their grades, the courses they've taken and the number and difficulty of the courses they've taken, we're stronger now than we've ever been."

"When you say a much smarter student body, those are the ways that you would measure that?" I asked.

"Well, those are the convenient ways to refer to it," Hayashi responded. "But one of the things we're thinking about now is: what do we mean when we say smart?"

"What *do* you mean when you say smart?" I asked.

"I mean a willingness and a capacity to prepare oneself intellectually to continue to learn. Actually, I've never been asked this question."

Hayashi related the fact that, during a recent meeting with a group of high school English teachers, one told him that, "Good writing reflects good thinking and a person who can't write well can't think intelligently."

Hayashi marveled that this statement "went completely unchallenged" by the group. He added: "And so I said, 'I don't begin with that assumption at all.' To what extent does a person's writing reflect the quality of that person's thinking? Put that way the answer becomes obvious, but much more complex, which is that: it depends. If you start with a person who has just arrived in the country and the person can't write a good coherent essay in English, you're not going to conclude, though many people do, that he or she is stupid. Once you start down that analytic track, then you realize that a person's ability to write has a lot to do with what opportunities a person had with respect to hearing his parents speak, what he's been exposed to, what he's read."

Hayashi explained to me that he had always had the view that "everyone can learn and everyone can be very, very smart. It's not measurable aptitude that determines achievement or equivalence to intelligence. It's what a person does. If a person really works, the person is going to get ahead."

I asked him whether his own experience had affected his view of intelligence. He replied that it had. "What most affected me was cultural observations. In grad school, I noticed that in a seminar if you were going to make a statement, you really had to plan on when you were going to begin to interrupt the speaker. If you didn't interrupt, you would never get a chance to speak. Coming from a Japanese family that was on the far end of quiet, even among the Japanese community, just being able to say something was very hard for me in grad school. In order to do it I felt I had to be rude. This was hard." Hayashi explained that he eventually "started to see that people really did have different . . ." He stopped there. Silence.

"Could you be thinking of different abilities?" I asked.

"Those abilities lead them to favor particular techniques," he said.

Racism and Academic Ability

"Would you say that this favoring of particular techniques breaks down by culture?" I asked.

"Less so than in the past," he said. "There is a sense of 'Asians are better quantitatively' but you don't know if it's because they get shut out of other fields or because they have a natural propensity for numbers. As an Asian who has no ability at all in numbers, I believe it's more the social factors—for example, widespread racial discrimination in certain fields—that lead to this distribution of preferences with respect to majors and colleges and careers, rather than cultural proclivities."

There it was again. Mention of racism, this time as "widespread racial discrimination in certain fields." In this case, my interviewee, Hayashi, explained aptitude differences and subject preferences in terms of "racial discrimination in certain fields" rather than "cultural proclivities." Whether or not pointing to racism as the central problem, Hayashi had suggested the presence of discrimination.

Recall that he had also suggested the reality of color grading, which can be otherwise interpreted, based upon the views expressed by Dr. Rey, discussed in the previous chapter, as an institutional or systemic sort of racism. Whatever the interpretation, color grading, stereotyping, and other developments behind the broken gate do appear related to increasing diversity on college campuses.

The Diverse, the Disabled, and the Average

The matter of diversity, by its very nature, cannot be closed. It must remain forever open, as diversity itself continues to diversify. Along the way, the debate intensifies; the polarity exacerbates, yet the basic issues stay the same. Are we overexpanding our definitions of culture and its components to the extreme point of fragmentation? Or, as professor emeritus of natural history at U.C. Santa Cruz Kenneth Norris asks, "Haven't we crammed a multivariate species into the peg holes of a single curve?" Are we defining our reality, our excellence, our standards far too narrowly?[12]

The wave of affirmative action debates of the 1990s may distract us from diversity itself. As Hayashi noted, all too often, ethnicity is the only dimension of diversity considered worthy of prolonged attention and economic investment. However, diversity is so much more. It includes age, gender, religion, aptitude, and, among other characteristics, physical condition. Each area of diversity places its own particular demands upon higher education.

Rights of the Physically Disabled

Consider physical disability as a form of diversity. The Americans with Disabilities Act (ADA) enacted in 1990 requires that (what it called) "reasonable" changes be made by colleges and universities (as well as other institutions) to ensure that people with disabilities have access to the same programs that those who are able-bodied have. This is a relatively simple mandate requiring that reasonable physical and practical adaptation and support be provided for the disabled. Yet, "reasonable" is a vague enough term to leave room for large discretion. For example, a typical supportive service is the provision of note-takers to assist persons whose disabilities interfere with their abilities to take notes in class. Even such a simple form of support is difficult to implement. The note-takers must take notes in a way that helps the student being served. Note-takers with the appropriate level of skill and commitment must be found. If they are volunteers, they must be organized. If they are employees of the university, they must be paid. At many colleges, disabled students are finding the note-takers' support inadequate, inconsistent, unreliable, and of poor or mediocre quality.[13]

Conditions are controversial enough that legal assistance has been called in for various reasons. In one of the broadest cases three disabled students at the University of Miami filed a class action suit in federal court against that university, asserting that the university had the responsibility to recruit and to pay, if necessary, qualified note-takers for manually disabled students. They also charged that the University of Miami was violating the ADA.[14] The university said that although this service could be found at a number of other colleges, it was not necessary that volunteers provide these services at the University of Miami and, moreover, that increasing expenditures on services for the disabled come out of other students' pockets.[15]

The students suing claimed that, unless they received all the assistance to which they were entitled, they would not have access to desirable graduate schools and occupations because their grades would be too low.[16] Again, the matter of access to opportunity arises. Is a university that does not provide excellent note-takers for disabled students obstructing the gate to graduate education for those students? How responsible should an institution be for the success of its physically disabled admits?

While the answers to these questions are still being debated, the civil rights of the disabled have been confirmed by governmental actions, at least to some degree. In 1992 alone, the U.S.

Department of Education found that forty-six colleges had violated the rights of students or employees with disabilities. Cases included discouraging disabled students to apply for admission, denying sign language interpreters to deaf students, and refusing to pay aides to disabled students.[17]

The Special Case of Learning Disability

If, in schools' efforts to diversify, ethnicity and physical disability have proven complex and controversial, they are merely the tips of some immense icebergs. What about the admission of students with learning disabilities to the university? This is a unique area of so-called disability, one that continues to be highly controversial.

Professors have reported that, continuing into the nineties, campus counseling departments have required them to adapt to the special needs of their learning-impaired students. As one professor explained, "The semester begins. Not long after, a student appears in my office with one of *those* letters." The following are two examples of "those" letters. This sort of notification to professors is usually a form letter filled in by a learning disability counselor. I have removed or changed all names to protect anonymity. To emphasize certain points, I break into the letters occasionally with my own comments:

> Dear Professor:
> Jane Doe has been identified through an extensive process as having learning disabilities. By definition, the term "learning disabilities" involves three major components: (1) average or above-average intelligence, (2) at least one cognitive processing deficit, and (3) severe discrepancy between aptitude and achievement.

Note that it is emphasized here that a learning disability is not a case of low or lower intelligence. It does, however, involve "at least one cognitive processing deficit."

Learning disabilities impact in different ways, including: auditory processing of information, visual processing, visual/motor integration, memory, attention/concentration, reasoning, spatial planning, and the like. Learning disabilities, unrelated to intelligence, are chronic conditions, which affect each person differently. Unfortunately, they do not disappear with age, but individuals develop coping strategies that help them compensate for the deficits.

Note that there is an effort to explain the nature of learning disabilities to the professor, who is informed that, in the learning-disabled student, "coping strategies" are developed to "compensate for the deficits."

As a Learning Disabilities Specialist, I have been working with Jane in developing an understanding of her disabilities and formulating strategies that will help her develop compensations for the difficulties she experiences in academic settings.

That Jane experiences "difficulties" in "academic settings" is acknowledged. Clearly, by the wording, the message is that Jane can and should be helped to "compensate" for her difficulties.

Jane is a student whose strengths are in the areas of logical reasoning, visual processing, and general knowledge. Her learning difficulties are in the areas of processing speed, visual/motor coordination, memory, and auditory processing. These disabilities impair her capacity to read and write at a normal speed, as well as to retrieve and order data stored in her memory.

Jane should be permitted to audiotape all classroom lectures. She should not be penalized for mechanical errors (spelling, punctuation, grammar) in work she completes in class. In addition, whenever possible she should be permitted to take all examinations at home, using an untimed, open-book format. If the at-home, open-book format is for some reason impossible, one of the following alternative exam formats should be selected:

- Frequent exams (perhaps monthly) instead of a midterm and final

- Exams given to Jane in two halves, with her being told in advance which course material will be covered in each half-exam.

If for any reason, it is absolutely necessary for Jane to take an in-class examination, she will require double the time given to other students, as well as a quiet, well-lighted room in which to take the exam.

A special exception is needed for Jane. This letter is based on the findings of the learning disability counselor that indicate to the counselor that Jane needs this special exception far more than the other students not identified as learning-disabled. Jane apparently requires what may sound like more lenient test conditions than do other students.

I note that Jane is scheduled to take two midterm exams on the same day: March 20 of this semester. Yours is the first of the two midterms. If Jane receives double time for your midterm, she will be unable to report on time for the beginning of the second exam. This problem could be solved by your permitting her to take your midterm at home. If this is not an option, I request that you, Jane, and the other professor confer to decide on an alternate plan.

More work for the professor? Extra attention to Jane and also time spent with her other professor are "requested." This is most likely to be heard as the greatest of all requests listed.

These recommendations should allow Jane fair compensation for her disabilities. Should you have any questions or concerns, please do not hesitate to contact me.

Sincerely,

Ms. —————————
Learning Disabilities Specialist

Note that the professor is asked to satisfy recommendations that should allow the special student "fair"—that four letter word again —"fair compensation for her disabilities."

> Dear Professor:
>
> Mr. Dan Smith has been identified through an extensive process as having a learning disability. By definition that was modified from Public Law 94–142 and used by the university, the term "specific learning disability" involves four major components: (1) average and above-average intelligence, (2) deficit in the processing of visual and/or auditory information, (3) severe discrepancy between aptitude and achievement, and (4) does not occur with sensory and/or physical impairment as a primary causative factor. A learning disability impacts in different ways (for example, auditory processing, visual processing of information, visual-motor integration, spatial abilities, and so forth).

Note that this letter includes the fourth category, further distinguishing learning disability from physical handicap.

> A learning disability affects certain specific cognitive abilities and is unrelated to intelligence. This is a developmental disability—from birth or a lifelong disability—and is not a progressive or degenerative disability. It is a chronic condition which affects each individual differently and, in most cases, does not disappear with age. Individuals develop coping strategies, which help them compensate for the deficits caused by their specific learning disability. Some of the usual procedures for working with learning-disabled university students are: strategies counseling (for example, to develop necessary compensatory skills) and course accommodation (taped textbooks, classroom note-takers, tutoring, test modifications, quiet room to enhance concentration, and sometimes consideration given to quality of ideas rather than to spelling and mechanics of language).

The letter reviews for the professor typical methods of assisting the learning disabled.

As a Counselor for Students with Learning Disabilities, I have been working with Mr. Smith in developing an understanding of his disabilities and using strategies that will help him develop compensations for the difficulties he experiences in the academic setting. Mr. Smith is a student whose strengths are in the areas of abstract reasoning and problem-solving and non-verbal receptive language.

His learning disabilities impact on the areas of auditory processing and on his visual perceptual processing. These deficits impede his auditory memory (both long- and short-term) and his reading rate, and result in an intermittent lack of motivation to learn in Mr. Smith.

Is "lack of motivation to learn" in itself a learning disability? Is it more severe in Mr. Smith than in other students? Do his other disabilities cause this lack of motivation? How can we tell? Regarding lack of motivation, what is a fair cut-off point in identifying this as a disability? Should we really go so far as to include this as a category deserving of special treatment when so many students are afflicted by motivational problems, and no one is forcing them to stay enrolled? This is not the Army in the time of a compulsory draft. College attendance is—at least to this day—voluntary.

It is recommended that Mr. Smith be given extended time on all exams involving time limits. In his particular situation, time-and-a-half should be sufficient. These accommodations vary with each learning-disabled student and are dependent on test material, presentation method, and type of test.

"Dependent on test *material?*"

The above recommendation should allow Mr. Smith compensation for his disability. Should you have any questions or concerns, please do not hesitate to contact me.
Thank you.

Sincerely,

Counselor/LD Specialist ⎯⎯⎯⎯⎯⎯
Services to Learning-Disabled Students

The professor is asked to "compensate" for Mr. Smith's disability. While on a single case basis, this may be possible, how does a professor manage to be just this sensitive to every one of her or his students' needs? What if many of the other students seem to suffer from at least intermittent motivational or other emotional problems? What is an overworked professor to do?

The Irreversibly Average

What if, in the interest of broader opportunity, we have imposed more on the system of higher education than it can afford to handle? As resources have been directed to meeting the special needs of an increasingly diverse student body, what has become of the student who is, by most measures, relatively average, not an addition to the diversity quotient of a campus? Who is attending to the special needs of the students who have not been officially identified as special: officially different, or disabled, or lacking in motivation due to some life problem not of their own causing?

While being done in the name of humanity, the addressing of special needs on college campuses has cost time, energy, and money. How do we evaluate such investments, especially when they are the taxpayers' investments? Of the students who have been identified as special, which of them have been actually supported by the university in such a way that their future opportunities are definitely enhanced by higher education? There are no easy answers. There is no fair solution. All special needs are special.

So it is that university systems have been and are being pulled in all different directions at once. Fragmentation, over-bureaucratization, and the consequent diluting of the college education is the result. Most students—whether special admits or not, whether additions to the diversity quotient or not—are subjected to benign neglect throughout their college lives. They are lost in the shuffle.

And the average students are hurting. Baby boomers may recall being told when they were children, "It hurts to be different." Yes, it does, especially when discrimination is involved. But these days, it also hurts not to be different.

From time to time during my interviews, a few students (who viewed themselves as average) wondered aloud whether it might not be more cost productive to invest the extra time, energy, and money in the average students, that the performance of average students might be more readily and inexpensively raised. This is a question to which there is no easy answer. Yet, it is plain for all to see that the student who is not the member of a special population has to emerge as the newly disabled. For a student on a diversity-sensitive campus in a diversity-oriented world, being irreversibly average can feel like a terrible handicap. It is the dooming confinement to a life of eternal invisibility and crippling insignificance.

The University Within: Responses to the Perceived Erosion of Intellectual Rigor

Something is going on; something is being whispered behind closed doors. What is it? Why the secrecy? Here is the answer suggested by a graduating senior at U.C. Berkeley: "The university has been the traditional site of the gathering of minds. I guess it still is, only these days, too many of the minds are too empty. They still gather, but so what? I'm not proud to be a student here. It's embarrassing."

A graduate student, who insisted upon remaining anonymous, stated, "I know there is a university within the university here. I'm in it. It's more obvious to me now that I'm a graduate student, but it was present during my undergraduate years on this same campus."

I asked her what purpose the *university within the university* served. She narrowed her eyes and replied in a strained but low voice, "To preserve what is left of a rapidly eroding intellectual rigor. The university within the university is informal. It's not underground. It's not a secret. Nobody plans it. It just happens."

"What just happens?" I asked, attempting to sound unaware.

She saw that I was feigning ignorance but chose to humor me: "The brightest professors see the brightest students looking bored, dragged down, impatient. They identify with us. They do something for us—mentor us, hold special discussion groups, meet with us in their offices or over lunch, give us special assignments. Sometimes they even deviate from what it is they are saying to the whole class and say, 'For those of you who are curious, let me add that. . . .' and then they get into whatever higher level of theory or abstraction or formulation they think we want to rise to."

"Do you see this often?"

"Only the brightest professors do this for us. And there aren't many of them. The general quality of the professors at this university is diminishing as much as the quality of the students. But the brightest professors identify with the brightest students and give them a little extra."

"Doesn't this bother the other students?"

"Most of them don't even realize what's going on. They just ask if the content of the more-advanced discussion will be on the test or not. If the professor says no, they space out."

Tiered System

The university within is hidden from view, but definitely present. Its existence is, perhaps, a natural consequence of tiered admissions policy. Chapter Three described the formal two-tier (once three-tier) system which was built into the liberalized admissions process at U.C. Berkeley and replicated in various forms at many other colleges. One of the likely consequences of a formally tiered admissions process is an informally tiered student body. Recall the reference to the controversial comments of Professor Sarich in Chapter Two. Amidst his more inflammatory comments regarding the possible diminished mental abilities of African Americans and females, Sarich also commented on the effects of U.C. Berkeley's then formally tiered, fair representation admissions system. Sarich argued that such admissions policies at the University of California at Berkeley discriminated against Whites. He also argued that the admissions policies aimed at diversifying the student body generated a "tribalization" effect in which students separated themselves by race. Moreover, said Sarich, another double-tiered system was indeed emerging, albeit informally, with Whites and Asian Americans in the top tier and African Americans and Hispanics in the bottom tier.[18]

However it is created and described, the informal tiering of the American student body is indeed taking place. It is, however, more complex and multisided than the informal double tiering described by Sarich. Yes, we have created universities with hidden tiers, undesignated levels of students, implicit academic strata. And among these strata is the most elusive one of all: a university within the university.

Why so elusive? Because no one wants to talk about it. This muffling, even denial, is occurring in an environment of not talking about all kinds of things. On the hot seat, Sarich maintained that someone must be willing to discuss controversial topics including race, gender differences, and intelligence in class in a nonconformist way. He said that where these topics are discussed, they are typically done so within the bounds of the prevailing liberal "political orthodoxy" and not in any form that has "been rendered taboo by a conformist mentality."[19] Not only was academic freedom called into question by Sarich, but, as he made clear, political and intellectual freedom have been jeopardized as well. There are things that one just cannot say without being persecuted for having done so.

The Plight of the Bright

One thing that apparently cannot be directly said is that the brightest students are being lost in the shuffle, if not purposely buried under the heap of what are considered more-pressing student needs. The tedium of participating in discussions far too elementary to hold their attention eventually quiets bright students. But it is not only the tedium that subdues the precociously bright, it is the negative reinforcement they meet when they are perceived to be "overly" enthusiastic during class discussions, when they are frowned at for speaking up a little too much, for arguing a point a little too forcefully, for blurting out answers to questions the rest of the class is reticent to attempt to answer or just can't get right. In many university settings, it just doesn't pay to be too obviously intelligent. It is frequently deemed best that the bright extrovert convert to a bright introvert—for social survival and also for academic well-being.

Slinking Toward the Mean

There is another aspect to this predicament of the too bright, and that is the difficulty in dealing with a less bright professor. "Don't tell anyone, but Professor X is not very sharp. He feels threatened by me, so I hold back a lot. It's a very strange position to be in." Indeed, the course chosen by many of the brightest students is to slink toward the mean in terms of visible, audible classroom performance. Even behind closed doors, in the professor's office, the dynamic of slinking toward the norm is operant.

In this era of attention to harassment and discrimination, we are very aware of what may be demeaning. Let us also take note of what may be *meaning*—forcing exceptional people downward toward average performance, toward the mean. The meaning of the brightest is one of the greatest casualties of our times. While, granted, elitism and discrimination in education must end, the implicit disapproval and iatrogenic neglect of those who are, by traditional definitions, our brightest, is catastrophic.

This is a silent yet powerful cry emerging from the broken gate. It is not merely one of being lost in the shuffle, it is one of having to allow oneself to be buried in the shuffle in order to fit in. While there is indeed a heterogenization of many student bodies, there is also a frightening pressure to homogenize the performance level of student bodies.

This is not an attempt to say who is at fault, to blame faculty or some particular faculty. Rather, my aim is to suggest that when the classroom is diversified, not only ethnically but in a host of other directions, there may be particular groups of students most likely to recede in importance, in visibility, even in value, while other groups of students gain, at least in terms of their rights for teacher attention. A concern for the average student was expressed earlier in this chapter. At the same time, we must not overlook the educational needs of the high-achieving students. The university is being pulled in so many directions that many a professor is treading the often treacherous crosscurrents of diversities from the sinking life raft of the podium.

Diminished Faculties

I asked professors about the plight of the bright and heard a broad range of responses ranging from denial: "There really is no issue here. The students tend to merge into one group with very few at either extreme"; to confirmation: "God yes, it's getting ridiculous. I feel pressed to ignore the good students in order to address the majority of students, who are not really good students"; to guilt: "When I take off on a discussion aimed at the few who can actually follow me and who deserve greater stimulation, I feel awful, as if I have committed a moral transgression for which I will eventually pay"; to challenge: "Yes, I now teach two or three classes within one class. It's a wonderful job—juggler. I'm proud to say that I rarely drop a ball."

Again and again, professors and their teaching assistants revealed that the traditional classroom feels increasingly like a three-ring circus or maybe a theatrical farce, a parody of education. One teaching assistant (TA) explained, "We assistants have become essential. There is so much catch-up, so much remedial work to be done. It's not becoming of the professor to do this kind of thing before the whole class, so we do it behind closed doors."

Another TA, who was in on this conversation, claimed, "We TA's are the ones who make the joke that this is still a great university work. We help keep the secret that there are people who shouldn't be here."

"Right," the first TA went on, "not only shouldn't they be here, but they shouldn't be taking these courses without several prerequisites first," he laughed "such as basic math skills, you know, multiplication, division, pre-pre-calculus, and even basic reading and writing skills."

The conversation continued with both TA's trying to convince me. Finally, one of them addressed the admissions issue: "We are truly the ones who have made affirmative action admissions policy work. The faculty can't handle this modernized student body alone. We are essential and very underpaid."

It is not only teaching assistants who report that, within classes, professors find students of a broad range of preparation and ability. Here is a quote from a memo sent by a departmental dean to his faculty: "It has been my experience that undergraduate performance is more variable than graduate performance. This is true at both ends of the distributions: the best students are as good or better than any in our Ph.D. programs, and the worst students make you wonder how they got into this university."

How can professors addressing such disparity function in the manner in which they, themselves, were trained? The classrooms to which they teach are significantly different from the classrooms from which they came.

Standard Shifting and Grade Inflation

I found that faculty and administrators responding to my questionnaire were well aware of shifting standards. Of all tenured faculty responding, 67.9 percent reported that standards had broadened. Almost all, 93.3 percent of the high-level administration and 82.1 percent of midlevel administration and management, agreed. Many tenured faculty (36.7 percent), all tenure track faculty (100 percent), most high-level administrators (86.6 percent), and over half of the midlevel administration and management (58 percent) felt that the classroom had been affected by changes in admissions policy.

Everywhere I went in my research for this book, I stumbled into the issue of "grade inflation." Clearly, grade inflation has come about as a way of compensating for the extended range of academic performance in the classroom. "After all," a White professor in his sixties explained, "there is nothing that says I have to apply the same standards for grading which I used at Harvard thirty years ago. It's my classroom. I give out the grades. I grade students the way I see fit. Why would I want to give D's and F's to students who are trying hard but who should never have been admitted to this university? I won't, so I inflate their grades."

Another professor, a White female in her forties, put it this way: "Grades are subjective. Formulas for calculating grades are selected subjectively. We can dress it up, making grading look detached and objective, but it's all a game. We now give out A minuses and B pluses and B minuses as if they were distinct grades. The scale has shifted up from F through A to C plus (which now sounds like failing) to B minus, B, B plus, A minus, A and an occasional A plus. We actually have more grading categories in more frequent use this way."

"Don't fool yourself," an African-American professor in his fifties warned, "these aren't all A and B students. We're just calling them that. It's an unofficial policy to upgrade. Makes the school look good. I sure didn't get treated this way when I was in school."

To wit, Garry Trudeau aptly portrays this problem to the public in his comic strip series on the plight of Professor Deadman in an era of grade inflation, of heightened concern regarding racism, and of institutional accountability. "B+ is a racist grade," the student tells Trudeau's Professor Deadman. "Racist? But . . . but you're White!" the professor exclaims. The professor later reminds the college president that "under student pressure" the school has "traded learning for success," to which the president responds, "The customer is always right." In a later episode, Deadman says, "Today, if a student fails a course, it's our fault." Trudeau sees how grade inflation has become an institutional survival skill. Bad grades make the college look bad. (See Figure 5.1 for a sampling of Trudeau's work.)

Cheating

While grades are inflating, cheating can still earn one an F. There is no direct evidence that changes in admissions policy led to any

Figure 5.1. Garry Trudeau's Doonesbury Comic Strips on Grade Inflation, Racism, and Economic Pressures Forcing Accountability onto Colleges.

Figure 5.1. Continued.

Source: Published in the *San Francisco Chronicle* December 21, 1993, December 27, 1993, and March 18, 1994, respectively.

Source: Reprinted with permission of Universal Press Syndicate. DOONESBURY Copyright 1993 and 1994; G. B. Trudeau. All rights reserved.

increase in cheating. However, it is worth noting that, whatever the cause, there have been reports of increases in cheating coming from all sorts of campuses. I was especially intrigued by this administrator's memo, which served to remove the professors' responses to cheating from their individual purviews:

There has been an unfortunate increase in the number of reported incidents of cheating on undergraduate exams. I am currently in the process of drafting a memo to the undergraduates regarding the problem, and in the future I plan to institute an honor code.

In the near term, I suggest that we take a harder line on students. Any arbitration of cheating cases is up to your discretion. However, I plan to tell students that anyone caught cheating will receive an automatic F on the exam.

I will also support you in any disciplinary action, and I strongly urge you to take cases of cheating up with the Student Conduct Officer. Clearly, this course of action can be unpleasant, but I would like to move toward a uniform cheating policy.

It has also come to my attention that a number of student clubs have access to instructor manuals for many standard textbooks. Some students have recently come to class armed with the answers to exams, since the questions were lifted directly from the instructor manual. If you make use of canned questions, please vary a few parameters in these questions to differentiate them from the instructor manual.

Thanks for your cooperation.[20]

Social Benefit or Personal Assault?

Universities within universities have come into existence at many leading institutions. The more fortunate, and perhaps more adept, students have managed to find each other and to be found by professors sensitive to their plight.

One of my interviewees, a professor of social science, demanding anonymity, states emphatically that this is true on many modern-day campuses, that such universities within are informal, and that they are conducted almost invisibly by particular professors who do this naturally rather than with any intent to undermine. He says, "The bright students do need and deserve much more attention than they are getting." However, he also claims, "It is good that our most able students are not lumped together and are instead dealing with fellow students of varying ability levels."

An admissions officer added an alternative perspective on this distribution of the brightest among so many colleges:

> If you're an American citizen and you believe as I do that one of the distinctions of this country—real distinctions, differences, between this and other countries—is that we have a handful (and I don't know how big a handful, but certainly a dozen or twenty) of great institutions, yours— U.C. Berkeley—included (some private and a few more public), you see that this is far more than other countries have. Elsewhere, there are one or two great institutions (if you can call them that) per country if they are lucky. And, one of the great benefits we have experienced as a result of our relatively large number of great institutions is that, since the Second World War, our able students have distributed themselves among these institutions.

Granted, the social benefits of broadly distributing our top-ability students are many. The brightest students can influence, inspire, motivate, be motivated by, even help those around them. The brightest students can share their ideas among a broader range of people than they could were they isolated, cloistered together, and protected. The mingling of intellects and intellectual levels can be a positive factor in everyone's life. It can do the country good.

Such mixing of abilities can be ensured by mixed admissions policies such as that modeled by the fifty-fifty mixed criteria admissions policy of U.C. Berkeley discussed in Chapter Three. As reported previously, the faculty and administration returning my questionnaire felt that the university classroom was affected by liberalized admissions policies. However, despite the probable growing neglect of the brightest students, the cover-ups reported by some teaching assistants, the struggles indicated by some professors, the problem of grade inflation, and the concurrent increase in cheating, most of the faculty and administration I questioned reported that they felt there was a redeeming social value to liberalized admissions.

In fact, the overwhelming majority of respondents to my questionnaire claimed that there was indeed a social benefit to liberalized admissions policies, as indicated by 66 percent of tenured faculty, 80 percent of tenure track faculty, 100 percent of high-level administration, and 82.1 percent of midlevel administration and management. Apparently, a significant portion of these persons found there to be some sort of positive trade-off between the increasing of social benefit and the decreasing of academic rigor.

But, they do say "trade-off." Indeed, it was over half of the faculty that, while noting the social benefit of liberalized admissions policies, were also noting a corresponding decrease in academic rigor. It is in this matter that faculty reports are most important, because professors are on the front lines—in the classrooms. These people, who make the university work and who, ideally, seek to keep the university ever more successful in an academically competitive world, are not finding U.C. Berkeley on the academic upswing.

If anything, a university in a society confronted with international competition would want to feed its brightest with the education they require to remain competitive; if anything, such a university would want to increase its academic rigor. However, unlike Hayashi, his views stated in Chapter Two, the majority of my respondents found U.C. to be either declining in academic rigor or, at best, remaining the same.

Testing for Admission into the University Within

And so has arisen the university within, and, with it, another complexity. Who gets into the university within? There are no tests for admission into this informal-but-elite mentoring circle. Admission is not only subjective, it is also subtle, almost invisible.

Perhaps the absence of testing is best in this situation. After all, what would be tested? High IQ? Selecting for high IQ does not guarantee outstanding achievement or great productivity. Furthermore, high ability levels are not organized along the high end of a single continuum. Although he has long been viewed as a proponent of the controversial support for IQ as a singular measure of intelligence, U.C. Berkeley professor emeritus Arthur Jensen differentiates between classifications of high mental ability. Of giftedness and genius, he says that these are "crucially different phenomena" and that "they are not simply different points on one and the same continuum."[21] Students, even the best students, are not necessarily rankable on one continuum.

We are thus haunted by an undeniable dilemma, by a question of truth, as asked by U.C. Santa Cruz professor emeritus of natural history Kenneth Norris: "If you rank minds according to a single scale and find that, for example, the races of the human species fall out in a regular order with so and so at the top and so and so at the bottom, does this really mean anything we can use to rank people by?"[22] No, it does not. In fact, the students admitted to the university within arrive there based on a highly subjective nontest ranking: instructor preference.

Gender Problems as a Model: Why a Woman Can't Be More like a Man

I initially thought that the brief discussion in Chapter Three on the early admissions of women to higher education was sufficient discussion of gender. I simply wanted to indicate that the gate had been broken several times, and that one of the earliest diversifications of the student body was the addition of women. The discussion of women in Chapter Three was originally included merely to draw parallels between the broadening of admissions criteria to encompass ethnic diversity and an earlier redefinition of admissions standards, which made it possible for women to earn real college degrees.

What Women's Rights Symbolizes

Naturally, this development reflected earlier historical pressures to extend the various rights of citizenship to women, including the rights to vote and to attend school. Most, if not all, historical movements that have sought equality for a disenfranchised subpopulation have argued that education is key. Denying education is denying power. Withholding knowledge is enforcing subordination. Yearning for knowledge reflects a desire to gain freedom from subordination. Angela Davis, political activist and lecturer, captures the political significance of the "yearning for knowledge" in her book, *Women, Race and Class*, wherein she details the relationships between oppression and forced ignorance and between African-American and White women's demands for education. Davis writes, "According to the prevailing ideology, Black people were allegedly incapable of intellectual advancement. After all, they had been chattel, naturally inferior. . . . But if they really were biologically inferior, they would have manifested neither the desire nor the capability to acquire knowledge. Ergo, no prohibition of learning would have been necessary."[23]

Davis details the relationship between the oppression of African Americans, specifically African-American women, and the oppression of White women, and the difficult but consequent meshing of their struggles for equal rights. She points to the battle against illiteracy in the South after the Civil War where "the history of women's struggle for education in the United States reached a true peak when Black and White women together led the . . . battle against illiteracy," contending that their "unity and solidarity preserved and confirmed one of our history's most fruitful promises."[24] The promise of equal rights, of equality itself, was tied to access to knowledge.

Women's Inferiority as a Concept

The backdrop against which modern women are provided education, even higher education, cannot and must not be forgotten. As noted in Chapter Three, it was not so very long ago that when women were provided a college education at all, it was merely a token education. Whether or not our founding fathers fully understood the implications of their design for a new egalitarian nation, their great American dream could not be realized without several battles for emancipation after the first one in 1776. The Civil War was fought for more than just the Black slaves. White women were still emerging from their European histories of "chatteldom," of intellectual oppression, and of starvation for knowledge. They still faced a line of thinking not unusual late in the nineteenth century—a line of thinking that teaches us a great deal about modern-day prejudices with regard to the many social subgroups who are now seeking enhanced educational opportunity.

Let's consider some of the important historical prejudices against women's mental ability and intellectual worth. Samples of such thinking are cited by Stephan Jay Gould in his brilliant book, *The Mismeasure of Man*[25]:

First: the controversial, then and now, words of Paul Broca, French professor of clinical surgery, who, in 1861, contended that as brain size increases, so does degree of civilization and intelligence and warned: "But we must not forget that women are, on the average, a little less intelligent than men. . . . The relatively small size of the female brain depends in part upon her physical inferiority and in part upon her intellectual inferiority."[26]

Second: In the 1879 words of Broca's colleague, Gustave Le Bon, who founded social psychology, and was a favorite of Mussolini's: "There are large numbers of women whose brains are closer in size to those of gorillas than to those of the most developed male brains. This inferiority is so obvious that no one can contest it. . . . All psychologists who have studied the intelligence of women . . . recognize today that they represent the most inferior forms of human evolution . . . there exist some distinguished women, very superior to the average man, but they are as exceptional as the birth of any monstrosity."[27]

Third: American evolutionary biologist E. D. Cope warned in 1890 of the possibility that "a spirit of revolt become general among women," stating that "should the nation have an attack of this kind . . . like a disease, it would leave its traces in many after-generations."[28]

All this, of course, was against the larger backdrop of the ongoing distrust of women based on their potential power over men, so pointedly expressed by eighteenth-century philosopher Friedrich Nietzsche, who warned of the dangers of women's affection: "The danger for artists, for geniuses . . . is woman: adoring women confront them with corruption . . . feminine love . . . is merely a more refined form of parasitism, a form of nestling down in another soul."[29]

Gender Issues as a Primer

As discussed earlier, historically staged, gender equity issues are a sort of binary (yes-no, male-female) map for other, more complex, multivariate, and multicultural equity issues. In any case, despite the inextricable relationship between women's access to higher education and the access of African Americans, Hispanics, and other subpopulations to that same higher education, I had planned no further discussion of gender. After all, the admission of women to colleges and universities has become a given. Women outnumber men on campuses by over one million.[30] And their graduation has become more a given than that of their male counterparts.

But then, several unrelated events took place and numerous memories resurfaced, converging in my awareness. One day, while teaching a course on mental health in the workplace, I was discussing the way variations in workplaces (occupations and settings) can exacerbate or dilute the issues we had covered. One of my students, who had grown up in East Germany before the fall of the Wall and who had special forces military training there spoke up: "It's not really whether women should be in the workplace or not. What we should talk about is that in some workplaces, men think they cannot count on women in times of danger. Whether they can or not does not matter. If men think women will not protect them, in the battlefield, then men do not feel safe having women as coworkers."

The class immediately took off in all directions on this one. I was inclined to let the discussion move freely for a while, and decided first simply to point out that this was indeed an example of how the intensity of the gender issue varies within different workplaces. Gender issues in a fast food restaurant are significantly different from those on a military battlefield. However, my German student, who had initiated this shift in the conversation, had more to say: "It's bigger than whether a man feels a woman will automatically take the same kind of risks a man will take in the heat of battle. It's whether a woman can even understand enough to teach us what this is really about." My student waved his arm at me.

A number of female students immediately jumped to my defense. I interrupted, saying that I could understand only intellectually the particulars of coworker interdependence in the battlefield, as I had never been there. Some of these female students were not pleased with my response. Others were. And then, it became clear that the male students were split on the issue as well. As I let the students hash it out, I could see that some wanted leadership from me; others wanted me to serve as a neutral party, a fair witness, or maybe even a referee.

As I silently postponed the remainder of my lecture in order to learn from the students' debate, I reflected on the fact that I had been teaching college students mental health in the workplace for about one-and-a-half decades, and times continued to change. By the mid-1980s, students and the university were asking professors to include discussions of the relevance of course content to ethnic minorities. About the same time, pressure to include the women's perspective grew. In the 1990s, concern for these areas continued, with an increase in the demand for discussion of sexual harassment. As we neared the mid-1990s, it became apparent that a semester-long course in mental health in the workplace could barely get by spending only four weeks on gender issues, especially sexual harassment. Despite my experience teaching the course, my awareness that these issues had been surfacing in college classrooms since the 1960s and my own experiences with harassment in my professional life, this was the first time I had ever heard one of my male students tell me that I, a female professor, could not teach this particular topic, because, as he claimed, it dealt with issues that were traditionally, and are still, for the most part, a man's experience.

I could not help but wonder how many times I had heard my male professors—and 95 percent of all the professors I had as an undergraduate and graduate were male—discuss, from a position of authority, things that were, traditionally, and are still for the most part, women's experiences. It was only halfway through graduate school that I finally began to wonder if men could be authorities on women's experiences. Was knowledge itself gender-based? What about knowledge of the experiences particular to one of the sexes?

So there I was in my own workplace, the classroom, being told that I could not teach something because I was a woman. I laughed to myself, as I thought about how it had been almost ten years since I had worn a dress or skirt on campus. Nowadays, I only wore pants. I often avoided laughing or smiling during my lectures to avoid appearing "girlish" and thus less of an authority. I wanted to be revered as much as I had revered my best professors when I was an undergraduate.

Then I recalled the behavior of some of those professors, several of whom were well-known writers, thinkers, leaders. Prior to my graduate work at U.C. Berkeley, I had been an undergraduate at U.C. Santa Cruz. In those unruly years of the early 1970s, it seemed as if professors were bound by no rules, no standardized morality. When a male professor, successful in his field and with a sizable following, made it clear that he wanted to take to bed one of his female students, the student was unprepared for the invitation, uncertain how to respond, and too inexperienced to predict what the consequences of her "no" would be. This indecision is not surprising. We are, even now, still adjusting to the fact of education for women and still learning how to deal with issues borne out of this education. Although, historically, one of the first breaks in the gate to higher education was the gender barrier, this break is no more than a century old, if that, depending on how it is measured.

I remember all too well the moment when a professor I had respected tremendously closed his office door and grabbed my breast. I was shocked. I had always found him quite physically unattractive. When he pulled me to him and tried to kiss me, I felt a new kind of revulsion inside me; yet, I found myself cautious. I pushed him away, rather gently. Then I saw his face change. By the look in his eyes, I knew that from that day on, I could never ask him to write a letter of recommendation for me. And I had counted on his letters.

Yes, the gate to admission can be broken. Hitherto uneducated or undereducated subpopulations can be brought into the university. They can even graduate, sometimes with honors. But what price must they pay? And how many gates must be broken in order for those hitherto closed out to be let in all the way?

The consideration of gender in higher education is virtually a primer for more complex diversifications of the university population. As Rey explained it to me, "Yes, we are all racists. But perhaps this point is more obvious when we talk about gender. We are all sexists." As he drew this analogy, I thought of age discrimination and what we call "ageism." Certainly, firing or not hiring someone based on age alone may be discriminatory, but what about the termination of an older worker who has become less physically coordinated or mentally alert in the workplace? What if this diminished ability or capacity is dangerous to the employee, the coworkers, or the customers? We must wonder who among us is not ageist in some way? Ageism can take many forms; we all make some decisions based on age. Who among us is ready to send our preschool children to war or place our adolescents in nursing homes for the remainder of their lives? We are all ageists in some way, perhaps with good reason. Does this logic justify sexism?

One would presume that—now that women make up half or more of most student populations, and now that professor-student relationships are more regulated, and now that sexual harassment has become a household term—women in the academic world are treated no differently than their male counterparts.

Alas, we know this presumption to be hasty. Gender biases and discriminations, and the emerging reverse biases and discriminations, not only persist but also take new forms over time. When all is said and done, gender issues will exist as long as there are two (or more) genders. (I say "or more" because transgender or "third gender" organizations have appeared on many campuses.) Put men and women together, and you have various issues particular to their intermingling. This is the case with all heterogenization of organizations, institutions, societies. The more obvious the differences among people, the more heterogeneous a group of people appears when groups are merged. The more heterogeneity, the more issues arise related to or deriving from this heterogeneity.

Gender is perhaps one of the simplest forms of human heterogeneity within the human species. This is because it is a variation of the first order—the most primary, most binary variation: male or female, or, as older renditions of the choice set would have it, male or not.

Student-Faculty Romance

One consequence of allowing women to go to college with men is that the sexes have been exposed to each other in new ways and in large numbers. Sexual attraction is unavoidable, even that between student and teacher. The problem lies in how the attraction is handled.

There are those who oppose warnings and prohibitions against faculty-student romances, some of whom have formed a group out of California State University, Long Beach, which calls itself, "Consenting Academics for Sexual Equity." Consenting Academics defends faculty-student romances, referring to its commitment to "the principle of consent regarding sexual relationships."[31] Responses to this group, which advertises for membership on the Internet (of the information highway), include requests for membership as well as criticisms, such as one that calls the organization a group of "aging men who demand the right to keep trying to seduce the undergraduate women as a privilege of office."[32]

Here, the freedom of association and relationship treads upon the freedom from discrimination and harassment. Which and whose freedoms deserve greater protection? Do policies that prohibit professors from engaging in romantic or sexual relationships with their students protect young women, or do they overprotect them to the point of infantilizing them? Can't a girl say no for herself?

Campus Rape

Sometimes "no" means nothing. This is ever more apparent as the problem of campus rape is unearthed. In fact, the problem is more prevalent than campus officials admit, according to Myra and David Sadker, coauthors of *Failing at Fairness: How America's Schools Cheat Girls*.[33] The Sadkers report that "more than one in every three college men believes that a woman who says 'no' to sex really means 'yes' or at least 'maybe.'"[34] The Sadkers cite a number of studies evidencing the appalling reality that about one-quarter of all college women in the United States have been forced into "having sex," and one-sixth of all American college women report having been raped. In 90 percent of these incidents, the force was inflicted upon the female coed by someone with whom she was acquainted.[35]

What is perhaps most relevant to the overarching issues in *Shameful Admissions* is the Sadkers' conclusion—after considering the data on campus rape, the responses of colleges to such rape, the ongoing prevalence of victim blaming, and the impotence of traditional rape prevention programs—that there is "a profound gender gap in perception but also a fundamental difference in campus entitlement and power."[36]

Gender-Based Grade Inflation

Again, entitlement and power underpin the disparate treatment of men and women on college campuses. While it is clear that women have reached parity in terms of their admissions to and enrollment in most areas of higher education, it is not clear that the fundamental differences in campus entitlement and power have been resolved among any of the student subpopulations, let alone in the arena of gender. In fact, overlaying the traditional male-female power struggle for equity are new variations on the theme of the battle of the sexes. The struggle for dominance takes on a new face with reports of gender-based favoritism, now frequently favoring female students. Male students now complain that females are benefiting from overcompensation, an overdoing of the effort to make them welcome and help them succeed in college. "I can compete with the female students, even the best of them, in an honorable way," a male senior at U.C. Berkeley complained, "but why should I tolerate the women students being graded less harshly than the men students? I really don't think they deserve any sort of special favors." This young man was alluding to the plague of grade inflation relating to gender. Although most of the reports of grade inflation—the giving of higher grades than are deserved—on college campuses appear to be unrelated to gender, I have been informed by some male students that they suspect the problem to be gender-based.

Originally, grade inflation was brought to light as something high schools were doing to raise their rate of college admissions by graduating more students with high GPA's. It has become a given that an A at one high school may only be a B at another. Where gender has become a central part of the discussion is in the high grading given girls in high schools, not only for academic performance but also as a reward for their classroom cooperation and docility relative to their more unruly male counterparts.[37] The damage is done when these girls graduate from high school with high self-esteem based upon their high grades, only to find that, by the middle of their college years, high grades are not so easily earned. This leaves some female students with serious questions regarding their abilities.

As complaints of sexual preference in college grading are trickling in, the picture grows increasingly complicated. Accusations of gender-based favoritism in grading are confounded by accusations of over-inflating certain favorite students' grades. And these accusations of grade inflation are in turn confounded by reports of grading-standard conflicts between high schools and colleges and also by the shifting of grading biases from one gender to the other almost as rapidly as we can speak to the issue. Confusion may be the most obvious consequence of efforts to bring about the nearly impossible dream of educational equality, at least between the sexes.

Ignorance Is Bliss

The enactment of this drama takes place against the backdrop of a troubled history not so very long in the past. It is readily obvious, as any fool can see, that physical rape is most likely to be perceived as rape. What we are less honest about are the more subtle levels of rape, which have persisted through history and which linger today, if for no other reason than that they are not very far back in our history. It was only a century or so ago that the purity of women was linked not only to their sexual purity but to their intellectual naivete as well. As author Andrea Dworkin states in her book on the centrality of women's right to human freedom, *Right-Wing Women:* "As a cultural symbol, the good female is innocent: innocent of sex, innocent of knowledge—chaste in both ways."[38]

Dworkin's thesis is a hard-hitting one, which maintains that male violence against women is pervasive and necessary in maintaining women's acquiescence to the fixed traditional patriarchal social order: the one in which the man is boss. Even when he appears to be sharing power, it is just possible that the male still reigns as king. Again, we must remember a yesterday of not long ago when, in Dworkin's words, "Historically, ignorance has been a form of grace for the good women; education was denied women to keep them morally good."[39]

The moral superiority of woman has been wedded to her oppression. Has she been slain by a two-edged sword of something other than her own design? Dworkin calls this a kind of "metaphysical paternalism," which constructs a "social model in which women need not experience their inferiority as a burden," fortunately for them. Instead, women are awarded such great social value as women "that their inferiority is of equal social worth to the superiority of men."[40]

This complex and crazy-making dynamic is the one that our parents and their parents and their parents' parents helped to preserve. Coming out of centuries of such a tradition, do we really expect that admission to colleges and universities will change the status of women overnight or even in one century?

Many women are discovering that the answer to this question is *no!* Furthermore, they are finding themselves, while racing away from the cultural psychosis of the old metaphysical paternalism, in a new double-bind: "the equality trap." In her revealing book by the same name, published in 1988, sociologist and attorney Mary Ann Mason tells it like it is: "Equality is a trap for women. Over the past twenty years, the condition of women has worsened, not improved."[41] Mason insists that the durable concept of women's rights must be updated "to deal with the new problems of modern women in a changing economy."[42] We must remember how this issue looked to pro-emancipation women of the early 1800s. In the words of "Matilda," written in her 1827 letter to *Freedom's Journal*, "I would address myself to all mothers, and say to them, that while it is necessary to possess a knowledge of pudding-making, something more is requisite. It is their bounden duty to store their daughters' minds with useful learning. They should be made to devote their leisure time to reading books, whence they would derive valuable information, which never could be taken from them."[43]

I certainly do not seek to reverse the marvelous opening of access and opportunity from which I have benefited tremendously. But I have certainly experienced the dark side of equality in the face of expectations placed upon me, while I was working and pregnant and while I was a student and pregnant, expectations that continued to seem absolutely blind to the differences between a pregnant woman or new mother and her male counterpart. Equality is just a word. I was told, "Well you wanted equality, now you got it." I learned the hard way that equal is meaningless if it says that we are all the same.

To this day, when I walk the campus of U.C. Berkeley with my daughter, I feel I need to repeat the words of Abby Kelly, advocate of women's literacy, as she spoke to a women's rights convention in 1850: "Sisters, bloody feet have worn smooth the path by which you came here."[44] I cannot help but think that women's demands for actual educational opportunities are a significant, although perhaps more simple, part of the overall process of diversification. I laugh when I remember being told, in 1970, by one of my several British (Oxford and Cambridge) undergraduate science professors, who had come to open the new University of California, Santa Cruz, "They should never have let girls into college. They are a waste of educational resources. They will destroy higher education by forcing us to lower intellectual standards."

Are we hearing the same sort of complaint with regard to ever more liberalized admissions today?

. . . .

Shameful Admissions:
Offering Less and Less to More and More

So we dare to ask ourselves, could it be that liberalized admissions policies have, despite their good intentions, manifested some undesirable effects? Could the cure be worse than the ill? I have heard some powerful ambivalence, as well as some resounding noes and some resounding yeses, to these questions. Certainly, liberalized admissions are not the only basis for complaints about the state of higher education. In fact, the intense controversy over the application of affirmative action preferences in admissions diverts our attention from the larger matters of the over-expansion and deterioration of higher education. We are looking away from the truth, distracted by mercurial and fashionable political debates. Nevertheless, liberalized admissions are pointed to as at least a significant source of so many of the effects discussed in Chapter One and throughout this book. This chapter lists these effects again, this time in reverse order, to see the trickling down, right into the college classroom, of political and social pressures.

On the *Political Level*, we find

- Distraction from the real issues

- The demise of the egalitarian ideal

- Old and new populisms in conflict

which affect the *Societal Level* in various ways, including

- Potential decline in the composite intellect
- Misuse and misappropriation of human capital
- Rising costs of higher education

which, in turn, have a marked effect on the *Institutional Level*, where we are witnessing

- Institutionalized (or systematic) racism
- Institutionalized (or forced) multiculturalism
- Conflicting policy goals
- Reverse discrimination
- Institutional irrelevance
- Institutional embarrassment

which translate into *Campus Level* developments such as

- Racial tension
- Emergent (newly learned) discrimination
- Ongoing gender stress
- Demands for compensation and support for special groups
- Failures of compensation and support
- Perceived decline in academic quality
- Graduation-rate problems
- Clandestine rise of the university within

which filter right into the *Classroom Level*, where we find

- Overcompensating biases

- Stereotype-based classroom management

- Color grading

- Classroom clusters

- Professor frustration

- Neglect of the average

- Neglect of the able

From this hefty list of negative outcomes whose cause is not entirely clear—outcomes of some mix of political and social developments and pressures, many of which *appear* to be related to the increasing multiculturalization of our society—one might surmise that the institution of higher education is indeed falling apart, even dying. However, these complaints are more productively viewed as growing pains. Higher education has outgrown its old model. As will be discussed in Chapter Eight, it is time for a new structure, one with new rules for admission and graduation, one having a new purpose.

Already, colleges and universities are feeling the pressure to evolve. They just have not quite understood how great a restructuring is needed. Instead, they want to remain what they describe as "great." Spokespersons for large universities are letting it be known that they are convinced that their institutions will live on in all their glory, while admitting that there lies ahead a large job. We hear this in statements such as this one—made amidst complaints about his decisions regarding allocations of funds and consequent calls for his resignation—by J. W. Peltason, past president of the University of California system: "The difference between an ordinary and a great university lies in the ability to make tough

decisions in the face of adversity, to raise and allocate the resources
we must have if we are to remain great."[1]

The Structural Parameters of Decline

Despite official proclamations of optimism, there are those who see
the institution of higher education, or at least its major operations,
as declining. One perspective on this decline is that our universities have outgrown or overgrown themselves. Let's call this the
parameter of size. This predicament is most adeptly described by historian and professor emeritus Page Smith, founding provost of the
University of California, Santa Cruz, in his book, *Killing the Spirit:
Higher Education in America*, published at the beginning of the
1990s.[2] Smith details the decline of higher education, suggesting
that in the "huge modern universities, some 75 percent of undergraduate students today receive inferior educations."[3] The modern
university, Smith writes in his critique of what he calls "academic
gigantism," is a huge institution, which has become "muscle-bound,
slower to respond to stimuli than the dinosaur."[4] It is a place where
"committees proliferate; the effort required to accomplish the most
modest reforms is out of all proportion to the results."[5] Smith notes
that the "principal (and perhaps only) argument for huge campuses
of from ten to forty thousand students is greater efficiency in terms
of research facilities, specifically libraries and sciences labs . . . that
one university of fourteen thousand is more efficient than, say,
seven of two thousand." The latter number, Smith suspects, is
already "at the upper limit of human efficiency."[6] As is true for any
overextended system, expansion reaches a point past which it
weakens all that has expanded.

Another parameter of decline we can call the *parameter of purpose*. According to Smith, it is not only a misappropriation of
efforts toward efficiency that undermine the modern university, it
is also the pressure on individual professors to publish or perish to
gain tenure, and on entire universities to produce research findings

to gain financial support from government and business.[7] Again, economic motivation results in overexpansion, in this case, in the income and reputation-producing arms of the university. Against the backdrop of overgrowth and overexpansion in size and purpose, the needs and the problems of the society being served by the university are changing. Being so overextended, the university is barely capable of contending with issues such as those discussed in this chapter.

Revolution in the Nature of Work

The 1980s and 1990s have witnessed a surge of concern regarding the intellectual preparation of the American workforce. Can American workers continue to compete on the international level as, more than ever, the new jobs demand thinking skills more than physical skills? We cannot deny the astounding shift in ability demand that we are experiencing at the turn of this millennium. Vocational education once was aimed at ensuring the employability of both the less-educated and the less-educable by teaching basic skills such as auto repair, carpentry, and the like. Now a greater level of academic competency is required of all workers, including those who once would have been able to achieve middle-class incomes in traditional blue-collar occupations. The traditional sources of vocational education, community and junior colleges, are not, as presently structured, large enough, funded enough, or prepared enough to bring about this new level of academic competency. Higher education *must* play a role in this transition.

As Thomas Toch, the education correspondent for *U.S. News and World Report*, who was quoted in Chapter One, writes of this "revolution in the nature of work": as this nation moves "into a post-industrial information age, more and more well-educated workers are required," and "[an increasing] proportion of the workers . . . must be drawn from the ranks of students that the public schools have traditionally educated least well: minorities and other disadvantaged groups."[8]

San Francisco Community College vocational director Chui Tsang claims that state and local budgetary "cutbacks have also hurt in ways not immediately felt. They've limited our ability to change courses to reflect what is needed now and in the future."[9] Tsang refers here to what he explains is the difficulty the vocational programs are having in keeping up with economic and technological changes. This is a condition faced by the vocational arms of many community college systems. For example, some vocational programs are still teaching students horseshoeing and ornamental horticulture. Although training in these areas may lead a few students into employment, those are not areas in which the job market is large.

The problem faced by vocational educators is not simple, however. There are many factors confounding the relevance of vocational education. One is the students' desires. Large numbers of students continue to sign up for courses that teach increasingly outmoded skills such as welding. This is even true in areas such as the San Francisco Bay Area, where the future job markets are in more technical areas such as electronics, computer programming, and biotechnology. This hints of a second, more complex factor: the difficulty in predicting local job markets of the near future. Community colleges, even when seeking to streamline and add muscle to their vocational education programs, do not presently have enough information to predict efficiently and then respond to the occupational demands of their regions, even a few years into the future. Moreover, a third, powerful, frighteningly important factor is economics. Cutbacks have left community colleges with reduced advisory teams, meaning that vocational students have even less direction than in the past, although they face a more ambiguous and changeable future.

Plight of the Educational Underclass

A fourth factor is that a significant segment of vocational students is a large educational underclass, including unemployed persons who have not been able to hold jobs, single mothers who require

job training to get jobs, and homeless people seeking enough training to find work that will move them off the streets and into
homes. On top of all these factors, the cost of community college
for students is rising. Consider the large community college system
in California, the home state of U.C. Berkeley, our flagship university. It saw a drop of 106,000 for the spring 1993 enrollment and
another 31,000 for fall 1993 enrollment, all due to fee increases.[10]
This accounts for some 9 percent of California's community college enrollment and represents a significant attrition of the educational underclass.[11]

While this economically motivated micro-exodus from community colleges is developing, another economically fueled exodus
is emerging—this one from California's first tier of higher education, the University of California system (which includes U.C.
Berkeley) and California's second tier of higher education, the California State University system. Due to fee increases, students are
leaving these systems. As a result, community colleges are swamped
with students who never before would have elected what they perceive to be the least desirable educational option. The community
college system, already under economic and population pressure,
is increasingly overcrowded by these immigrants into the educational systems of the communities they once would have chosen
to leave. The educational underclass is thus being pushed out of
any form of higher education, at the time in history when it most
needs it.

So here again, California reveals the troubled world of our over-
burdened, overcommitted, and underfunded tomorrow. The nation
cannot help but take notice. Although the *Master Plan for Higher
Education in California* called for an open enrollment system, which
turns no one away from an opportunity for higher education, community colleges have been unable to be the bottom-line backup
guarantor of this wonderfully egalitarian policy. California faltered
in the implementation of its most democratic promise—an equal
opportunity education—a promise to provide any resident of the

state, regardless of race or income, college-level job training and/or academic preparation.

Legislators scramble to rectify the situation, often with plans more costly to the state and, consequently, more difficult to budget than existing policies. A case in point was the proposal by California Senate Education Committee chair, Santa Barbara Democrat Gray Hart, which encourages University of California–eligible students to attend a community college for their first two years in exchange for a waiver of all U.C. fees when they transfer into the U.C. system for the education that is rightly theirs.[12] This may be the best answer to the problems we face, but without increased community investment, a reallocation of state resources, or funding from heaven, someone or ones will lose out in college. At present, it will be the underclass. The average members of the middle class are next.

Educational Outsiders

Already, a generation of people who do not or will not fit the system exists. Will there be an institution of higher education to receive them? Consider the comments of Bobbie Groth, former director of admissions and professor at Shimer College, Waukegan, Illinois, a small liberal arts college, which he says is generally referred to as an "alternative" college: "Whatever the reason, there is a whole sector of the population which has been educated in and out of school in a manner which does not fit them into the mainstream of the 'higher education' chronology or content in the United States."[13] Among this group, Groth includes applicants who are the products of home schooling or alternative elementary and high schools. He also lists students who left high school as young single mothers and who, some years later, decided a college education would provide them a way out of poverty, as well as students who are entering college "late" by traditional definitions, after having served in the military or having entered the job force immediately after high school and who now feel that "education is the avenue to the next phase of their lives." Groth notes that these older students are "so far away from the targeted population for standardized testing that even if they have taken the tests—their test scores make no practical sense."[14] On the other end of the age spectrum are the "early entrants," who either graduate from high school early or leave high school before completion and are seeking college courses.

Intensified Racism on Campuses

Higher education struggles with in-house problems. The difficult matter of free speech on campus has been framed and reframed in the decades since the 1960s. While antiestablishment speeches and civil disobedience rallies were the source of tension in the 1960s and early 1970s, the 1980s and 1990s brought a new twist. The presence of ever-stronger ethnic constituencies on campuses has resulted in vocalization of racial competition, conflict, and even hate. The latter, so-called "race hate," has exacted new hate speech codes from college administrators. Under the watchful eye of the courts, universities are redefining their codes of conduct as they pertain to hate speech, downplaying references to speech as much as possible. It is ironic that, despite the intent to control hate speech, campus speech codes must favor vocabulary referring to action, to behavior rather than to speech. In this way, constitutional protections of the freedom of speech are less in jeopardy. Speaking to this point, Lawrence White, university counsel for Georgetown University, writes: "First Amendment jurisprudence recognizes an important distinction between speech and action and allows a greater degree of latitude when action is being regulated."[15] Yet, even with this guidance, many colleges and universities are opting out of the struggle to control hate mongering and racism on campus to avoid constitutional questions. This avoidance is dangerous. White referred to the warning expressed by Charles Lawrence, a law professor at Stanford University, who wrote that, by framing the debate "as one in which the liberty of free speech is in conflict with the elimination of racism—we have advanced the cause of racial oppression and have placed the bigot on the moral high ground, fanning the rising flames of racism."[16]

Could it be that we have entered a trap, a trap in history, a social quagmire, a Sartrian hell from which there appears to be no exit? Can there be no way out of the enigmas of diversity on campus— or on the globe? There is no turning back.

So, the egalitarian dream has its rough passages. To enhance and protect freedom, we must reduce and even deny freedom. The rising flames of racism on campus have been fanned by policies that bring face to face social groups who might otherwise have had to see each other only from a distance. These are not people from other sides of the world or the country or the town or the track, who one reads about or sees while driving by. These are fellow students, who share dormitory rooms, dining hall tables, professors. A brand-new level of social intimacy must be conjured: an intimacy that rips down the old barriers of protection, isolation, denial, and stratification. We have yet to see whether it will manage to rip away bigotry and prejudice.

So now what have we? Greater interaction, greater proximity, greater potential for multicultural and cross-social camaraderie, and more tension on campus. This tension should be embraced. A good campus can withstand tension. In fact, how can the examination of the ideas and issues of our times take place in an atmosphere that avoids tension?

This, of course, is a statement less easily made in the face of inflammatory speeches such as those given on campus by Khalid Abdul Muhammad, in which he, representing the Nation of Islam, has accused Jews of being major traders of Black slaves.[17] This line of thinking has inspired a whole new set of racial tensions on campuses.

In the fall of 1993, a professor of Black studies, Christie Farnham Pope, was threatened by one of her students with a "jihad" or holy war. This student accused his professor of brainwashing African-American students with material that undercut the teachings of the Nation of Islam. Although it was the chairperson of the department who removed the student from that class, sit-ins protested his removal and called for the professor's removal from courses teaching Black history. The administration agreed to accept the sit-in, thereby legitimating, in Pope's words, "the presence in my class of unenrolled persons whose purpose was to collect evidence to use in pressing for my removal."[18]

While the situation was more than likely aggravated by the fact that the professor was a White female, Pope pointed to the problem of radical Afrocentrism in an article she wrote for the *Chronicle of Higher Education*. Pope, professor of Black Studies at Iowa State University, claims that Afrocentrism is an intellectual movement that "rightly exposes the Eurocentric manipulation of the past by historians and other scholars."[19] She points out that, "like any vibrant intellectual movement, Afrocentrism contains within it a wide spectrum of positions."[20] However, Pope was confronted, in her own classroom, with a radical form of Afrocentrism, one taught by the Nation of Islam, which she describes as being "intent upon developing a heroic myth that not only claims most of the accomplishments of the ancient world for Black Africa, but that also links these accomplishments to the skin pigment melanin, producing a new essentialism in which race is destiny."[21] Pope was eventually exonerated, but the conflict her case represents continues.

More Crime on Campuses

What may be the most discouraging of all the indications of the decline of higher education is crime on college campuses. Awareness of this condition has crept into the collective consciousness of the nation. As Anne Matthews, who teaches nonfiction writing at Princeton University, wrote in her 1993 article for the *New York Times Magazine*, "The Campus Crime Wave": "Only a generation ago, American campuses were tranquil enclaves in both image and fact . . . but, since the early 1980s, image has less and less to do with reality. From ax attacks in libraries to shootings at dances, violence on urban, suburban and rural campuses has transformed many schools into discreetly armed camps: electronic passkeys for dormitories, cold-steel mesh on classroom windows, computer controlled cameras in stairwells, alarm strips in toilet stalls."[22]

Although Matthews reminds her readers that such violence is nothing new, pointing to thirteenth-century riots at Oxford, and nothing restricted to the United States, noting recent armed clashes on college campuses in Bangladesh, she emphasizes that the intensity of violence on our campuses has "radically increased."[23]

While it may be, in a perverse way, reassuring that most (about 80 percent) of the campus crime is student-on-student, Dorothy Siegel, professor and vice president at Towson State University in Baltimore,[24] reminds us that our students themselves are now the criminals. And we are no longer talking about plagiarism and library theft. A significant proportion (on some campuses, estimates run as high as 90 percent)[25] of campus crime is alcohol-related.[26] The first annual crime statements, submitted in 1992 (as required by the then new Federal Campus Security Act) by almost 2,500 institutions of higher education, reported a total of 30 murders, 1,000 rapes, 1,800 robberies, 32,127 burglaries, and 8,981 motor vehicle thefts.[27] These are most likely underestimates of the crime rates, as campuses prefer to generate as little bad public relations for themselves as possible.[28]

Government will say it is not avoiding the problem. However, the Campus Security Act, requiring disclosure of crime rates on campuses, applies only to campuses receiving federal funds and does not include the crimes of larceny, arson, vandalism, and disorderly conduct.[29] Both this act and the 1992 Campus Sexual Assault Victims' Bill of Rights came out of campus assaults on female students by male students.

Siegel claims that the Towson State study of campus crime "reveals a distinct subculture, common to campuses nationwide, of victims and victimizers."[30] The perpetrator profile is a discouraging one: perpetrators often commit multiple crimes rather than one, usually have low grade-point averages, drink heavily, and are, in sad disproportion, athletes.[31]

Alcoholism on campus is a critical component of the overall rise in modern campus crime. A 1992 Harvard study of 1,669 college freshmen reported a radical increase in student drinking, with a radical increase in students drinking with the intention to become drunk, and with female student drinking also rising significantly.[32] The old adages, "boys will be boys" or "kids will be kids," become a sorry recital.

As Matthews reports, "In the campus-crime world, as in many aspects of American life, California functions as an early warning system, a canary in the academic mine. Campus bomb threats, sniping, arson, rape, murder are all crimes with which the Berkeley administration has experience."[33]

In the face of shifting labor force demands, diminishing funding, increasing numbers of students, mounting racial tension, and growing rates of campus crime, what chance does higher education stand? Its fundamental parameters of size and purpose are already overextended, thus undermining the American system of higher education. What purpose does higher education now serve? By virtue of its overextension in politically and culturally fragmented times, its value could be diminishing beyond repair.

The University May Now Be Truly Irrelevant

Or maybe, as Dr. Rey, former admissions committee director at U.C. San Diego, said, "The university is irrelevant."

Confounded by his dismissal of this great American institution, and struck by the absoluteness of his statement, I found myself drawn to hear more from this man. I believe that Americans must engage in conversations such as this at this time in our history.

"So what would you do with universities, Dr. Rey?"

"Leave the universities alone," he replied. "Let them go back to teaching the classics. Let them all learn to speak Latin and do basic research, et cetera."

"And let them admit what type of students, Dr. Rey?"

"All who want to become academics can go to a university."

"And what would the others do instead?" I asked.

"People who want to work in the community, teach them to work in the community."

"Teach them, but where? At the junior college?" I pressed.

"No. As a rule, junior colleges are worse than universities," he replied.

"Where would you teach them then? By what mechanisms would we transfer adult-level skills and knowledge?" I queried.

Rey's suggestion was innovative: "You create educational programs in the community and you hire people to work in them. You give them computers and give them information and bring in experts to show them what they need to know."

"Would these be public programs?"

"Well, right now they are public programs," Rey noted. "If there were some way to fund them from within the community, that would be even better. We need learning and information enterprises in minority communities. We need people willing to risk time and money to provide the needed services. We have grocers, laundries, auto repair, why not computers and computer instructors?"

Several times during this interview, Rey returned to his central point: the educational establishment is unable to address minority concerns. His basic reason for this: "Education furthers social realities that oppress minorities."

I asked him if he was calling for an entirely new model. "Dr. Rey, it sounds as if you are actually calling for a whole new mechanism of training and educating—one we don't know yet. Not the workplace, not the school, not the community college, not the university."

"About the only thing left—the only mechanisms with any possibility of integrity—are the community centers. But churches and small businesses can work too."

So the community center would be the source of higher education in Rey's approach. Had his vision changed since he had served as an admissions officer for a major university? "In thinking about your work in college admissions in the early 1970s and comparing your current attitude, I surmise that your dreams have shifted, Dr. Rey. Is that because making them come true was too difficult, or because you found a better way to make them come true, or because you found better dreams?" I paused, but he was silent here. I went on, "So you're really talking about a community-based intervention that would be educational but would also be vocational and very community-oriented?"

"Yes, that's exactly what I'm talking about," he agreed. "That's right. You train them to read and write because the schools aren't going to do it. Or you augment the school curriculum so as to actually help them survive in the public schools all the way through to graduation. And then you provide them with post–high school technology, and with resource and information access so that they can do something where they live."

"And how do you define community, Dr. Rey? Geographically? When you do a community-based intervention, which is what you are describing here, what are you talking about? A geographical community?"

Rey paused and then continued, "Well, to be funded you have to have a geographical entity. In the old days of social work, this was called the 'catchment area'—in other words, a target area and a target population. And, the target population often has shared demographic characteristics—low income, shared language, shared ethnic identity."

"Would you target a specific ethnic group with this?"

"Yes, we do."

"In other words, you would target the Hispanics within this geographical area?"

"Exactly. Culturally relevant programs run by culturally relevant people."

"Would a program such as you're describing work if it went past one ethnic group or if it targeted everybody? Do we already lose the quality?" I asked.

"No, that's the next move. We already have a Black project and we have a Chicano project—two separate projects. The third one we want to have would be a cross-cultural one," he told me.

Cross-Cultural Competence

Rey proposes a model designed to prepare what he calls a "cohort" —a generation of children. He says that we should train leaders to create a cohort, the members of which are cross culturally competent, but who "retain their identities and connections to their own communities, who learn to rely on each other, with respect for their elders, and care about people regardless of color," he says. This cross-cultural competence "wouldn't include being able to access the system of the higher education or some type of occupational strata . . . it wouldn't entail learning to play the admissions game."

I asked Rey whether this community-based education might end up leading to even greater segregation and greater exclusion.

"Perhaps so!" he answered. "But within these communities would be a sense of self-reliance and respect for differences, unlike today where the myth of equality masks racism and *de facto* segregation."

I asked if Rey had completely abandoned the equal opportunity admissions dream of "creating broader access, lending a hand to the Hispanic community in the U.C. system."

I could hardly finish the sentence. He wanted to speak to this immediately. "Just forget about this stuff. They're not being educated at universities!" he protested in a friendly but firm voice. "There is a 60 percent Hispanic drop-out rate. They're not being taught what they need to know to be empowered. Or to be free. They are being taught to submit to institutional authority. And that means White authority or the vestiges of White authority myths. No one buys White authority. Even White males think they are oppressed."

Access to Opportunity

Where does this leave us? I wondered and started to ask, "These cries from the broken gate, these cries saying, 'I'm not getting this opportunity' and 'This opportunity doesn't look so great now that I'm here,' could be. . ."

"Irrelevant." Rey used that word again: *irrelevant*.

"But you see that many shed tears over it anyway, even though it is not necessarily the opportunity to get."

Now he agreed.

I went on. "You are telling me that this whole 'liberalization' of admissions policy has not done as much as it was intended to do. But, have there been some minority groups that have benefited?" I asked.

"I think not," he said, shaking his head.

"Does this mean that you, if you had to do it again, would skip your own college education?" I tested him.

"Absolutely," he said without missing a beat, "I would have done what all the smart guys that I grew up with did. They went out and made a lot of money."

"You wouldn't go back and get your doctorate if you had to do it all over again?" I asked.

"If there was any way that I could have known then what I know now, I would never have gone to college," Rey insisted.

"Well that's just about as important as everything else you've said here. . . . Now, getting back to your admissions work at UCSD, you said you were a convenient political ideologue."

"Politically correct ideologue. My ideology matched their ideology. People work under systems of shared ideas, ideologies. If you're a feminist or a Communist and you go into a place where that is not acceptable, you don't get the job. So what I'm saying is that, when I went down to U.C. San Diego, I was naturally politically appropriate. I didn't have to pretend to be anything," he answered assertively.

"Were your ethnic characteristics also appropriate?"

"Perfect."

"Dr. Rey, do you feel that you were brought into the Admissions Office, admitted to the committee, because of your ethnicity?"

"Absolutely, without any doubt. And every student I recruited, I recruited because of his or her ethnicity."

"Well, that is *differential policy*, in a sense, to recruit, to select, or to turn away somebody based upon his or her ethnicity, isn't it?" I asked.

"I'm not against differential policy. I'm against negative differential impact," he responded.

"In other words, it is acceptable to treat people differently in selection processes?" I asked.

"It's okay to tax somebody who makes a million dollars ten percent. It's not okay to tax somebody who makes $1,000 ten percent."

"This is how the same policy can have a different impact," I noted.

"Exactly," he agreed. "Ten percent from somebody making $1,000, you break their back. Ten percent from somebody who's making $1 million, you inconvenience them temporarily while they make a couple of phone calls to another accountant."

"This is an instance in which the same policy has a differential effect—one on the rich and one on the poor. Another type of picture—I am now referring to what was done at U.C. Berkeley— emerges when you have an admissions policy with 50 percent being admitted in one way and 50 percent in another. That was really two subpolicies, each of which had different impacts. Some accused U.C. Berkeley of maintaining a quota system, although officials denied that it was one."

"I have never objected to quota systems," Rey said here.

"In other words, in your view, Dr. Rey, race-based or at least race-relevant selection is acceptable. It's almost necessary to rebalance or to make reparations?"

"Of course, but it is also irrelevant!" he emphasized. "Admissions policies—academic hand-wringing—the real issue is academic indifference to the learning needs of humanity. The real issue is another generation of White racists imposing their obsolete curricula on people in pain, then finding clever ways of blaming the victims for hurting."

"In my interviews, many students, professors, and administrators are referring to racial tension. Some professors claim students cluster together by race."

"It's going on all over the country," he nodded.

"So that tension is very present in your eyes," I went on, "but what about it?"

"Competition over scarce and limited resources," he explained. Rey closed with these words, which are still ringing in my ears:

> Our universities are stale, musty warehouses where once-bright students died and became professorial zombies. Academics fear learning, so they use all of their resources to control and limit it. You won't find Darwin, Copernicus, nor Freud at a university. Thomas Edison, Henry Ford, Mao Tse-tung, Ho Chi Minh, et cetera, et cetera, et cetera, studied in the real world not the library tower. Their work had immediate practical value. We must learn in order to free our human spirit. The academic concentration camps of the late twentieth century stifle everyone and people oppressed by color and gender the most. Those who run public and higher education should be indicted for crimes against humanity.

The Case for Class Action

Crimes against humanity! Rey has leveled a heavy accusation here. He describes universities as "academic concentration camps" which "stifle everyone," identifying "people oppressed by color and gender" as most stifled.

Few would go so far as to say that the American system of higher education is this evil. In fact, researchers tell us that a large percentage of Americans are apparently unconcerned about the quality of higher education or the multicultural and political problems on campuses. They are relatively unconcerned, except for its cost.[34]

Yet this lack of concern is measured among a general public that knows little about what goes on in college classrooms, what is taught on college campuses, how professors are hired, or how tax money filters into college bureaucracies. This is not surprising, considering the fact that 75 percent of this general public does not hold a bachelor's degree,[35] and therefore has little direct experience with higher education, let alone with the college campuses and classrooms of today.

Is this unconcern lack of exposure? Lack of awareness? Lack of information? Perhaps the shameful admissions and candid firsthand observations contained in previous chapters can be shared with those who are among the unconcerned citizen group. In the meantime, according to researchers, this unconcerned group does report that it feels that colleges and universities do not do much of any importance.[36] And here lies the catch. If the general public feels that colleges and universities do not do much of any importance, why would the general public want to continue paying for higher education through taxation?

It is important to remember that 75 percent of this unconcerned group has no B.A. Perhaps the mere experience of attending college renders a citizen more concerned. This fits the original understanding of egalitarianism, discussed in Chapters One and Two, which required an educated citizenry to help maintain our democracy. There is, however, another, less palatable but more likely explanation for why the quiet unconcerned generally have not been to college and the vocal concerned generally have: a loud and visible portion of those who have seen what is going on in higher education are, and cannot help but be, concerned! These citizens, representing a broad range of cultural and political perspectives, have become quite vocal about the pitiful shortcomings and the insidious flaws of academia.

With at least some, and a quite vocal some, of taxpayers, parents, and students increasingly dissatisfied with the education their tuition dollars buy; with most every racial, ethnic, gender, disability, and special group bringing charges against some element of some college or university somewhere; with so many highly qualified students being turned away by the top-cut universities for which they are highly qualified: higher education is a logical target. Citizens could, hypothetically, take the system of higher education to court in perhaps the grandest of all class action suits: the American citizen versus the American university.

The most obvious flaw in this reasoning is the most significant part of this story: there is no unified class to bring action, for the overwhelming majority of complaints against the university are based upon competition among subgroups. The class we would call the American citizen is now, more than ever, a collection of very different and competing sociocultural and socioeconomic subgroups. Even among students and their parents who feel that they have purchased a falsely advertised vehicle, which does not really run, who feel that the baccalaureate degree they have paid and worked for is looked down upon by employers and even by graduate schools in that it fails to ensure the levels of literacy, writing ability, analytic ability, numeracy, cultural exposure, responsibility, and general competence we need in our college graduates— even among these consumers of higher education, there is no cohesive class.

In this sense, our preoccupation with diversity has divided us. United, we could take a stand against the fragmentation and deterioration of higher education, which now has reached the point where the B.A. it awards is inconsistent, unreliable, and hollow. However, divided, caught up in the pros and cons of affirmative action and other diversity policies, we can only take a series of stands against each other and the institutions appearing to favor only some from among us. We can only see discrimination and reverse discrimination and not the problems with the larger picture, the conditions that fuel these waves of tension and backlashes. Perhaps the best motivation for unity among citizens, a unity bridging but not denying specific ethnicities and other distinguishing characteristics, is that such unity would increase their power and their potential for such class action.

Still, as things stand today, with us so divided, there could be another hypothetical case for class action: the American citizen against the American dream. Here, if we try, we might be able to make the university the basis of our complaints—or at least the official scapegoat. After all, our universities have indeed failed to serve everyone, every single citizen, let alone equally, and have therefore been instrumental in weakening the citizenry, dividing us into competing social subgroups. Somewhere along the way (maybe even in a college classroom), we were led to believe that higher education should, would, and actually could manage to serve us all.

7

Can We Serve Them All?

These shameful admissions reflect the hazards of war. College applicants and college students have been hit by flying shrapnel. While they have never really been the target of the war of ideals, they have indeed been the cannon fodder. Once admitted, college students must understand that they are not enrolling in a demilitarized zone, but instead they are heading into a very real conflict in which the weapons are concepts and policies and administrations and curricula and even professors and classroom seating arrangements. It's an all-the-more-difficult war to comprehend because the real problems shield themselves behind the handy targets of multicultural pressures, ethnic competition, and old and new racisms.

Now, finally, we are persuaded that we cannot have it all, that we cannot please everyone all the time. We learned this from the great social experiment we conducted via the affirmative action programs originated in the 1960s with President Johnson's Executive Order 11246 and the Nixon administration's U.S. Department of Labor regulations, which followed this order.[1] Not only were these programs difficult to design and to enforce, they were difficult to implement successfully. By the mid-1990s, we learned that these programs were also difficult to fix, to redesign, and, should we want to, to deconstruct.

Affirmative Inaction

From the start, affirmative action policy encompassed far more than college admissions. Government agencies were required to report the percentage presence of women and minorities in the labor force. All federal agencies and government contractors were required to make equal opportunity clauses part of their recruitment advertising. Any underrepresentation detected was to be reported and corrected.

The ideals behind this policy were noble: give disadvantaged Americans an extra boost through the gates of opportunity, gates that should be open to all Americans. As President Johnson explained the motivation for affirmative action back in 1965, "You do not take a person who, for years, has been hobbled by chains and liberate him, bring him up to the starting line of a race, and then say, 'You are free to compete with all the others,' and still justly believe that you have been completely fair."[2] Instead, based upon affirmative action directives, we created corrective race- and gender-based measures to be applied in hiring, awarding contracts, and college admissions.

We have seen how such measures can work toward a fairer representation, at least within universities, of the surrounding population. We also have seen how a university's admission of a freshman class with a particularly diverse ethnic profile does not guarantee that this will be the profile of either the corresponding enrolling or the corresponding graduating class. We also have seen how affirmative action policies often resulted in the turning away of highly academically qualified applicants of some races, while admitting less academically qualified applicants of other races. No one really disagrees that these are some of the difficulties inherent in the implementation of affirmative action policy. The disagreement is more in the arena of value. Are these difficulties worth it?

Advocates of affirmative action say yes. U.C. Berkeley sociology professor Troy Duster points out that a historical perspective, one acknowledging that we have experienced many generations of racism in America, is essential in evaluating affirmative action: "Affirmative action is deeply flawed. . . . It's abused. It is sometimes ridiculous," Duster admits; however, he adds, "You can't overturn the caste system by treating it as if it doesn't exist. You have to treat a social problem with a social solution."[3]

Sure enough, where the debate has flared is around the value of this social solution. Are the gains in minority enrollment and graduation worth the exclusion of highly qualified applicants of other races? There is no single correct answer. The trade-off is viewed from a host of personal, political, cultural, and practical angles. What is clear is that affirmative action, this "social solution" to a historically generated "social problem," is neither a simple nor a pure solution. This solution has proved to be one of the most controversial, complex, and problem-generating solutions in modern times. We must wonder whether more or less complication, confusion, and disappointment would have come out of a decision on the part of the federal government to leave the wrestling with fair representation issues to each campus independently of the others. Such a decision to do nothing, for better or for worse, might be described as *affirmative inaction*.

Harvesting the Top Crop?

Still, for better or for worse, our society has taken action. In fact, as I said earlier, cries from the broken gate of opportunity are not all sobs of sadness and strife. Messages of strength, success, competence, excellence, and optimism have also been quite audible in the responses to my questioning and interviews. There is also a great deal of institutional learning taking place, even at the private universities where the pressures of citizens, social policy, and the media are likely to be fewer.[4] My interviews with admissions and administration officials of elite private schools verified this.

Although, in keeping with the current tendencies of private universities to maintain a low profile during national flare-ups of equal opportunity debates,[5] most of them chose to have their names left out of this book, they did share some valuable information with me.[6] I inquired of them, "Do you feel that, over time, the type of student you have admitted has changed? Are you seeing a shift or an evolution of the profile of the student body?" Although I always was told yes, the yes was qualified like this: "In superficial ways, yes," one official replied. "What I mean by superficial is with respect to inborn characteristics . . . which are not trivial but which don't seem to me to get to the heart of the matter."

Recruiting for Diversity

I also was told that the matter of recruiting for diversity has most definitely been addressed at private universities. One official explained:

> We have certainly succeeded at this university in the past couple of decades, in the ethnic diversity of our applicant group and therefore of our student body. For [many decades] we have been actively recruiting a diverse group of students, using our alumni and every other means at our disposal, so the idea that we would recruit a pool that would be not homogeneous is not new to us. For at least twenty years, we have been very successful in diversifying along ethnic grounds. So this effort isn't new to us. In fact, for most of the century, we have been working very hard at diversifying among geographic and, to some extent, socioeconomic backgrounds.

Of course, some of this century-long recruitment trend reflects the socioeconomic shifting that has occurred in the general population. An Ivy League admissions director reminded me, "A number of significant changes have occurred in the typical educational profile of American families—many more college students have parents who have been to college now. And, nowadays only a few percent of the college-going population has a father who didn't go to college, unlike decades past."

I asked several private university officials whether or not the academic quality of their schools had been in any way compromised by their efforts to recruit for cultural diversity. Most did not think so.

Several admissions officials told me, "The big issue in admissions is financial aid. Everyone knows this." Again, the touchy matter of financial support for students surfaces. Indeed, the capacity to admit people without regard to financial need—admit need-blind—guarantees a university the capacity to say to a family, "We'll help you afford it." As it was explained to me, the ability to admit the best qualified students need-blind, "allows us to attract many other students who pay full freight, full-paying guests who know that when they come here they will be joining a place where everybody got in only for talent and not because somebody could afford it and somebody else couldn't."

However, in the lingo of one admissions officer, this sort of personalized case-by-case selection process "burdens the choice." This weighs the admissions decision-making process with the knowledge that "every time you make an admissions decision you turn away some five who really could do the work, and some other people in that five are also going to have great contributing futures. So we've got a responsibility we feel very heavily."

What about discrimination? I ventured to ask my interviewees in a most delicate way, "Everywhere across the country there are noises being made—I know you're hearing these too—about turnaways being discriminatory by race."

To this, I received a range of responses including chuckles, shrugs, grimaces of frustration, and flat out comments such as, "Well, we don't do that," and, "We go out of our way to recruit a racially diverse group of applicants." Several private Ivy League officials explained that their schools have purposefully produced a generous leeway for choice within a highly academically qualified group. As one official put it, "To get in here you have to convince the full admissions committee that you've got exceptional promise in the future. Certainly we weigh positively differences in background whatever they are, including ethnicity and experience in your local community. We certainly can use, and have for twenty years or more, race as a positive tip. It doesn't get anyone in, but it can certainly help make a case that's on the way to being made."

Institutional Interests in Diversity

I was also told that a top-cut private Ivy seeks to include "a range of talent from different kinds of backgrounds, as well as talents in different areas. So we have every interest in the mix." I was also reminded by an administration official at one of the top private Ivys, "We have no 'institutional interest' at all in taking a candidate who isn't very good and turning away somebody who is. That isn't good for our school. It's not a matter of some social policy."

Most of these elite school officials insisted that they address the matter of ability disparity prior to admission. They claimed they were not running into the problem that some professors at other colleges are reporting—the situation in which they walk into a classroom that's already too large, maybe seventy students, and find that they really have young people so far apart academically that it's hard to fit them on the same grading curve. This is the kind of serious complaint that some of the professors at U.C. Berkeley and other top public universities have made. As discussed in Chapter Five, these professors claim that, when this happens, the grading curve they produce by the old formulas sometimes breaks down by color. Some of them feel they have to shift criteria for different subgroups of students within their classes, and they find the whole thing frustrating and embarrassing. Others think this is fine; this is a sign of the times, and this is good.

My private university administration interviewees admitted that they often hear complaints regarding student performance such as,

"How did so-and-so get in?" and that they do occasionally make admissions errors: "Very often it's somebody who, when you go back and look at the folder, was absolutely, undeniably academically qualified—it was some other type of problem, which would also be an admissions mistake." One official admitted, "So, we certainly do get individual complaints, but I don't think anybody here has observed a broad pattern of unevenness broken down by race."

"Do you hear comments such as, 'The B.A. from the Harvard, or the Stanford, or the Yale, or from your institution doesn't mean what it used to'?" I asked.

"That's golden-age mentality," one replied, alluding to the things-were-better-in-the-good-old-days line of thinking. "The fact of the matter is, our students—you know, I hate to say this but it's just plain true and I can prove it several ways—the students who come here are much brighter than they were fifteen or twenty years ago. The people we're turning away today are people who would have walked in ten years ago. And everybody knows that."

"This is good for your university, isn't it?" I asked this administrator. "It supports your reputation. And it says that your institution addresses the educational needs of the most able."

"It's disgusting in some ways though," I was told by this same concerned administrator, "because it means that you're turning away people who, in bigger numbers, could really be super here."

At the same time, private Ivy admissions officials are quite concerned about lower education: "My worry, looking around the country, is that, in secondary schools, the students who are the most promising academically are not the focus of their schools or their school boards depending on whether it's a private school or municipal system concern. I think there is an increasing tendency to assume those kids will be fine, and to focus on the kids who need more remediation." Another comment: "There are not really fewer of the very brightest, it's just that they're not as well-developed and as easy to spot, and we haven't taken as good advantage and therefore won't of their talent, which we need at least as much as we ever did."

Officials from elite universities tend to share concerns about the impact of rising educational costs, the feelings and perceptions that families have about rising costs, the general willingness or unwillingness of families to invest in their children's education, and the ability of families to pay. The economics of education cannot be dismissed as trivial. Families are increasingly less able to pay full fare, whether for private or public education. Bright students who cannot afford tuition may disappear, may never even begin to apply.

Therefore, to buttress socioeconomic, ethnic, and talent diversity, need-blind recruitment is key, at least for some of the leading private universities—thereby enabling active recruitment for both excellence *and* diversity. Once top-cut applicants are recruited, selection of an excellent and diverse student body from among the pool of applicants—a pool that has already been molded to be excellent and diverse—is a natural sequel.

The recruiting for both excellence and diversity, which is conducted by elite private colleges, runs an astounding and yet confounding parallel to the motto (implanted by chancellor Tien) of U.C. Berkeley, "Excellence *through* diversity." Given that such a motto contributes to the public image of a university, then this motto in itself is an effort to recruit for just what it says it stands for: excellence through diversity. Are great institutions, the most well-known public and private, arriving at the same conclusions, desiring to recruit the same sort of student body, having come up very different paths to the same juncture? Are their intentions actually the same?

Maintaining Standards of Quality and Humanity in a Changing World

Excellence and diversity: natural or forced bedfellows? It all depends upon one's perspective. Certainly, our university of tomorrow, U.C. Berkeley, is a testing ground, a highly visible laboratory in which the chemistry of this balance has been tested by a fifty-fifty admissions policy: fifty for merit, fifty for diversity. Whereas a private university is relatively free with regard to public dictation of its admissions practices and formulas, a public university has far less autonomy. Compromises such as U.C. Berkeley's fifty-fifty policy were deemed necessary by the public sector, at the state level.[7]

It all depends on what we choose to call "natural" with regard to bedfellows. Donna Shalala, President Clinton's secretary of health and human services and past chancellor of the University of Wisconsin, Madison, cast another light on this matter: "The new leaders of great institutions have to have more than great academic skills. They have to understand outside constituencies—the business community, minority groups and women's groups, social services, school systems."[8] Could this be the driving force behind the emergence of the "excellence through diversity concept"?

Numerous constituencies, both inside and outside its number-one testing ground, U.C. Berkeley, argued against diversity as a driving ideology. The late professor of political science, himself a professor at U.C. Berkeley, Aaron Wildavsky, contended, "If excellence in education is replaced by an ideology whose supreme value is 'diversity,' then the primacy given to gender, ethnic, and racial composition will have produced catastrophic consequences."[9] Proponents of such seemingly pessimistic views point to the many conflicts of the 1990s as evidence of such catastrophic consequences.

Community is Diverse

Central in the discussion of the diversification of student bodies and thus of college admissions is *community*. What of the community— the sense of identity, belonging, and participation felt by its members—a college manifests? Can such a community withstand the tremendous and often centrifugal pressures posed by diversity?

Supporters of diversification claim that not only is such survival possible, it is the only option. They say that the university of tomorrow, especially when supported by public funds, must represent the community of its constituents. Only a fair representation of this increasingly diverse community of taxpayers will work. They say

that the vital essence of academic life is not its institutional structures. It is not the schedule or the course list, nor is it the organizational structure of the various departments and administrations. The
spirit of the academic community is not located within these specific structures of the college or university. This spirit is not a static
component of the institution. Instead, it is a continuous process, an
explicitly desired product and an implicitly and often undesigned
by-product that results from the meshing of the many components
within and around the institution.[10]

Viewed historically, this is a relatively new way of seeing a university. The more traditional guarantors of community in academic
life have been a socioeconomic homogeneity of the student body, a
faculty composition running parallel to that of the student body, and
a curriculum focus structured to traditional standards, and/or, in the
case of professional schools such as those preparing students for
degrees in law or medicine, a narrowly defined set of requirements.
Name recognition, athletic success, famous alumni, and the history
and reputation of a particular institution all have been integral parts
of the community in which it stands: the status of the college or university adds to the status of the town. For many a university, the task
of creating status is primary.[11]

Simply attending and graduating from a university such as Harvard, Stanford, or University of California, Berkeley has opened
many a door for a young graduate who might otherwise have been
lost in the shuffle of competition and demand for opportunity. As
Julius Getman sets forth in his book, In The Company of Scholars,
the diverse and frequently competing missions of higher education
have included the creating of status, as well as the providing of
opportunity, and the maintaining of a class of intellectual elites,
missions examined from several angles in this book.[12] These missions are frequently cast at odds with one another, and in so being,
generate an inextricable tension. The foundations of community
can be compromised by the exacerbation of such tensions. In our
time of multiculturalism, the mission of creating status is interro-

gated by fundamental questions such as status for whom? Status in the eyes of whom? Status as an opportunity awarded by what means?

Parallel but Diverse Dreams

So much of the pressure of multiculturalism is described in terms of the egalitarian ideal. However, we tend to overlook another critical angle on this matter: the subtle and most Machiavellian issue of parallel but diverse dreams. In the highest sense, we may be on the brink of acceptance of diversity. Prodded by science fiction and the New Age–human potential movement, the modern American mind is ever-growing in its acceptance of the notion that experiences and perceptions of reality differ among individuals, among gender and age groups, among political parties, and among cultural groups.

We are all here. We see each other on television, in magazines, at work, at school, and in the streets—but do we really live in the same world? The diversity of human realities is so extensive that it suggests that there is no *here* here—at least no communal here.

Yet, I have visited a number of universities where students insist that they are "very pleased to be here," "proud to be here," "privileged to be here," and that they "worked very hard to be here," "deserve to be here," and even "have a right to be here." For these students, there is a university here. They identify with the place. They became a piece of the place and will take it with them forever as they journey on through their lives.

In this respect, *community happens*, regardless of the disparate forces at work upon it. A university that functions well is one that learns to live with its multiple personalities. We may as well accept diversity, because, in the words of Sheldon Hackney, chairman of the National Endowment for the Humanities (NEH), "We are all members of different communities and groups at the same time."[13] We are diverse.

What does this given, this undeniable existence of a diverse community, mean to the university? Once accepting this reality, how do we move from our traditional and narrow definitions of excellence, intelligence, and merit to a new and improved model of society? "Is it the job of a university to define intelligence? . . . Or is it," as professor Kenneth Norris suggested, "to take the diversity of minds that stream through the admission process and allocate them, or let them allocate themselves, to places in the smorgasbord of the educational establishment where they find they best fit, and are most likely to succeed?"[14]

In Search of Excellence Through Diversity

It was with the burden of such questions that I embarked upon the most optimistic and, at the same time, brow-raising, interview I conducted in writing this book, and that was with chancellor Chang-Lin Tien of the University of California, Berkeley.[15] I arrived a few minutes early at the grand old California Hall, where Tien's office is located. As I waited at the entrance to sign in with security, I could not help but remember various scenes, including student demonstrations, at the entrance of California Hall. So much of the pageant of modern American history had enacted itself here. My reverie was interrupted when the official asked me for my name and purpose. When I said I had come to see the chancellor, there was an "oh yes," and I was directed up the stairs. I landed in a large waiting room where I had only a few moments to read through the various books on the various achievements of this university, which I found displayed on the waiting room table before I was ushered in to Tien's large but unpretentious office. I was waved into a comfortable seat in the sitting area. Tien sat near by.

He shifted in his seat, appearing to make himself comfortable for what would be a long and fruitful conversation. I said, "You have been quoted as saying that we can achieve 'excellence through diversity.' What a wonderful motto. Would you tell me something about what it means?"

He said, "The demographic transformation, not just in the state, but in the country as well as in the whole world, is accelerating in many ways. And so, it follows that now, in order to build excellence in this changing world, we have to broaden the pool of resources."

Note that Tien talks about the global trend toward the merging of populations, or at least the diversification of populations, as "the demographic transformation." Note also that he says the university must broaden its "pool of resources." This is reminiscent of the comments made by administrators at the top elite private Ivy League universities, who explained that applicant pools were purposefully cultivated. I therefore wondered and asked the chancellor, "How would you define excellence?"

He was ready for this question, I assume because he had been asked many times, and went on immediately, "Excellence is very subjective . . . different people have different views. The excellence I'm actually talking about in the motto is institutional excellence in terms of academic contributions, scholarship, and so on."

I was ready with the next step of my inquiry: "Now, I'm sure you've heard some of the professors' comments that, within some of their classrooms, there is this ever broader, ever-stretching, range of academic ability and performance. According to this viewpoint, the end of this range looks like excellence, and the other parts of this range do not. Do we need diverse definitions of excellence to deal with changing classrooms? Is this a reality that we must accept?"

"First, I don't maintain the premise that we have different levels of preparation among the students. For instance, at Berkeley, there are very talented students coming from all different backgrounds. Their talents vary accordingly. I am completely *for* our maintaining a very high standard of excellence. That is always my goal. We have to stand firm on that. However, we need to provide opportunities for disadvantaged groups, for developing their talents, mentoring them, and providing opportunities for them to develop and to compete on the same level of standards. That's what I am striving for."

"It is commonly thought," I said, "that the state spends approximately $11,000 a year per student, that it costs about that much to educate a student here at the university. Would you say that, for us to pull the students who are not academically talented for some reason—perhaps simply because of inadequate high schools—up to the standard that you are talking about, we need to spend more of our resources on those students than we do on more accomplished ones?"

Tien leaned forward and smiled. "First, you quote the number of $11,000. That's been debated. People all have different views on how you calculate the cost of instruction. Also, different schools and different institutions vary tremendously."

He went on, "Second, what is required to maintain the level of excellence, to develop students' talents to a particular level, is not related only to monetary—financial—resources. Providing a caring and humane environment in which people can interact and build confidence, providing the sense that one is being cared for—many of those things do not require financial resources. It is more attitudinal than economic."

I continued, "Of course, I do hear from some students that, at least at times, they feel they are being charitable when they sit back in class and tolerate fifteen to forty-five minutes of listening to material that is much too basic for them to be sitting through. Many of them are positive about this and feel that this is their contribution to the effort that the university is making. Occasionally, I am told by students that this is a waste of time and that they are angry about it. What would you say to these students?"

Ability Distribution Is Not a Racial Issue

Tien nodded affirmatively. "Maybe there is a certain degree of truth in this; maybe this happens sometimes, but I want to emphasize, that even in a very homogeneous society, in its homogeneous institutions, you have the same kind of distribution; you have students bored while others require fifteen to forty-five minutes of explanation. *This isn't really a racial or multicultural issue.*"

Tien was offering another explanation for the seemingly broad range of ability in university classrooms. He was saying that this range is typical even where there is little ethnic diversity. Tien further emphasized this point. "In the 1950s, 90 percent of this student body was Caucasian. At that time, when 90 percent was Caucasian, the graduation rate was less than 50 percent. But now we have 55 percent students of color. Our graduation rate is, on the average, say 65 percent or 70 percent."

"When you say students of color, do you include everybody who is not Caucasian?" I asked.

"Not Caucasian . . . yes."

"So you are including Asians?" I attempted to find out whether the graduation rate for people of color was buttressed by the inclusion of Asian Americans into the large amorphous group.

He knew what I was getting at. "Yes, Asians, and others, including Blacks, Native Americans, and Hispanics," he said.

"Maybe you can help me with this issue." I went on, "When we talk about excellence through diversity, are we talking about excellence along many new continua or by the old, more single standard of whatever that old excellence was?"

Excellence Is Not Absolute

He replied, "I understand what you mean. Let me answer this way: excellence is not absolutely standard. You have to judge excellence within the social and economic environment. These environments are changing. What we mean by excellence today could be very different from what we will mean fifteen years from now. And the same thing happens when people measure intelligence." He continued, "We have to be very careful about using traditional measurements and distribution curves. We have to be open-minded enough to accept and explore new thinking, new directions."

This open-mindedness, with regard to excellence and intelligence, is the forging of a new standard of merit. However, at the time of this interview, 50 percent of UCB admissions were determined by academic merit largely based on old definitions of such merit. Even so, critics of liberalized admissions policies claimed that the quality of the resulting student body was deteriorating. I asked the chancellor about this criticism.

He answered, "Some people say Berkeley students are not as good. But Berkeley is among the top universities."

I wanted to get to the bottom of this matter. "So what do you think is going on? Why the attacks on Cal? Is this all some sort of rugged public relations competition, or are we witnessing some kind of anti–U.C. Berkeley phase?"

Tien answered:

> Many people say Berkeley has a discrepancy of talents. They attribute this discrepancy to its large number of students of color. However, if you look carefully at some other leading universities, they have much larger discrepancies in terms of academic preparation, but because of other criteria. They are more homogeneous in terms of race and other ethnic composition, so nobody criticizes their discrepancies. Nobody even raises the issue. Some of them accept a lot of students for other than their academic talents—for legacy, family background. They also use athletics as a way to bring people into their schools, because if you only use family background, there will be questions. So they create other criteria by which to admit students, and when you get all those people in by all those other criteria, you find the number of students ranked in the top 10 percent of the high school graduating class is no longer as high as it is here at Berkeley.

"Would you say that people tend to look at great educational institutions such as Harvard, Stanford, Yale, U.C. Berkeley, and say that when the degree of selectivity is greater, we have a guarantee of more excellence? Does Berkeley appear to be less selective in the eyes of the public?" I asked.

Diversity Policy Can Maintain Selectivity

This is, quite probably, the presumption, the general perception; however, Berkeley certainly is not far behind the private elites in terms of selectivity. I do think Harvard gets the very best students, in terms of high school rank, many more than Berkeley does. . . . Harvard gets not just the top 1 percent, but maybe one-tenth of the top 1 percent of graduating high school students. Also, keep in mind image. Image influences general perception. Harvard is a university that is 315 years old. U.C. Berkeley is 127 years old. So Harvard has had graduates for a much longer time, who have graduated with the great prestige of Harvard. However, Berkeley is not really far behind. In terms of training and educating the future leaders of the United States, I would say Berkeley is probably the best place because of its tremendous diversity.

Then I inquired, "Do you see U.C. Berkeley as the university of tomorrow?"

He was certain he did. "Oh, absolutely. I've told that to many people. I feel that the U.C. Berkeley educational environment is the best in the country and the prototype."

"I understand that you were on the Board of Trustees at Princeton. I assume then that you are very aware of the differences and the pressures on the private Ivy Leagues versus what are called the public ivys?"

"Oh yes," the chancellor replied, "the pressures are very different. But this is also the great strength of this country: we have diversity. Even among the higher education institutions—tremendous diversity. We have large schools, small schools, private schools, and more specialized schools like Cal-Tech, or MIT, or Georgia Tech, and so on. Then you have general universities. . . . We need this diversity of institutions."

"Tell me, Chancellor Tien," I asked, "how Princeton fits in to the spectrum of universities."

"Princeton is very different from Harvard. It is much smaller. Princeton is about one-third of Harvard's size and has no professional students other than engineering. Princeton has no medical school, no law school, no business school, and it is very liberal arts oriented, and very small . . . very elite in many ways."

"Does a person in your position here, versus the one in your position at Princeton or Harvard, have more or less autonomy than you do?"

Tien went on to explain that the autonomy did not so much vary in degree as it did in character. "Again, I would say that, by ordinary standards, maybe a chancellor at a public university has less autonomy because he or she has to deal with the governor, the legislature, and the board of regents, and because he or she must be more responsive to public opinion. Yet, on the other hand, I can see, since I'm on the Board of Trustees at Princeton, that although the president over there has more autonomy than we do, he also has much stronger legacy, alumni, and other private pressures."

"It's a different kind of autonomy," I mused.

"Yes. Again, all things are relative," he told me.

Now I shifted forward in my seat. It was time for political philosophy. I probed further:

We talk about egalitarianism in education, how slowly we opened up elementary and then secondary and now higher education to a broader range of people. We talk about populism winning out over classicism as a philosophical model defining the purpose of the university— the classicist view being that the university should be preparing an elite representation of society to take the elite positions, the populist view being the opposite, which is, at least in part, the explanation of what we are doing here at Berkeley. What would you say the future of our relatively egalitarian, populist, liberalized admissions policies will be? Where are we going with all this?

Larger Historical Trends

Tien paused a moment here and then explained:

> You cannot change historical trends. You cannot turn back the forces of democracy, the forces of diversity, or the forces of accelerating the pace of change. I think we will continue to see more and more diversified constituencies and communities, not just in terms of students, but among faculty, alumni, campuses, towns, and government influences. Many people don't see that dynamic nature of their environments. All this is very natural. This and every university are part of the larger picture. This diversification is an evolutionary process. The more this process goes on, the more people like me and others should try to cooperate, to show we care, to participate instead of becoming even further isolated. That's my view.

But I was troubled. "But what of all the conflict that comes with this?"

Tien was not troubled. "Conflicts will resolve. We will find more ways, new ways to build common bases, commonalities, new ways to share together. In many ways, this is an Asian philosophy: conflict/resolution—the so-called yin and yang."

"I like the idea that you are able to bring that philosophy to your work here."

"I try," he chuckled, unassumingly. "We must exercise mutual respect, mutual understanding. The more we build on that, even when we disagree, the better we can work together. And in this sense, I feel extremely blessed. The professors have been very supportive of me. Many of them disagree with me. In fact, when

I was appointed, many said that I would probably lower the standards, push only affirmative action. But they find it not so. I have shown I stand firm on many of the academic standards issues, and that I nevertheless believe that we have to give people opportunity."

We shook hands and I said goodbye. The chancellor had given me some thought-provoking answers. As I wandered across the campus, I tied Tien's comments to the mix of stories, opinions, and cries I had heard coming from the broken gate:

- First, the trends that are upon us are macro-trends and cannot be reversed. They are here to stay and we do best to work with them.

- Second, the sense of fragmentation and dissolution, of increasing entropy, which arises in the process of diversification is natural. All this is part of evolution.

- Third, differences should be valued, not ironed out or melted away. We can disagree and nevertheless work together.

- Last, yes, U.C. Berkeley is indeed the university of tomorrow, marching boldly and with strength into the future. -

Is Wisdom but Balance?

So, we continue to wonder, can we have it all? Or can we just talk as if we are having it all, appeasing our longings with mottoes such as "excellence through diversity"? The jury is out. Time is watching the great test playing out on leading college campuses around the world: the weighing of egalitarianism—or whatever we believe that to be—against the drive for excellence—or whatever we believe that to be. This weighing has to be, by its very nature, a process laden with debate and challenge. This is a necessary part of our evolution toward a reasonable equilibrium.

In fact, the basic stance of the fascinating policy-analysis document referred to so many times in this book, the *Karabel Report*—a UCB document that captured so much of the essential dilemma of our times—was that a "fair and equitable admissions policy is not . . . a neutral one."[16] Instead, it is a policy that establishes "a reasonable equilibrium among legitimately competing goals, values, and interests."[17] Nevertheless, we must question even equilibrium and any path that appears to be leading to it. We instinctively know this. The *Karabel Report* thus also required that those who alter admissions policy continually monitor the "social consequences" of that policy and alterations of it.[18]

But, we continue to wonder, can we really have it all? What about educational quality? Can this be preserved? The *Karabel Report* maintained strong support for academic criteria: "As an institution of international renown and as one of the nation's leading research universities, Berkeley has an obligation to admit students with exceptionally distinguished academic records."[19] Yet, the following goals explicitly stated in the *Karabel Report* burdened this obligation with numerous other responsibilities. Read them and see the sorts of restrictions that were placed on academic criteria. Ask whether or not there has been and will continue to be an elaborate double-talk spoken behind the face of many a well-intended admissions policy:

- As a taxpayer-supported public university, Berkeley must strive to serve all of California's people.[20]

- Berkeley should actively seek diversity—socioeconomic, cultural, ethnic, racial, and geographic—in its student body.[21]

- In its admissions criteria, Berkeley will recognize outstanding accomplishment in a variety of spheres, including (but not limited to) art, athletics, debating, drama, music.[22]

- The admissions process should include a human element and must not be based on grades and test scores alone.[23]

At the same time

- Berkeley will absolutely not tolerate quotas or ceilings on the admissions or enrollment of any racial, ethnic, religious, or gender groups.[24]

- Berkeley should accept only those students who have a reasonable chance of persisting to graduation.[25]

The balance sought by the *Karabel Report* and other recommendations of the late 1980s and early 1990s required subtle but definite shifts in several facets of policy. Particular fancy terminologies were dropped, and particular new and supposedly improved ones were adopted. Doubletalk? Try to make sense out of these "changes":

Parity was dropped. The extremely populist policy principles of the 1960s, 1970s, and early 1980s, once described and justified as necessary "preferential treatment," "parity," and "total protection of special groups," were retired (at least temporarily) in favor of "flexible" and "increased emphasis" on academic merit.

Broad representativeness replaced parity. The implementation of the *Karabel Report* was supposed to represent a so-called "general departure" from the previous stance taken by admissions policy. The drive to "reach" explicit "parity" began to recede, moderately shifting emphasis to "broad representativeness," which, as quoted in the report, called for higher education to "strive to approximate . . . the general ethnic, gender, economic, and regional composition of recent high school graduates." From the standpoint of this approach, the old "parity" was, at least on paper, more exacting. To reach parity meant to achieve an enrollment on a U.C. campus that is the same as the high school graduation rate for any given group. What parity called for was a university student population that would match almost exactly the pie graph of the graduating high school population of California. Because the old pre-*Karabel*, Tier-3 targets were specific and aimed at achieving this explicit parity, the critics of this tier of the admissions system argued that it was actually a "quota system," and no one wanted to hear that.[26]

Quota was a bad word. To avoid accusations of quota filling, these specific targets were replaced with so-called "flexible" targets, "ranges" based on the availability of qualified students as well as the desired balance of the student population. The *Karabel* recommendation in this area aimed to protect the campus's ability to meet its mission to serve the "full spectrum of the California population" and at the same time not have its process legally jeopardized as a quota system might. The old Tier-3 process, as described in Chapter Three, was replaced with a more holistic review of a would-be, Tier-3-type student application in which the applicant was evaluated in a multidimensional, gridlike manner rather than on just a few variables, which were subordinate to the dominance of specific targeting.

Looser, politically safer, terms were adopted. New targets for "secondary review" were defined as having "rough" upper and lower bounds, with enough flexibility that even lower bounds of targets were not to be met if the number of qualified applicants was insufficient, and with upper bounds being exceeded if there was an unusually strong pool of target applicants in the secondary-review category. In fact, during each admissions cycle, targets were to be adjusted based on the "relative strengths" of applicant pools. Sheer eligibility (or "total protection" policy) no longer would guarantee any particular applicant group admission: "total protection," therefore, ended.[27]

Total protection? Which citizens ever felt totally protected? Has anything of substance actually changed in all this effort to redefine college admissions? No. Will anything of substance change amidst efforts to repeal affirmative action-type policies? Perhaps not. But then, we just cannot have it all. Buyer beware. You pay with your tax dollars for all these revisions and rewordings of a confusing and divisive social problem, whether or not anything is actually accomplished.

Rethinking Pathways
to the American Dream

None among us is unaffected by what is reported in this book. Whether or not you are going to college, applying to college, paying someone's way through college, a college graduate yourself, a parent of a young child who will come of college age in the new millennium, a taxpayer, an educator, someone who votes, or an entirely disinterested party, you face the emergence of a new global reality, in which intense diversity—not just of cultures but of competing ideologies and desires—is a given. The challenge for you, and for all of us, is to see the larger picture and your place within it. Your—our—survival as a free people depends upon all of us coming to this awareness.

Sleepwalking through the gates of time, we have tumbled blindly, ever closer to liberty and justice, opportunity and education for all: ever closer and yet ever further away. Now we must wake up. Something about the American dream is inevitably unrealizable. Just when we think we almost have achieved it, we come to see that the same dream looks very different through the eyes of others. We don't know how to share. We don't really want to share with others when we are worried that our own may not be getting what they need. We don't know how to make room at the top and still preserve the excellence we let ourselves believe is waiting there. We don't know how to open the gates of prosperity to everyone, especially as multiculturalism becomes a global reality. The old cultural hierarchies are threatened. The new are as yet unstable. Citizens of all races, creeds, and cultures want the opportunities they believe they have a right to, with education being the primary determinant of these opportunities. All contend they have a right to admission to opportunity and should not be deprived of this right.

So we make the college campus the stage for the enactment of a drama that does not really belong there. More and more, as a last-ditch effort, we admit our young people to colleges and universities, assuming that the great rebalancing of all social inequalities can be accomplished there. This is the last stop before the realization of the dream. Here is where life chances are ultimately determined. Get that degree and have a good life. When colleges fail to serve us, to fill in all gaps, and to correct all flaws in our great system of opportunity, colleges become the sick ones, the identified patients and the bad ones, the culprits. Everything is wrong because colleges have failed to right it all.

The greatest irony is that the demand for higher education is burgeoning, even in the face of the serious limitations of this education. We sense that something is wrong with this picture; however, seeing no other or clearer path to prosperity—or even socioeconomic survival—we send hoards of young people, from all backgrounds and with all ability levels, through college. To accomplish this, in recent decades, we have created educational opportunity, affirmative action, race-based scholarship, and other structures to make certain that young people from all walks of life are admitted to college. Even as new, more heated debates emerge, debates regarding the utility and constitutionality of some of these structures, the demand for higher education continues to grow.

It is unfortunate that the difficulties of multiculturalism have taken center stage. We are allowing these to distract us from a larger and even more problematic development: as the opportunistic megalith we call the higher education industry expands to phenomenal proportions, we close our eyes to the fragmentation, dilution, and deterioration of higher education. We try not to see how inconsistent and unreliable higher education has become in terms of its quality, content, intellectual level, and contribution to the workforce. We try not to see, as part of this general deterioration, the stereotyping, cultural clustering, color grading, and newly emergent forms of discrimination going on in classrooms. We try not to recognize the inconsistencies in quality and efficiency, the misappropriation of our tax and tuition dollars, the resulting hollow quality of today's college degree. That we look away from all this is not surprising. These are such shameful admissions.

Healing the Split Society and the Fractured Dream

Heed the advice offered by attorney Gerry Spence in his book, *From Freedom to Slavery: The Rebirth of Tyranny in America:* "The first step toward freedom is to recognize our enslavement."[1] Such recognition is a major undertaking. It requires that we all slow down and look carefully at what we expect of our political system and the institutions, such as colleges and universities, that it supports and that support it.

We have become slaves to a set of ideals. Now we must free ourselves of the dream and examine the reality. The catch here is that it is the sound education of as many citizens as possible that facilitates this sort of examination. As author Fukuyama reminds us, "The effect of education on political attitudes is complicated, but there are reasons for thinking it at least creates the conditions for a democratic society. . . . Educated people are said not to obey authority blindly, but rather to think for themselves."[2]

Examine the Idiosyncrasies

Thinking for ourselves involves taking an overview of the issues. We would do well to make the first point of our examination the effects of racial and multicultural pressures on higher education. If we allow ourselves to be caught in the changes of the political tide or the wave of major backlash without understanding what is happening, we are merely pawns in the process. So let's return to the concepts set forth in Chapters Two and Three, those of the old and the new populisms, and see how major political trends are influencing and maybe even dictating our thinking.

By the start of the decade of the 1990s, it was apparent that a backlash was well under way. This backlash against affirmative action, diversity policy, and other elements of the new populism was inevitable, as political swings always are. Many will, in fact, argue that the backlash had been under way for at least a few centuries, since the very moment in history when the concept of egalitarianism first emerged.

What came as more of a surprise were some of the idiosyncrasies of this most modern backlash. First of all, the backlash was not, for the most part, a 180-degree swing. Egalitarianism was still the heralded ideal. So, the swing was not away from this ideal but rather away from one unit of analysis and back to another. Although many of its proponents did not recognize the unit of analysis as the focal point of their rebellion, the backlash was indeed against diversity policies such as liberalized college admissions. Such policies had forcefully injected our old populism with a unit of analysis beyond the individual: the ethnic or other social group.

Somehow, instinctively, most everyone forgave the new populism for its powerful shifting of American focus. After all, the obstacles to progress of the old, more individual focus, on "liberty and justice for all" in a nation where "all men are created equal" were discriminations not against particular individuals who had homogenized into the melting pot but against entire social groups such as African Americans, Jews, and females, who had somehow remained identifiably different.

This was the second idiosyncrasy of the new backlash: the intuitive understanding of the built-in, tragic flaw—the knowledge that it was the failure of the old populism to refrain from discriminating against entire social groups—that brought about the new populism. This understanding promoted a prolonged tolerance of the tension between the old and the new populisms and a sense of guilt among political liberals and intended benefactors of the new populism about addressing the tension aloud.

A third idiosyncrasy, as viewed in Chapter One, was that although the backlash constituted a turning of the tide, we found ourselves at more of an ebb tide, with attitudes and constituencies washing in myriad directions. The American dream was fragmenting before our very eyes. We were awakening ourselves with the sounds of our own tormented cries from the mad nightmare of the broken gate: seemingly broken but never breaking barriers to human equality.

This is a rude but good awakening. Our humanity is at stake. Few organisms in nature, if any, can be precisely measured as being exactly equal. The closest we have to equal organisms are equal machines, and even then we do not find our own manufacturing methods successful in rendering exact replication. Fortunately, humanity does not wish to become a herd of organic but programmable, equal drones, easily controlled lookalike machines, which our exact equality could render. What wells up within our hearts is the sense that perfect equality is undesirable. We value the freedom to vary, to differ. This is the fourth and perhaps most heart-wrenching idiosyncrasy.

This is where an insidious psychosis, a social level of psychosis, creeps in. We discover that our most basic values, equality and freedom, are in abject conflict. This, the fifth idiosyncrasy, is the discovery of the sanity-threatening double-bind.

Studies of the mentally ill indicate that families who create inescapable double-binds around their children can generate schizophrenia in them. How? By creating lose-lose situations to which there appear no resolutions other than madness.[3] "Put on the red coat," a child is told. When she complies, she is scolded, "No, I said put on the blue coat." When she races to correct herself and comply with the new order, she is scolded again. "No, I said put on the red coat." There is no succeeding, no pleasing the parent, no way out.

Old and new populisms are the two voices of the same parent, of the United States Constitution, but somehow, they sound as if they are delivering opposing directives. In *The Evolution of Racism*, Pat Shipman captures this deep conflict in our awareness when she acknowledges, "We are collectively responsible for the appalling conditions under which so many live, for opportunities not offered, for chances not received, for the training never made available. These disasters are our fault, which we must acknowledge and redress." She then adds the counterpoint note, "But we are also deeply and individually responsible for our own failures of potential . . . for the moral laziness that makes us lower our standards for ourselves to the point of failure."[4] Recall the words of Marian Wright Edelman of the Children's Defense Fund in her book, *The Measure of Our Success*, which bring us a poignant imperative that we must "remember and help America remember that the fellowship of human beings is more important than the fellowship of race and class and gender in a democratic society."[5]

We are giving ourselves so many mixed messages these days. How can we please our founding fathers? How can we ever realize the dream? What is it that we have struggled to achieve for all these years? Do we see a reasonable way out of the growing American double-bind?

We feel trapped: populism nouveau, with its group-level unit of analysis, with all its good intentions, is now running at crosscurrents with the original goal of equality among individuals. Lose-lose. No apparent escape.

And so we compromise with compromise policies such as the half and half, fifty-fifty admissions policy in place for several years at U.C. Berkeley. Some of us are philosophically prepared to transcend the juxtaposition of values represented by such an official double-bind. Certainly, Chancellor Tien is, with his beautiful analogy to yin and yang, the necessary balance of opposing forces in all the cosmos. And clearly, the California state legislature, a body composed of individual politicians, did arrive at the official mandate, the fifty-fifty compromise, as its way out, at least for a while. Making an explicit policy statement that incorporates political tension acknowledges and relieves some of the underlying tension.

Legislative action is less driven by Eastern philosophy and more by perceived political necessity, but it sometimes arrives at the same point: admit half of all students based upon individual academic merit, as the old populism would have it, and not as the old classicism would have it, with only a small group of elite White males attending college at all. Admit the other half of all students based upon academic merit mixed with other criteria, which, as the new populism would have it, allows for the possibility of proportionally representing the state's ethnic-social profile.

And so we arrive at the controversial proportionality of populism nouveau. The social psychosis stirs. Communication is confusing. Quotas may be a more honest term, but they are not politically correct. Proportionality, less adherent to specific numbers and percentages, leaving room for approximation, is safer. Arguments against ethnic proportionality or fair representation warn of the demise of excellence. Already, they say, we reduced purely merit-based admissions to 50 percent.

Arguments in favor of proportionality contend that it is not at all a threat to excellence. After all, the only way excellence is threatened by proportionality is if not all ethnic groups are endowed with the trait of excellence. It is either a great irony or a fallacy-ridden construction of reality that finds the dominant ethnic group claiming or even insinuating that it is the sole or at least the primary source of excellence.

Proportionality Has a Troubled Implementation

Either proportionality is a threat to excellence or it is not. However basic this argument may sound, with its neatly and diametrically opposed pro and con, some analysts contend that this is not at all the issue. Rather, it is the time frame and the means of bringing about fair representation that these analysts see as critical.

When procedures such as admissions, faculty hiring, and curriculum development become procedures for the actual implementation of general diversity policies and specific proportionality ratios, they can be more of an implementation nightmare than a direct threat to excellence.

Taking the adversarial role in this line of argumentation, author of the classic *Art and Craft of Policy Analysis*, UCB professor Aaron Wildavsky, during his term as president of the California Association of Scholars, contended in 1993, "The belief that only modest harm will come from gender and racial preference is based on the unwarranted assumption that the measures that caused this decline are only temporary expedients. I believe these views drastically underestimate the consequences of pursuing the path on which almost all higher education has embarked."[6] Because of his long history of examining social policy for its pitfalls, the views of Wildavsky on the implementation of proportionality are an important contribution to the discussion of its value. (As he passed away prior to being interviewed for this book, I am referring to issues he addressed in certain of his writings, which he felt were particularly relevant to my work.)

Wildavsky specified his concerns regarding the implementation of proportionality in both college admissions and faculty hiring. He highlighted the importance of not having a single social goal—such as proportionality—preclude all others: "When the egalitarian critique of our universities changes from being only partly true, as in the past, to entirely true in the present, when, in brief, power *will* determine content, all that universities should be in an open society will be lost."[7] With these warning words, Wildavsky was underscoring his point that, as faculty hiring and student admission are ever more tied to proportionality, curriculum content will shift too far in one direction, will shift in such a way that the new "dominant doctrines will be those which claim that real knowledge does not exist, that it is only constructed by dominant forces in society to serve themselves and to put other people down." Wildavsky valued checks and balances. He was concerned about their waning to a point of imbalance. It is out of imbalance that distortions arise and take control.

Wildavsky warned that knowledge may end up being "held to be equivalent to group identity so that some groups have it and others don't by virtue of who they are, not what they know."[8] Of course, it is exactly this that is claimed by those who disagree with Wildavsky. They contend that proportionality is necessary to shift the arbitrary definitions of knowledge and intelligence and excellence, which have been set forth by the dominant, heretofore White, culture.

Let's link Wildavsky's concerns to Tien's yin-and-yang analogy. Yin and yang mean balance. Balance is essential. However, by its very necessitating of opposing forces, this model is equipped with its own tragic flaw: the potential for imbalance! But would we have it any other way? One extreme or the other, completely eliminating all opposition, while certainly eliminating the potential for any imbalance, would be entirely totalitarian. No freedom there. Equality maybe, equality of oppression, but not freedom.

Endangered Species of Knowledge

Perhaps cultural diversity is as essential to life on Earth as is ecological diversity. Not only evolution, but survival depends upon diversity. If this be the case, we are at great risk when we fail to cherish, address, protect, nourish, and educate diversity. The demise of linguistic diversity serves as an example and a forewarning. Already, linguists predict that half of the world's 6,000 languages will die out during the first half of the next century.[9] Linguistics professor Michael Kraus, director of the Alaska Native Language Center at the University of Alaska, Fairbanks, warns us, "Every time a language dies, surely it impoverishes us all. The death of any language diminishes the store of ideas, of different ways of looking at the world. It may diminish our very freedom to think in different ways."[10]

California is, in fact, a region in "the final stages of language attrition."[11] At one time, when Europeans landed on the North

American continent, California was what has been described as "one of the most linguistically diverse spots on earth," with some 100 languages spoken by Native Americans in the region, many as different from each other as English from Chinese. Today, only one of these indigenous languages is spoken by children.[12]

Could the store of ideas be diminishing? Once we are no longer able to think in the different ways thousands of different languages afford us, we are no longer able to think differently. The diversity of intellectual activity, and even of free thought, may be becoming archaic, an anachronism. It may be slipping away the way grains of sand leave a hand, imperceptibly, until enough is gone for an observer finally to notice the difference—if the observer remains mentally equipped enough to notice the difference. As intellectual diversity and, thus, free thought leave, there is an increasing lack of awareness regarding their loss.

How many of us have in some fashion endured such a loss, as well as a lack of awareness of this loss? We cannot really tell. Various forms of this diminishing of intellectual diversity are taking place on our college campuses. To wit, historian Page Smith describes the emergence of a new sort of "academic fundamentalism." Narrow-mindedness, the prejudice exhibited by professors when confronted with ideas that do not conform to their own theoretical credos, whether right, left, centrist, or other-leaning, fuels this growing and dangerous academic fundamentalism. Here Smith infers the existence of not one but a diversity of truths: "Academic fundamentalism is the issue, the stubborn refusal of the academy to acknowledge any truth that does not conform to professorial dogmas."[13]

It is in the pressures to expand, to profess for tenure, to sell out to government and business, and to face diversity with ideological rigidity that the "killing of the spirit" of higher education is proceeding. The acknowledgment of diverse truths is difficult for huge universities saddled with financial pressure and increasing institutionalization. Yet, it is in these very institutions of higher education that the pressures to acknowledge diverse truths are emerging most forcefully, as admissions policies shift to open the gates of higher learning to a more diverse representation of the world today.

An ever more heterogeneous student body arrives at the university with an ever more heterogeneous preparedness to absorb an ever more heterogeneous composite truth. We are beckoned to sit up and take notice of the demand for what we might call a *multiposite truth* rather than what we should admit is a *uniposite truth*. The demands for cultural diversity, which have arisen on campuses where the student body is ever more culturally diverse, reflect this craving for *multiposity*.

Anger

How can our old institutions, especially those that profess to teach truth or at least the methods of seeking it, meet such a demand? Institutions are by nature threatened when confronted with change.

Again, the social psychosis! This time it surfaces through fear of change conflicting with fear of staying the same. As my colleague and early mentor in the science of observation, Kenneth Norris, stated: "We humans are deathly afraid of being ranked, classed, and with good cause. The most luminous example of what can happen is the Holocaust, where people of all sorts, frail gentle old ladies, intellectuals, little children and the rest were labeled and killed for bearing the label. . . . And yet, beneath this fear we do rank each other. Constantly. Ponder the unexceptional statement: 'The University of California accepts the upper 12.5 percent of California's students.'" Norris again highlights the irony and hypocrisy of our present predicament. He does not, however, suggest that we dismantle our ranking system. Instead he says, "We must, in fact, perform such classification if our populace is to be trained and selected for the vastly diverse mental needs of our society. We must classify if we are to direct this or that young person into the places where he or she can succeed. But," he concludes, "unless we know what we mean by intelligence, or what performance in a test signifies, we are surely engaged in a crudely defined process that will fail to do justice to many young people and to our society more broadly. For many of them the anger may never leave."[14]

Norris detects, even attests to, the presence of an anger, an anger stemming from invalidation. This is an anger we all feel on some level, an anger the species inflicts upon itself, whenever it traps itself in the double-binding of *diversity resistance* and *diversity insistence*. This binding, this stagnation, this confusion, can wreak upon a society and its institutions madness and breakdown. This is what is happening in our society today.

A way out of the social psychosis of the populisms must be mapped. I suggest an escape route, both philosophical and pragmatic, in the following sections of this chapter.

Toward "Higher" Education

I like the scenario painted by Mary Catherine Bateson in *Peripheral Visions*: "Systems of education are everywhere in ferment, visions of promise countered with proposals for increasing rigidity . . . many proposals have too narrow a focus . . . when [it is] the entire concept of education [that] needs to be rethought."[15] Indeed, it is the major job of rethinking that we are either unwilling or unable to do.

Instead, we fund and cut funding, as if we are certain of the outcome of these distinct actions. Public expenditures represent either public priorities or public naiveties regarding how and why elected officials appropriate tax dollars into particular categories. By the fact that the United States, on the average, spends (in 1991) some $33,000 per criminal prisoner per year,[16] we might surmise that imprisoning criminals, whether it be to change their behaviors, to keep them off the streets, or to scare potential criminals by example, is a high priority.

Compare this $33,000 with the 1992 U.S. annual average of $5,466 per pupil in daily attendance in public elementary and secondary schools,[17] the 1992 U.S. average annual appropriation of $4,321 per student in public institutions of higher education (not including the average annual net revenue of $1,529 per student usually paid or borrowed with intent to be repaid by the student or the student's family),[18] the 1991 national average Head Start expenditure per child per year of $3,159,[19] and the 1990 average annual cash payment to a welfare family (of four) of $4,620 per year or $1,620 per single recipient living alone.[20]

While we are already spending six or seven times as much (on a per-recipient basis) maintaining criminals in incarceration as we are on providing higher education to young adults, we are looking for ways of further economizing on higher education expenses. At the same time, we are trying to make *more* room for prisoners, build them more jails, improve the programs available to them in jail, and help them earn college degrees while incarcerated. Perhaps we should admit the folly of our misappropriations and encourage high school graduates to apply directly to jail. Our distorted priorities, or at least our perceived necessities, are clear in both our funding and our attention.

The Lurking Technological Imperative

It is out of both economic pressure and technological imperative that college by television has arrived.[21] This development says more to us about the future than almost any other shift in education in recent centuries, if not in the entire history of mankind. "Telecollege" will revolutionize higher education, making it entirely possible and affordable to earn a degree while sitting at home watching television. Telecollege, composed of "telecourses," containing instruction provided by the leading professors at the most prestigious universities, represents a tremendous cost savings and, at the same time, the greatest leap in access in the process of universalizing education and in taking what was once reserved for an elite group and distributing it to the masses.

Not only is telecollege by far the most affordable means of providing education, it also has in its favor adaptability in terms of time and place (tapes of lectures can be rerun repeatedly) and uniformity of exposure (a topic can be taught by the same marvelous lecturer to the broadest number of citizens).

With this mass producing of the college experience already well under way, we are at a critical juncture in the evolution of higher, and all, education. Telecollege, with all of its economic and distributory advantages, represents the greatest depersonalization of education we have yet encountered. Come and get it! No direct human contact required: a college degree!

This is, of course, a natural sequel to the trends we have witnessed over the past centuries. There was a time when knowledge was transferred on a one-to-one or one-to-small-group basis. Eventually the classroom became the site of most teaching. Originally, classes were small and still reserved primarily for the elite. Universalization brought with it an ever-growing class size. And television brings with it the ultimate extension of size, which enables the ultimate universalization of experience. It is exactly this highly egalitarian—and in that sense most laudable—experience that we must interrogate for meaning. Letting our interrogation of telecollege lead us, we would be wise to monitor carefully any and all efforts to mass produce and bureaucratize education further, inquiring

- What of the *human element*?

- What of the inspiration of *creativity*?

And, we must ask, when the personal contact—the energy exchange between student and teacher and among students—is omitted from higher education, what happens to the mind; how is the development of the intellect stimulated? Can a television-trained mind adequately prepare itself for the demands of the era? We must also be ever-inquiring

- What of the most delicate mental functionings of the students—how will we train their intellects for the challenges this rapidly changing world will bring, the necessity to *quickly learn new technology?*

- What of the *realization of human potential?*

Coupled with the demise of the human element in education is the decline of the college community and, with it, the potential for decline of the societal community. Without community involvement and identity, what becomes of civic engagement? It is essential that we continue to ask

- What of *identification with the community?*
- What of *civic responsibility and contribution?*

In asking these questions, we must demand not only conceptual answers but also structural responses. As we press for the above values to remain in, to reenter, or to arrive for the first time in higher education, we are producing a new university, one that must be available to all citizens, its foundations being humanity, creativity, learning technology, potential realization, community identity, and civic contribution. Let us call this new institution the *communiversity.*

The Human Element

It is not that learning by watching television is impossible. It is not that television lectures cannot be made interactive. We can indeed turn on, tune in, and learn. However, the human exchange, the interchange of energy, expression, and engagement is radically transformed when the teacher is electronically communicating. What is most precious about the teacher-student interchange is most elusive. It is most human and personal and, at the same time, virtually immeasurable. There are those who argue that we have already lost most of this interchange as class sizes have crept up to the point that many professors never learn their students' names. Some never even come to recognize their faces. Even prior to the advent of telecollege, education has become all too impersonal.

It is not only class size that has depersonalized education. It is the general approach of our educational process. Our modern Western definition of education is "the transmission—from the adult generation to the young—of several basic intellectual skills" and a "curriculum of selected facts," skills and facts that are selected based upon "the economic, technological, social and political goals of those in positions of authority."[22] There is, however, a long and respectable history of opposition to this definition, a history peopled by a long line of social thinkers including Rousseau, Emerson, Alcott, Parker, Montessori, Steiner, Neill, Goodman, and Holt. These people can be called "holistic educators," because "they have all defined education in terms of wholeness—the whole, integrated person; a whole, democratic, community life; and a respect for the whole cultural, global, ecological, and even cosmic context of human life."[23] These and others who have propounded another view of education have, in their own ways, viewed education as being closer to what the Latin roots of this word suggest it to be: "Educare" or "ex ducere"—the "drawing forth" of the "human possibilities contained within the soul of every child."[24]

Holistic education is, then, the antithesis of contemporary, mainstream education. It is not what we are providing. It is unfortunate that "holistic thought" has developed the reputation of being a less strenuous, less intelligent mode of analysis, one on the fringes of all science and all respectable intellectual discourse. Holistic thought has been dubbed a "New Age" approach, which, in its eagerness to counter the catastrophic myopia of increasingly fragmented specialization, fails to demand of itself conceptual clarity and theoretical rigor. Given this prejudice against it, holistic education and its theorists can barely erect a case against the establishment.

Somewhere along the line, higher education has been entirely misunderstood and its evolution quite warped. Education cut off from context is flat learning—if learning at all. As The Carnegie Foundation's Ernest Boyer, former U.S. commissioner of education, insists, "The great obstacle to general education is the fragmentation and specialization of the academy . . . we simply cannot afford to graduate students who fail to place their knowledge and lives in perspective."[25]

Creativity is the Life Force of Learning

We also cannot afford to neglect, understimulate, and perhaps even force out of existence, creativity. This may sound impossible. After all, learning in any form is a creative process. It is also a selective process. The mind *creatively selects* information to be thought about and then stored. Once information is stored, it has been learned and can be used again.

However ubiquitous human creativity may seem to be, the purposeful stimulation of creativity is not everywhere. In fact, it is sorely lacking. Students' minds can be trained to become more attentive to the remarkably creative process of information selection and storage, of learning. Students' minds can thus learn to learn.

Intelligence finds its way into expression via creativity. We often overlook the role of creativity in the expression of mental, ethical, and spiritual activity. Instead, we see only the most obvious signs of creativity: the most innovative inventions, the newest science-fiction films. We notice children's wildest stories, brightest paintings, and loudest projections of their creativities. Quieter creation is unseen.

Maria Montessori, upon whose work the Montessori Method of education, which encourages the child to learn at his or her own pace—to shape him or herself, is based, suggested, "The newborn child should be seen as a 'spiritual embryo'—a spirit enclosed in flesh in order to come into the world." Montessori described the child as an "incarnate" or an enfleshment of the spirit, and explained that, "the incarnation comes at the cost of great inner difficulty, and around this creative work unfolds a drama that has yet to be written."[26]

Education must see the student—at any age, including adult, middle, and old age—as being continually and creatively engaged in the expression of the spirit through the mind and body that he or she is developing. We are most in touch with our reverence for the mind of a young or an old person when we think in terms of the spirit it expresses. The creativity involved in this expression is something we can encourage, nourish, and educate. However, whatever specific activities we undertake with the goal of encouraging creativity in our students, we must be driven by a prevailing respect for the spirit housed within the body of the student. This spirit is always creatively working to express—to manifest—itself.

Higher education must be, by explicit intention, a creativity-enhancing environment. If it fails in this, we are sacrificing the greatest of our human resources: the creative mind, the warehouse of untapped answers to as yet unasked, future, questions.

Toward Wisdom

A true school insists upon intellectual rigor as a backdrop to its wisdom. Such rigor includes not only content specific to particular fields of study but also, and more importantly, the skill of knowing how to find, recognize, take in, and use information. (These days, while students must learn mathematical computations and formulas, they also must learn to use adding machines, calculators, and computers, in addition to learning how to read instructions and how to teach themselves to use any new technical items that may come their way now or in the future.) To keep up with the demands of our rapidly changing world, modern and post-modern minds must be taught to absorb new information, new skills, rapidly and efficiently. We must focus on the ability of the mind to learn, and we must train the minds of all our citizens in advanced techniques of learning.[27]

Institutions of higher education must become true schools of thought, offering a curriculum designed to teach science of mind:

specific learning, thinking, problem solving, and creating processes. The purpose of such a curriculum should be fourfold:

1. To develop fully the intellectual, creative, and civic potentials of all students

2. To generate in each and every student strong awareness of and appreciation for the creative, problem-solving, reasoning, and specific metacognitive (higher level) abilities of one's own mind

3. To train students to use regularly the metacognitive understanding and awareness gained in academic work and to find applications in daily and community life

4. To motivate all students to realize their mental potentials both individually and as part of the global community of humanity

Among the many specific classroom activities that must be included in a *consciousness-technology curriculum* at all levels of schooling, from grade school through college level into all levels of continuing education, are

- Lessons in identifying and absorbing new information thoroughly and rapidly—with a distinct dependence upon each of the following areas of instruction

- Lessons in the process of overcoming problems and meeting challenges, which include an explanation of the process of transcending them

- Lessons in the recognition and appreciation of intellectual and emotional struggle: as mind-strengthening, personality-strengthening, and community-strengthening

- Lessons in reading, understanding, and following instructions

- Lessons in task analysis in which students are taught to analyze instructions, assignments, and other tasks in order to break them down into specific sets of steps in specific order

- Lessons in temporal relations in which the sequence of particular sets of events in time are carefully observed and recorded in the form of pictures, words, and numerical data

- Lessons in memorization in which students are taught memorization techniques and are given many, many opportunities to practice

- Lessons in concentration in which students are trained to focus and are tested again and again in settings that provide numerous distractions from what they must concentrate on

- Lessons in detecting large and small differences and similarities among objects, colors, sounds, notes, bits of information, pieces of grammar, concepts, theories, and cultures

- Lessons in the identification of information or data that is irrelevant in the answering of particular questions, the completing of particular assignments, the building of particular models, and so forth

- Lessons in categorization in which students group like objects or concepts together and then organize them by level of generality, with the biggest categories being the most general and containing the most subcategories

- Lessons in formal debate in which students learn to find and argue the strengths and weaknesses of information and theory of a scientific, philosophical, ethical, and political nature

- Lessons in visualization in which students use their imaginations to generate an image of a real object or geometrical form in their minds

- Lessons in the manipulation of actual and conceptual objects and images in which students learn to see or sense the way things will fit together or relate to each other in space, with the aim of improving visualization skills

- Lessons in the detection of patterns in which students learn to tell the difference between noise or random signals and real information, which is generally pattern-based

- Lessons in specific forms of metacognition in which students study themselves thinking, creating, and solving problems: watching closely the way their own minds work

- Lessons in actually getting mental work done, such as homework, class work, and studio work—art, music, writing—in which students learn to organize and focus their energies, beginning with basics such as keeping their work spaces and binders neat, organizing their time, planning their activities in the now and in the future, prioritizing their activities, and then implementing their activities with a singleness of focus that facilitates the ultimate expression of their work

- Lessons in the fundamental arguments of many different philosophies and religions, including philosophical metaphysics as well as the basic Western version of the rationalism-versus-empiricism debate, building in regular practice in discussing all these concepts with clarity

- Lessons in the application of one's talents to high citizenship: the definitions, requirements, responsibilities, and expressions of this citizenship on local, regional, national, and global levels

It was the introspective seventeenth-century philosopher Rene Descartes who wrote, "I think, therefore I am." Whether or not one absolutely agrees with this absolutism, it is increasingly apparent that the *way* I think—and the *power, clarity, and ethics* with which I think—determine much of what I have and can become, and much of what humanity is and will become.

That a Mind Is a Terrible Thing to Waste

Yes, we have heard it said that "a mind is a terrible thing to waste." Yet, how often do we avoid the implications of this adage in our own lives? *A student's mind will develop (regardless of his or her age) as far as it thinks it can develop.* This means that for students to realize their own mental potential, they must be

- Led to believe that the potential exists

- Encouraged to develop and realize this potential

- Provided the stimulation to develop this potential

- Provided the awareness that mental challenges and life's struggles help to develop this potential

- Provided the consciousness technology, spiritual structure, tools, training, and education to develop this potential

- Engaged in real-life situations that call for structured thought

- Taught to see the rewards, the value, of mental development and of realizing one's mental potential

We are all students and we are all teachers. We must guide our students to fuller realization of themselves. We must teach them to believe in their unlimited abilities. They must come to know that their abilities are worth developing. We all must come to know exactly this, which we must teach. To meet the challenges of the future, our world needs all the wisdom it can generate. Higher education must model this philosophy in an academy format designed to motivate citizens to become teachers and leaders in the services, the sciences, the humanities, the philosophies, and in the emerging and reemerging politics of the world of the new millennium.

Forging a New Social Justice

Our starving intellects and thirsting creativities long for communities of learning—true schools—schools of thought in which we can share the experiences of feeling ideas come alive, of seeking knowledge for its underlying wisdom, of rising beyond the limitations of our day-to-day perceptions, of manifesting the creative forces within us, and of making a difference in the world. Each of us can be inspired by synergy, by the community of others, to reach within our hearts and our minds beyond the artificial yet often rigid boundaries of our self-imposed and socially imposed realities. What is needed is more than just a school, but rather, a school of thought, a community of learning and learning to learn, a place of meaning. What we must now create and imbue with life is the communiversity.

Too many people, young and old, have come to feel themselves alone in the realization of their potentials. Too many eventually abandon entirely the exploration of their mentalities, their intellects, their souls, their lives. And their lives grow empty and meaningless with the flatness of their self-denials. They live far too close to dead. A true school prepares students for what can otherwise be the *dis-inspiration*—the spiritual and intellectual quicksand—of turn-of-the-modern-millennium adulthood.

Elders as Teachers

Children, while young and finding the world new, are least likely to feel so dis-inspired. While young, they have us, their parents and teachers. They have us for but a few years before they become us.

But they do have, as all of us have, our elders. It is in the wisdom of the elders that the wisdom of time—time, that sacred terrain—is housed. Young people must have opportunities to integrate their intellectual resonances with those of the elderly. Such opportunities are not meant to force "old" ways upon the young, but instead to share—to combine and to contrast—time-tested methods of pattern recognition and information processing with the young.

But what is an elder? How do we recognize a "true elder?" How do we cultivate the elders among us? How do we prepare the young to grow into our future true elders? These are questions a true school continues to ask its students, because they must learn to make such determinations.

As a species, we are increasingly focused on the now, to the point that all past and future is trivialized, diminished in our post–high-high-tech, nouveau modern, increasingly networked but very compartmentalized reality. In a learning community—a modern school of thought—time must be a loop rather than a segmented line. The older cultures, the invaluable yet fragmented vestiges of them, which remain on Earth today, are the elders of our civilization, the forebears of our times. The height of technological understanding must be taught and taught well and, concurrently, must be cast against ancient knowledge in order to ferret out and to fashion true wisdom. Old and young alike must learn together. A true school is thus a grade school, a high school, a university, a vocational school and what we can call an *elderversity*. A true school teaches wisdom via the conscious integration of time and ideas: of age groups, philosophies, intellects, and arts.

Service

The spirit of service must be built into education at all levels. Without this element, learning is dry, irrelevant, myopic, self-centered, and devoid of spirit.

Civic responsibility implies some form of involvement, some form of activity in the community. To teach civic responsibility both from an intellectual and an experiential standpoint will place new onus on "scholarly activity." The contradictions contained in this phrase have been noted by a number of scholars, including Ann Lieberman, codirector of the National Center for Restructuring Education and Teaching, and professor of education at Columbia University.[28] Lieberman refers us to the dictionary to read that *scholarship* is defined as "a quality of knowledge and learning which is systematic, attempting accuracy, critical ability and thoroughness," while *activity* is another endeavor entirely, "requiring action, producing real effects as opposed to theoretical, ideal or speculative."[29] The spirit of giving "voice to both activism and knowledge building,"[30] which Lieberman calls for in her writings on university involvement in elementary and secondary school restructuring, can be invoked in the communiversity. In her effort to generate a greater contribution by universities to K–12 education, Lieberman calls for a change in the very organizational structure of universities, one that improves upon the university's ability to interact with the community in which it exists. The "technological rationality," which has dominated the university (particularly in the teaching profession, notes Lieberman) throughout its disciplinary fields, is one which holds that "the highest form of inquiry, the best research, is the product of those in the university removed from the contexts of practice."[31]

We can expand upon Lieberman's thinking. Technological rationality is actually an insulating mechanism, a formidable barrier. After the journey on which *Shameful Admissions* has taken me, I can see that this is the wall that must come down, the gate that must be broken. Technological rationality is isolating the intellect. While it supposedly protects the sanctity of intellectual reverie, it is failing the institutions which house it.

The context in which the university exists, the world in which it lives—*the community*—is being allowed in (or forcing its way in, depending upon who is reporting this action). If the university will not come to community, will not live and breathe fully of its surroundings, then the community will come to the university. Here, the metaphorical breaking of the gate can be reduced to a single effect. This is the real cry: give admission to the community.

Students must be taught the meaning of service from the standpoint of community: regional, national, and global citizenship. It is unfortunate that so much of modern education overlooks this aspect of schooling. The nurturing of citizenship and civic responsibility must permeate all aspects of curriculum. We are planetary citizens and must accept the responsibility of being so. Only when the teaching of such civic wisdom takes place is there a true school.

And now we are at a crossroads in human history, a time when our systems of thinking, of educating, and of financing and administering this education, have become unwieldy and threaten to become ever more impersonal. Now it is time for higher education to merge with the community, to focus on the holistic origins and creative aspects of education: the intellectual needs and incentives to realize potential required by citizens in a rapidly changing world, and the civic role that education must play. We must restructure our junior colleges and community colleges, building upon the foundation that we have already laid so well, instituting true communiversities everywhere.

Reviving and Revising the Dream

We are by no means finished with the American dream. It is still forming. The simple matter of applying for, paying for, and acquiring a college education is fraught with ever-emerging philosophical and political complexities of the most profound degree. By taking a close look at college today, we see the face of our history and the future of our notion of equality. Paulo Freire describes what he calls a "very obvious truth" in *The Pedagogy of the Oppressed*, in which he explains that we are "beings in the process of becoming" in a likewise "unfinished reality."[32] He also points out that "just as the oppressor, in order to oppress, needs a theory of action, so the oppressed, in order to become free, also need a theory of action."[33]

If we are to be a free people, we must have such a theory of action, a way to forge social justice through education. The persecuted, the Pilgrims, the founding fathers, the White slave owners, and the tired, the poor, the teeming masses, all came to America—the land where the Native American once lived free—to be free. They brought with them their chattel—their women, children, and slaves—and tried to make the American experiment in liberty and equality work. Only now, at the reflective time of the new millennium, do we see that we actually came here *to learn to be free* and *to learn to share freedom*. Now that we know this, it is best that we restructure our educational institutions to enable us to do so: to learn freedom—its rights, responsibilities, and options.

A rethinking of higher education is essential. Why refrain from a major revision simply because traditional definitions of "college" and "university" have been accepted for a long time?

Society is outgrowing its established model of school, of both lower and higher education. A new education is needed in this newest of new worlds. Our old model of schooling, once aimed at supporting as well as serving as a corollary to the ideal of egalitarianism, is now caught in the crossfire between the old populism and the temperamental populism nouveau. New designs of school must be designed to bolster new models of society, new respect for diversity, and new understandings of justice and equality.

Colleges must also recognize that today we are teaching a far more sophisticated population of students. The intellectual potential is tremendous and largely overlooked. We already have at our disposal the learning technologies that can induce a leap in the evolution of the individual, regardless of race, creed, or color, and thus of the societal, *composite human intellect*. The early stages of this mega-experiential leap in human awareness are only now becoming apparent.[34] We can encourage this, or stifle it.

Concurrently, adulthood is finally being examined as carefully as childhood. Child development has been carefully mapped, analyzed, defined in terms of recognizable stages and substages. Now, as we begin to live longer, shift careers more frequently, and care about the phases of adult life, adulthood is emerging as more than one very long midlife (twenty-something through sixty-something), and then old age (everything after that).

Now we understand more about our learning curves. Yes, there are times of life when the brain best absorbs particular kinds of information. And yes, there are times in life when one does more to learn particular sorts of things. These times do not always mesh. And it may be that, presently, we not only fail to teach the right topics at the prime times, but we also tend to force topics on students at the wrong times.

It has been said that youth is wasted on the young. It has also been said that higher education is wasted on young adults. Although we cannot address the former matter, we can and must continually consider the latter: who should learn what when? And where should they go to learn whatever it is they must learn? And who are best prepared to be their teachers?

Educating the Self

There is another, very minor question, the littlest one of all. Ironically, because of its almost boundless immensity, the monumental proportions of its relevance, the littlest question may remain very, very small: who goes there—who are you?

The superficial distinctions among members of the human race are shields. Yes, each of us is a particular gender and ethnicity. Each of us is our own parents' descendant. Yes, we are all of the sex-race-class-nationality-ideology identifications that we either chose willingly or surrendered to have imposed upon us. But these shields are barriers. They are barriers between us and our true selves. The problem of discovering who we really are, both as individuals and as life forms, is so much greater than is reflected by our current efforts to be represented within our chosen, or appointed groups—so much bigger than those we dance out in the name of diversity. This identity crisis belongs to all of humanity.

A lifetime can be spent dealing with political issues. This is not to disparage such a choice; many outstanding women and men have elected to spend the time of their lives in this arena of human endeavor, and many of us have benefited in innumerable ways.

Still, the politic of the self remains primitive, embryonic, almost preconceptual. This politic, having a life of its own, is metamorphosing in and out of conscious state, as if calmly marking time, awaiting the opportunity finally to seize center stage and steal the focus. The twentieth-century self, as loud as it has been about its rights and the expression of its potential, is nevertheless obscured by its own cries from its own broken gates, gates to its own arbitrarily formulated territories. Could all this egalitarianism, populism old and new, be mere distraction?

I, for one, am ever grateful for the opportunities the breaking of the gates has given me. The egalitarian ideal has promoted the distribution of opportunity and knowledge and freedom, and I would have it no other way. It would have been impossible for me even to write this book without the historical drives toward greater emancipation and opportunity.

Only now that I have listened so closely to so many cries from the heretofore locked gates, do I sense that we are all pounding on a far more formidable wall. We are all knocking on heaven's door, and there, the admissions criteria are profoundly unclear. In fact, we cannot say for certain whether or not there is a heaven. If there is, we cannot know if there is but a single heaven with a single set of entrance criteria. Who gets in?

What is clear is that no matter what your social status, the death of you in your current form is coming to you at some time. Death is, prima-facie, an equal opportunity. All this noise we make this side of death, is it heard on the other side, in another dimension? In the end, we must wonder what it is we humans are trying to resolve as we pass through our earthly journeys. What is it that all our efforts to distribute or not to distribute opportunity will achieve in the longest of long runs? The painful truth is that educational institutions, entering the new millennium, are hollow, relatively sun-less shrines to the twentieth-century mind, a mind so dwarfed by truths it is too shallow to know.

Proposing the New "Communiversity"

I may seem to be ending this commentary, this recounting of the cries at the broken gate, on a negative note. I do say that the modern university, in most of its manifestations, is dead, or in the process of dying. But this is not negative. This is good. Higher education as we know it has overextended and overcommitted itself. The system is dissipating, weakening, and becoming ever more vulnerable. Higher education as we know it has outlived its focus, its purpose, its efficiency. The winds of change are upon us, and our institutions of tradition, eroded to their skeletal profiles, are now houses of cards creaking, shuddering, crying in that wind. Let them fall. Let them go. Invest no more in their preservation, but instead spend money on their orderly dissolution. And then

- Empty our colleges and universities. Then determine which of these facilities should become think tanks and research schools, which should become trade and professional schools, and which should become community education programs.
- Rethink community education. Adapt or redesign its institutional structures to serve as communiversities. All junior colleges and community colleges should become communiversities. They should serve all citizens, without ethnic, gender, or age restrictions, making national and then specific local citizenship the entrance requirement. Many emptied universities (and perhaps also many empty school buildings and military bases) should do the same.
- Let these communiversities serve local people, the communities, and regions in which they are based. Allow these communities to diversify the elective- and community-service portions of their curricula according to local preferences. Exempt no students,

no matter what their socioeconomic status or career goals, from community service.

• Allow pre-college-age young people to enroll (by student request and teacher recommendation) in communiversity courses and to receive dual credit for these courses: credit at both their K–12 schools and their communiversities. Enable the more advanced K–12 students to complete their communiversity requirements at a younger age, thereby investing fewer tax dollars to hold them unnecessarily in their basic schooling. Some of the most able young people should matriculate into think tanks and advanced professional training as early as the age of fifteen. Allow this to become acceptable.

• Concurrently, allow adults of all ages to return to school whenever they can demonstrate a desire or need to develop new skills or to gain further education. Make returning in midlife and learning in old age an acceptable norm. Require compulsory service, with tutoring and teaching as an option, of all these adults. Encourage the elders to design and teach courses, as part of their service requirement.

• When an adult can demonstrate that trade school is the best direct route to enter a renewed labor force, allow that adult (if she or he has graduated from a communiversity in years past) to go directly into a trade school.

• Assume that the bulk of first-time-through communiversity students will range in age from eighteen to twenty-five. All basic education beyond high school, all standard general requirements now required at vocational schools, trade schools, law schools, medical schools, colleges and universities, and all education aimed at filling in the gaps left by high school education should take place at the communiversity. While anyone can enter the communiversity, only those who meet all basic national requirements can leave with communiversity certification. Make this certification authentic by guaranteeing that those who earn it have the clearly specified skills it represents. No one who seeks this certification should be exempt from having to prove that all required skills have been learned.

•   In addition to certifying those who meet nationally specified academic requirements, make the work of the communiversity to generate and maintain an educated and technologically up-to-date populace—in essence, a collection of citizens. Each citizens' group is diversified by locality, each representative of its immediate local environment, and each imbued with civic responsibility it gains through completion of compulsory community service as part of its required coursework.

•   Distinguish between general educational requirements and specialized training and/or research. Once all general educational requirements are met, allow this more fully informed, civic-experienced, work-experienced, and well-educated populace the opportunity to self-select for training and specialized education in social service, government and military positions, trades, professions, or scholarship.

•   Self-selection must involve a trial number of years, possibly two, of low-paid apprenticeship in the selected area of training prior to testing for admission into the specific educational program that will lead the individual into her or his chosen work.

•   From among all who graduate from communiversities—all having met strict national graduation requirements; all having completed a solid, community-service course requirement and then satisfactorily completed a postcommuniversity apprenticeship program—allow those who have self-selected for application to further higher education to be tested rigorously and held individually responsible for their own test results, with no special accommodations for age, gender, ethnicity, or race.

•   Send our scholars to think tanks, armed with corporate, philanthropic, and federal support. Identify these top intellectual minds from among the top 5 percent of all communiversity graduates, based on national achievement test scores, specialty tests, written tests, oral tests, demonstrated research ability, and recommendations following the required pre-application think tank apprenticeship. All applicants must be willing to commit to a lifetime of scholarly endeavor. Strict payback agreements must be signed by those accepted, agreements committing them to pay back the cost of their scholarly training should they not complete or stay in the scholarly field. Award these people doctorates upon completion of a rigorous think tank doctoral program and initiation. No one else needs a doctorate.

• At the same time, increase the esteem we award our tradespeople. Redefine *trade* to include a broader range of professions. Not only beauticians, sanitary engineers, plumbers, and electricians are tradespeople but also architects, doctors, attorneys, domestic engineers, public health officials, and many others. In truth, all *practitioners* are tradespeople and can be awarded some new, glowing certification, which applauds them for being so. Send our students to newly respected trade-professional schools, armed with commitments from the schools who train them to place them in jobs or not to admit them in the first place. In return, demand from these students signed contracts, which require them to work in the fields for which they have been trained for several times the number of years they have spent training.

• All advanced training, including the trades, must follow communiversity graduation. The communiversity should take on the role of equalizing all social subgroups in terms of preparedness for competition. Allow a new sense of equality—equality of qualification and of time in service—to take form.

We can thus prepare citizens to contribute to a new, more vigorous society, one in which we are finally prepared to ask not what our society can do for us, but what we can do for our society. However we came into the world, whatever life chances we have been given, we can become stronger by negotiating the challenges with which we have been confronted. The communiversity education and service program will provide all citizens a launching pad. The take-off point, the time and trajectory, and the meaningfulness of one's life is then up to the individual.

This is the new social justice, one imbuing people with pride and responsibility, one empowering each and every citizen with the education and civic training required to bring that citizen into the work of society and to provide that citizen greater say in this work. The new social justice is one in which the young are helped fully up to a certain age, the young adults are required to serve their communities in exchange for their higher education, and the adults are enabled to make their lives work and their contributions ongoing.

A Solid Tier and a Theory of Action

A broad national effort to bring the communiversity tier of education into being will breathe new life into our citizens, into our communities, and into our country. Diversity will flower as a characteristic of locality, with most young people remaining in their communities long enough to complete the local communiversity requirement and its related community-service requirement before considering departing from that community. Many young people will elect to remain in their home communities to do their apprenticeships and to live among the people with whom they identify. Eligibility for low tuition at one's local communiversity must be tied to several years of pre-enrollment residence in that community and ongoing enrollment in the community-service requirement. Payback of public support for one's education is made through this service. Absolutely no one should be exempted from the service requirement. This is not something a well-to-do student can opt out of. It is a "required course." For those going into advanced training past the communiversity, post-training, pay-back requirements will be scaled down for those who commit to a decade or more of work in their own communities or other communities in need of particular trades and professional people.

And why not pay back to society the cost of our educations? And why not contribute to the world from which we take so much?

And why not learn the meaning of citizenship? These are the rightful expectations of justice: justice to society. The gates have been broken. We teeming masses have poured in. Now let's make this place our own: do justice to ourselves.

Beyond our old and new egalitarianisms and populisms are our actual realities—unfinished, perpetually becoming. Let us teach, educate, and distribute an individual and a communal mastery over the elements affecting our destinies. Let us make this the new, living, breathing theory of action, empowering us to shed the shackles of our own oppression. Breaking the gates is not enough. Taking responsibility for building a world beyond the gates, a world that really works, must come next.

Our new pedagogy must be the pedagogy of the socially responsible. The foundation of this educational strategy must be the *social cell*. This cell is both a level of organization and a level of awareness. It is in no way a model that is representative of either the political left or the political right. Our old politics just won't work here. We have to evolve new models. We must find new ways to get out from under the increasingly rigid and stagnant layers of bureaucracy, which prevent us from bringing about true change.

Teach, by demonstration, that this social cell is the community component of the synergistic *cellular society*, which we are evolving. Each social cell is distinct from all other social cells in its special cultural and ethnic profile, in its economy, its products, its schools. Each social cell is a member of a diverse array of communities: a large colony of social cells, which come together to make a new nation, conceived in a new understanding of liberty and dedicated to the new proposition that all persons are created and then must return the gift of creation to the world in which they find themselves, taking responsibility for helping the world to evolve. Our survival as free beings, who can live together and allow for differences, depends upon this attitude, this new civicism, this revived and modernized *civitas*, the essential *politic of human survival* in the new millennium.

Endnotes

Chapter One

1. A statement from the 1892 National Education Proceedings quoted in T. Toch, *In the Name of Excellence: The Struggle to Reform Our Nation's Schools, Why It's Failing and What Should Be Done*. New York: Oxford University Press, 1991, 42.

2. Toch, *In the Name of Excellence*, 43.

3. Toch, *In the Name of Excellence*, 43.

4. Boyer, E. quoted in J. Evangelauf, "A New 'Carnegie Classification'." *Chronicle of Higher Education*, XL(31), Apr. 1994, A17.

5. Fukuyama, F. *The End of History and the Last Man*. New York: Avon Books, 1992, 116.

6. Edelman, M. Wright *A Measure of Our Success: A Letter to My Children and Yours*. New York: HarperCollins, 1983, 54.

7. I describe a technology that I teach, demonstrate, and document in A. Browne-Miller, *Learning to Learn: Ways to Nurture Your Child's Intelligence*. New York: Insight Books, 1994.

8. Quoted with permission from an interview with David Siggers conducted by the author on Apr. 21, 1995.

Chapter Two

1. Lazarus, E. "The New Colossus." 1883, is cited in D. J. Boorstin, (ed.). *An Advanced Primer*. Chicago: University of Chicago Press, 1966, 458–462.

2. Kaus, M. "The End of Equality." *New Republic*, June 1992, 21.

3. Clinton, W. quoted in Kaus, "End of Equality," 21.

4. Kaus, M. *The End of Equality.* New York: Basic Books, 1992, 63.

5. Sommerfeld, M. "28 States to Cut Higher-Education Budgets." *Education Week*, Feb. 12, 1992, 8.

6. Brown, R. cited in D. E. Blum, "The Undaunted 'Kook': An Agitator for Athletes' Rights Finds His Ideas Gaining Acceptance." *Chronicle of Higher Education*, Apr. 1994, A33.

7. Kaus, *End of Equality*, 58–77.

8. Quoted with permission from an interview with Debra Chermonte, Director of Admissions, at Oberlin College of Arts and Sciences in Oberlin, Ohio conducted by the author on Sept. 26, 1994.

9. Brown cited in Blum, "The Undaunted 'Kook'," A34.

10. Lubman, S. "A 'Student of Value' Means a Student Who Can Pay the Rising Cost of College." *Wall Street Journal*, Jan. 5, 1994, B1–B2.

11. Lubman, "Student of Value," B1–B2.

12. Lubman, "Student of Value," B1–B2.

13. Lubman, "Student of Value," B1–B2.

14. This director of admissions at a private Ivy League university, interviewed in the fall of 1994, preferred to remain anonymous.

15. Moll, R. W. "The Scramble to Get the New Class: Is the Dean of Admissions Now Outside the Academy?" *Change: The Magazine of Higher Learning*, Mar./Apr. 1994, 11–17.

16. Moll, "Scramble to Get the New Class," cover.

17. McDonough, P. "Buying and Selling Higher Education: The Social Construction of the College Applicant." *Journal of Higher Education*, July/Aug., 1994, 432.

18. Quoted with permission from an interview with Debra Chermonte conducted by the author on Sept. 26, 1994.

19. Trudeau, G. "Doonesbury Comic Strip," *San Francisco Chronicle*, Mar. 9, 1994, Comic section.

20. Shea, C. "Squeezing the Calendar." *Chronicle of Higher Education*, Mar. 1994, A35.

21. Shea, "Squeezing the Calendar," A36.

22. Rush, S. quoted in J. L. Nicklin, "The Layoffs Continue." *Chronicle of Higher Education*, May 1994, 37.

23. Harvard Graduate School of Education Editorial Board. "College: Getting in Versus Staying In." *Harvard Education Letter*, Jan./Feb. 1993, IX(1), 1.

24. Shea, C. "A Flood of Applications." *Chronicle of Higher Education*, Apr. 1994, A31.

25. Shea, "Flood of Applications," A31.

26. Shea, "Flood of Applications," A31.

27. Dimensions. "Going to College," *Education Week*, Apr. 1, 1992, 3.

28. Evangelauf, J. "A New 'Carnegie Classification'." *Chronicle of Higher Education*, Apr. 1994, XL(31), A17.

29. Evangelauf, "New Carnegie Classification," A17.

30. Cage, M. C. "Enrollment: Ups and Downs." *Chronicle of Higher Education*, Nov. 1993, A34.

31. Cage, "Enrollment: Ups and Downs," A34.

32. Cage, "Enrollment: Ups and Downs," A34.

33. Evangelauf, J. "Tuition for 1993–94 Climbs Sharply." *Chronicle of Higher Education*, Sept. 1993, A33.

34. Evangelauf, "Tuition Climbs Sharply," A33.

35. Evangelauf, "Tuition Climbs Sharply," A35.

36. Evangelauf, "Tuition Climbs Sharply," A35.

37. Quoted in "Money Guide: Dartmouth 'Worth the Price'." *Dartmouth Life*, Oct. 1993, 2.

38. Dimensions, "Going to College," 3.

39. Dimensions, "Going to College," 3.

40. Parkin, M. *Microeconomics* (2nd ed.) Reading, Mass.: Addison-Wesley, 408.

41. Parkin, *Microeconomics*, 408.

42. Parkin, *Microeconomics*, 51.

43. A situation I have explained in A. Browne-Miller, *The Day Care Dilemma*. New York: Insight Books/Plenum, 1990.

44. *Education Week,* Nov. 27, 1991, 7.

45. Hiss, W. quoted in *Education Week,* 7.

46. Murphy, S. quoted in *Education Week,* 7.

47. Cameron, R. quoted in *Education Week,* 7.

48. Gifford, B. "The Allocation of Opportunities and the Politics of Testing." In B. Gifford (ed.), *Test Policy and the Politics of Opportunity Allocation.* Vol. I. Boston: Kluwer Academic, 1989, 22–30.

49. De Witt, K. "U.S. Eases College Aid Stand, but Not All the Way." *New York Times,* Dec. 10, 1990, A1 and A16; See also Pitsch, M. "A Month Later, Educators Are Still Seeking Final Word on Race-Exclusive Scholarships." *Education Week,* Jan. 9, 1991, 1 and 26.

50. Zook, J. "Black and Tribal Colleges Exempted from Student Loan Default Rules." *Chronicle of Higher Education,* Apr. 1994, A40.

51. Zook, "Black Colleges Exempted from Loan Default Rules," A40.

52. Zook, "Black Colleges Exempted from Loan Default Rules," A40.

53. Nighthorse-Campbell, B., U.S. Senator. Stated in a fundraising letter for the American Indian College Fund (central offices in New York), undated, mailed early in 1994.

54. Sarich, V. quoted in E. Marshall, "The Raging Bull of Berkeley." *Science,* Jan. 1991, 251, 369.

55. Marshall, "Raging Bull of Berkeley," 369.

56. Blauner, B. *Daily Californian,* Berkeley: University of California, Nov. 26. 1990, Op-Ed section.

57. Blauner, *Daily Californian,* Op-Ed.

58. Quoted with permission from an interview with Patrick Hayashi, associate vice chancellor for admissions and enrollment, University of California, Berkeley, in an interview conducted by the author on Jan. 26, 1994.

59. A predicament I have documented and analyzed in A. Browne-Miller, *Intelligence Policy: Its Impact on College Admissions and Other Social Policy.* New York: Plenum, 1995.

60. Anwi, A. G., Tanner, L., and Leyden, M. "The Changing Roles and Needs of Students." *Higher Education in Europe,* 1985, X(1), 10–13; "Third Conference on European Academic Mobility (Rome, Oct. 23–26, 1984)." *Higher Education in Europe,* 1985, X(1), 131–164;

Pakhomov, N. N. "Higher Education and Development: The Experience of the USSR." *Higher Education in Europe*, Nov. 1986, XI(3), 36–39.

61. Committee on Admissions and Enrollment. *Freshman Admissions at Berkeley: A Policy for the 1990s and Beyond. (Karabel Report)*, Berkeley: Berkeley Division, Academic Senate, University of California, 1989, 55.

62. Karabel, *Freshman Admissions: A Policy for the 1990s*, 55.

63. Hayden, T. quoted in "Plan to Reform College Budget: Assemblyman Hayden Proposes Linking Fees to Income." *San Francisco Chronicle*, Jan. 22, 1992, A12.

64. Hayden quoted in "Plan to Reform Budget," A12.

65. Hayden quoted in "Plan to Reform Budget," A12.

66. Patrick McCallum, executive director of the Faculty Association of Community Colleges, provided this data for use in the article by J. Tepperman, "Why Johnny Can't Work." *San Francisco Bay Guardian*, Mar. 23, 1994, 17.

67. Tepperman, "Why Johnny Can't Work," 17.

68. Tepperman, "Why Johnny Can't Work," 17.

69. Pister, K. quoted in J. McNulty, "Fee Forum," *Banana Slug*. University of California at Santa Cruz Alumni Bulletin, Spring 1994, 5(3), 8.

70. Gardner, D., president of the University of California. "Gardner's Letter of Resignation." Nov. 13, 1991 speech addressed to Meredith Khachigian, Chairman of the Board of Regents. *Cal Report*, Winter 1992, 4.

71. Quoted in "U.C. President Gardner to Step Down." *Cal Report*, Oct. 1992, 4.

72. Peltason, J. W. "A Look at the Challenge Before Us." *U.C. Focus*, Mar. 1994, Special Edition, 8(4), 1.

73. McNulty, "Fee Forum," 8.

74. McNulty, "Fee Forum," 8.

75. McNulty, "Fee Forum," 8.

76. This director of admissions chose to remain anonymous.

77. Gardner, D. quoted by P. Hayashi, associate vice chancellor for Admissions and Enrollment at the University of California, Berkeley, in Letters, "Admissions Explained." *Cal Report*, Winter 1992, 2 and 20.

78. Anderson, L. "From the Air." Musical composition in *Big Science* album, Warner Bros, Laurie Anderson and Roma Baran, producers, 1982.

Chapter Three

1. Peltason, "Challenge Before Us."

2. Wayne Greene, quoted and referred to by name later in this book, with permission to quote from interview conducted by author on Dec. 14, 1993.

3. The Tennessee and Alabama Female Institute (1853). *1853–1854 Catalogue of the Mary Sharp College of Tennessee*, quoted in J. M. Taylor, *Before Vassar Opened: A Contribution to the History of the Higher Education of Women in America*. Freeport, N.Y., 1972, 27. (Originally published 1914.)

4. Taylor, *Before Vassar Opened*, 9.

5. Taylor, *Before Vassar Opened*, 12.

6. Taylor, *Before Vassar Opened*, 6.

7. Taylor, *Before Vassar Opened*, 4–5.

8. Gilchrist, B. B. *The Life of Mary Lyon*, 207–208, cited in Taylor, *Before Vassar Opened*, 7.

9. Oberlin College (1834). *Catalogue of 1834*, 6, quoted in Taylor, *Before Vassar Opened*.

10. Taylor, *Before Vassar Opened*, 6.

11. Taylor, *Before Vassar Opened*, 6.

12. Taylor, *Before Vassar Opened*, 235.

13. Solberg, W. U. *The University of Illinois, 1867–1894*. Urbana, Ill.: University of Illinois Press, 1968, 160.

14. University of Illinois, *1871–1872 Catalogue*, 52.

15. Solberg, *University of Illinois*, 160.

16. Solberg, *University of Illinois*, 161.

17. Lipset, S. M., and Riesman, D., *Education and Politics at Harvard.* New York: McGraw-Hill, 1975, 135.

18. Lawton, M. "Schools' Glass Ceiling Imperils Girls: Study Cites Barriers Erected in School That Prohibit the Advancement of Girls." *Education Week,* Feb. 12, 1992, 1 and 17.

19. "Schools' Glass Ceiling," 17.

20. "Schools' Glass Ceiling," 17.

21. Browne-Miller, A. *Intelligence Policy: Its Impact on College Admissions and Other Social Policy.* New York: Plenum, 1995.

22. Adams, W. *The Test.* New York: Macmillan, 1971, 183–184.

23. Adams, *The Test,* 184.

24. Karabel, *Freshman Admissions: A Policy for the 1990s.*

25. California State Department of Education. *Master Plan for Higher Education in California. 1960–1975.* Sacramento, Calif.: Liaison Committee of the State Board of Education and the Regents of the University of California, 1960, 72–73.

26. Department of Education, *Master Plan for Higher Education,* 72–73.

27. Commission for the Review of the Master Plan for Higher Education. *Master Plan Renewed: Unity, Equity, Quality and Efficiency in California Post Secondary Education.* Sacramento, Calif., 1987.

28. Karabel, *Freshman Admissions: A Policy for the 1990s,* 1–2.

29. Karabel, *Freshman Admissions: A Policy for the 1990s,* 4.

30. Karabel, *Freshman Admissions: A Policy for the 1990s,* 1.

31. Karabel, *Freshman Admissions: A Policy for the 1990s,* 4 and 35 on the tension.

32. Karabel, *Freshman Admissions: A Policy for the 1990s,* 11.

33. Karabel, *Freshman Admissions: A Policy for the 1990s,* 22 and 36.

34. *Ethnic Distribution of New Freshmen at U.C. Berkeley, Fall Term, 1979–1983.* Berkeley: Office of Student Research, University of California.

35. Karabel, *Freshman Admissions: A Policy for the 1990s,* 1–4.

36. Joint Committee for Review of the Master Plan for Higher Education. *California Faces, California's Future*. Sacramento, Calif., 1988, 19.

37. Office of the Chancellor—Budget and Planning. *Freshman Admissions at Berkeley*, a paper released by the Chancellor's Office, Berkeley: University of California, Feb. 1988, 3–4.

38. Office of the Chancellor, *Freshman Admissions at Berkeley*, 3–4.

39. Karabel, *Freshman Admissions: A Policy for the 1990s*, 22–23; See also Office of the Chancellor, *Freshman Admissions at Berkeley*, 3–4; See also "An Inflated S.A.T.—Test Scores: Going Up!" *Newsweek*, June 20, 1994, p. 77.

40. Karabel, *Freshman Admissions: A Policy for the 1990s*, 22.

41. Karabel, *Freshman Admissions: A Policy for the 1990s*, 22.

42. Karabel, *Freshman Admissions: A Policy for the 1990s*, 23.

43. Karabel, *Freshman Admissions: A Policy for the 1990s*, 23.

44. Karabel, *Freshman Admissions: A Policy for the 1990s*, 25.

45. Karabel, *Freshman Admissions: A Policy for the 1990s*, 25.

46. Karabel, *Freshman Admissions: A Policy for the 1990s*, 25–26.

47. Karabel, *Freshman Admissions: A Policy for the 1990s*, 43.

48. Karabel, *Freshman Admissions: A Policy for the 1990s*, 46.

49. Karabel, *Freshman Admissions: A Policy for the 1990s*, 46.

50. Karabel, *Freshman Admissions: A Policy for the 1990s*, 46.

51. Karabel, *Freshman Admissions: A Policy for the 1990s*, 46–51.

52. Karabel, *Freshman Admissions: A Policy for the 1990s*, 51–52.

53. Cesa, T. A. "Using Logistic Regression to Model Whether Admits Will Register." Berkeley: Office of Student Research, University of California, Apr. 1993, 9–10.

54. Browne-Miller, *Intelligence Policy*, 22 and 182–183

55. Cesa, "Using Logistic Regression," 9.

56. Cesa, "Using Logistic Regression," 8–10.

57. Hayashi, P. "Affirmative Action: A Personal View," *College Board Review*, Winter, 1991–1992, 162, 31.

58. Hayashi, "Affirmative Action," 31.

Chapter Four

1. While preferring to remain anonymous, this student insisted I write this statement down.

2. Watters, E. "The New Politics of Race." *San Francisco Focus*, Apr. 1992, 58.

3. *U.S. News and World Report* "America's Best Colleges: 1994 College Guide." Washington D.C.: U.S. News and World Report, 1993, 85.

4. *America's Best Colleges*, 85.

5. Data for this table collected from *America's Best Colleges*, 1993, and table composed by author.

6. Data for this table collected from *America's Best Colleges*, 1993, and table composed by author.

7. Carpenter, A., and Provorse, C. (eds.). *The World Almanac of the U.S.A.* Ramsey, N.J.: Funk & Wagnalls, 1993, 33.

8. Carpenter and Provorse, *World Almanac*, 85.

9. Data for this table collected from *America's Best Colleges*, 1993, and table composed by author.

10. Karabel, *Freshman Admissions: A Policy for the 1990s*, 27.

11. Commission for Review of Master Plan for Higher Education. *Master Plan Renewed: Unity, Equity, Quality and Efficiency*, 7.

12. Quoted with permission from an interview with Wayne Greene conducted by the author on Dec. 14, 1994.

13. Hallinan, V. cited in "Official Accused of Unethical Conduct." *San Francisco Chronicle*, Dec. 27, 1969, 2.

14. Freeland, R. "1992–93 Student Retention Update." *Report OSR 93–002*, Berkeley: Office of Student Research, University of California, May 1993, 1.

15. Freeland, "Student Retention Update," 2.

16. Freeland, "Student Retention Update," 1.

17. Freeland, "Student Retention Update," 1.

18. Freeland, "Student Retention Update," 1; See also Office of Undergraduate Admissions and Relations with Schools. "Introducing University of California Berkeley, 1993–1994." Berkeley: University of California, 1993, 1; See also Office of Student Research. "Under-

graduate Statistics for the University of California at Berkeley, Fall, 1993." *Report: OSR 93–007*, Berkeley: Office of Student Research, University of California, Nov. 1993, 3.

19. Freeland, "Student Retention Update;" Office of Admissions, "Introducing University of California Berkeley, 1993–1994;" Office of Student Research, "Undergraduate Statistics for the University of California at Berkeley."

20. Interviewed in late 1994, this director of admissions at an elite private university chose to remain anonymous.

21. Interviewed in the summer of 1994, this director of admissions chose to remain anonymous.

22. Interviewed in the fall of 1994, this director of admissions at an elite Ivy League university chose to remain anonymous.

23. Pascarella, E. T., and Terenzini, P. T. *How College Affects Students: Findings and Insights from Twenty Years of Research*. San Francisco: Jossey-Bass, 1991, 504.

24. Pascarella and Terenzini, *How College Affects Students*, 504.

25. Pascarella and Terenzini, *How College Affects Students*, 504.

26. Pascarella and Terenzini, *How College Affects Students*, 504.

27. Smark, J. "College Influences on Graduates' Income Levels." *Research in Higher Education*, 1988, 29, 41–59.

28. Smark, "College Influences on Graduates' Income Levels," 41–59.

29. Pascarella and Terenzini, *How College Affects Students*, 510.

30. Pascarella and Terenzini, *How College Affects Students*, 510.

31. Pascarella and Terenzini, *How College Affects Students*, 510.

32. Pascarella and Terenzini, *How College Affects Students*, 512.

33. Pascarella and Terenzini, *How College Affects Students*, 512.

34. Quoted with permission from an interview with Michael Goldberger, Director of Admissions at Brown University, in a telephone interview with the author on July 11, 1994.

35. Quoted with permission from Goldberger.

36. Quoted with permission from Goldberger.

37. Quoted with permission from Goldberger.

38. Sowell, T. quoted in Watters, "The New Politics of Race," 58.

39. Berkeley: Office of Student Research, University of California. Freeland, R. "1992–93 Student Retention Update" and "Undergraduate Statistics for the University of California at Berkeley, Fall, 1993.

40. Parker, C., and Schmidt, J. "Effects of College Experience." In H. Mitzel (ed.), *Encyclopedia of Educational Research*, Vol. 2, New York: Free Press, 1982, 535–543, esp. 541.

41. Karabel, *Freshman Admissions: A Policy for the 1990s*, 33.

42. Browne-Miller, *Intelligence Policy*.

43. Watters, "The New Politics of Race."

44. Browne-Miller, *Intelligence Policy*; See also Watters, "The New Politics of Race," 68.

45. These hotly contested data are presented in D. D'Souza, *Illiberal Education: The Politics of Race and Sex on Campus*. New York: Random House, 1992, 3.

46. Watters, "The New Politics of Race."

47. Watters, "The New Politics of Race," 55.

48. Jaschik, S. "Doubts Are Raised About U.S. Inquiry on Harvard Policies." *Chronicle of Higher Education*, Feb. 1991, A19 and A22.

49. Jaschik, "Doubts Are Raised," A19.

50. Jaschik, "Doubts Are Raised," A22.

51. Jaschik, "Doubts Are Raised," A22.

52. Collison, M. "Colleges Have Done a Bad Job of Explaining Affirmative Action to Students, Critics Say." *Chronicle of Higher Education*, Feb. 1992, A37.

53. Steen, M. "Undergraduate Admissions and the Politics of Race: How the Decisions are Made." *Berkeley Graduate*, Sept. 1993, 18; See also Karabel, *Freshman Admissions: A Policy for the 1990s*, 29 and 35; See also D'Souza, *Illiberal Education*, 28–31.

54. The "Pledge of Allegiance" is attributed to Francis Bellamy by a Congressional report in 1957. It was first published in 1892 in the *Youth's Companion*, cited in *The World Almanac*, Ramsey, N.J.: Funk & Wagnall's, 1994.

55. Quoted with permission from an interview with Antonio Rey, past member, Admissions Committee, University of California, San Diego conducted by the author in Tiburon, Calif. on Jan. 7, 1994.

Chapter Five

1. Gottfredson, L. "Societal Consequences of the G factor in Employment." *Journal of Vocational Behavior,* Dec. 1986, 29(3), 403.

2. Rohranbacher, D., U.S. Rep. "Evidence of Asian American Discrimination in College and University Admissions: Fact Sheet." June 1989.

3. D'Souza, *Illiberal Education,* 3.

4. D'Souza, *Illiberal Education,* 27.

5. D'Souza, *Illiberal Education,* 28.

6. D'Souza, *Illiberal Education,* 28.

7. D'Souza, *Illiberal Education,* 31.

8. Karabel, *Freshman Admissions: A Policy for the 1990s,* 15.

9. Karabel, *Freshman Admissions: A Policy for the 1990s,* 15.

10. Karabel, *Freshman Admissions: A Policy for the 1990s,* 15–16.

11. Quoted with permission from an interview with Patrick Hayashi, vice chancellor of admissions, University of California, Berkeley conducted by author on January 26, 1994.

12. Norris, K. in "Foreword" to A. Browne-Miller, *Intelligence Policy,* ix–xii.

13. Jaschik, S. "Colleges and the Disabled." *Chronicle of Higher Education,* Apr. 1994, A38–A39.

14. Jaschik, "Colleges and the Disabled," A38.

15. Jaschik, "Colleges and the Disabled," A38.

16. Jaschik, "Colleges and the Disabled," A38.

17. Jaschik, S. "46 Colleges Found to Have Violated Rights of Disabled, U.S. Documents Show." *Chronicle of Higher Education,* Apr. 1993, A18.

18. Sarich quoted in Marshall, "Raging Bull of Berkeley," 368.

19. Sarich quoted in Marshall, "Raging Bull of Berkeley," 368.

20. Memo released by an anonymous university administrator in an anonymous department in 1993.

21. Jensen, A. R. "Giftedness and Genius: Crucial Differences." Paper presented in Symposium in Honor of Julian C. Stanley: From Psychometrics to Giftedness. San Francisco, 1992, 3.

22. Norris, in "Foreword" to *Intelligence Policy*.

23. Davis, A. quoted in K. M. Stampp, *The Peculiar Institution: Slavery in the Antebellum South*. New York: Vintage Books, 1956, 2; See also Angela Davis's insightful discussion of the relationship between Black and White women's liberation in *Women, Race and Class*. New York: Random House, 1981, in which she also cites "Matilda," 58.

24. Davis, *Women, Race and Class*, 109.

25. Gould, S. J. *The Mismeasure of Man*. New York: W.W. Norton, 1981, 104–105.

26. Broca, P. "Sur le Volume et la Forme du Cerveau Suivant les Individus et Suivant les Races." *Bulletin Société d'Anthropologie Paris*, 1861, 2, 139–207, 153.

27. Le Bon, G. "Recherches Anatomiques et Mathématiques sur les Lois des Variations du Volume du Cerveau et sur Leurs Relations avec l'Intelligence." *Revue d'Anthropologie*, 1879, 2nd series, 2, 27–104, 60–61.

28. Cope, E. D. "Two Perils of the Indo European." *The Open Court*, 1890, 3, 2070–2071.

29. Nietzsche, F., writing in 1888, "The Case of Wagner." printed in Kaufmann, W. (ed.). *Basic Writings of Nietzsche*, New York: Random House, 1992, 617.

30. Dimensions, "Going to College."

31. "'In' Box: Professors Who Date Their Students. . . ." *Chronicle of Higher Education*, May 1994, A14.

32. "Professors Who Date Their Students," A14.

33. Sadker, M., and Sadker, D. *Failing at Fairness: How America's Schools Cheat Girls*. New York: MacMillan, 1994, 183.

34. Sadker and Sadker, *Failing at Fairness*, 183. See also the articles cited by the Sadkers: Koss, M. P., Gidycz, C. A., and Wisniewski, N. "The Scope of Rape: Incidence and Prevalence of Sexual Aggression and Victimization in a National Sample of Higher Education Students." *Journal Consulting and Clinical Psychology*, 1987, 55:2, 162–70; and Adams, A., and Abarbanel, G. *Sexual Assault on Campus: What Colleges Can Do*. Santa Monica, Calif.: Rape Treatment

Center, 1988; and, Russell, D.E.H. *Sexual Exploitation: Rape, Child Sexual Assault, and Workplace Harassment*. Beverly Hills, Calif.: Sage, 1984.

35. Sadker and Sadker, *Failing at Fairness*, 183.

36. Sadker and Sadker, *Failing at Fairness*, 185.

37. Sadker and Sadker, *Failing at Fairness*, 156–160.

38. Dworkin, A. *Right-Wing Women*. New York: Putnam, 1983, 205.

39. Dworkin, *Right-Wing Women*, 205.

40. Dworkin, *Right-Wing Women*, 204.

41. Mason, M. A. *Equality Trap*. New York: Simon & Schuster, 1988, 48.

42. Mason, *Equality Trap*, 48.

43. "Matilda's Letter." *Freedom Journal*, quoted in Davis, *Women, Race and Class*, 58.

44. Kelly, A., speech cited by B. Glassman Hersh in "The Slavery of Sex." Urbana, Ill.: University of Illinois Press, 1978, 33; also cited by Dworkin, *Right-Wing Women*, 49.

Chapter Six

1. Peltason, "Challenge Before Us," 1.

2. Smith, P. *Killing the Spirit: Higher Education in America*. New York: Penguin Books, 1991, 299.

3. Smith, *Killing the Spirit*, 299.

4. Smith, *Killing the Spirit*, 298.

5. Smith, *Killing the Spirit*, 298.

6. Smith, *Killing the Spirit*, 298.

7. Smith, *Killing the Spirit*. 298.

8. Toch, *In the Name of Excellence*, 3 and 40.

9. Tsang, C. quoted in Tepperman, "Why Johnny Can't Work," 17.

10. Tepperman, "Why Johnny Can't Work," 18.

11. Tepperman, "Why Johnny Can't Work," 18.

12. Tepperman, "Why Johnny Can't Work," 18.

13. Groth, B. "And Then What? Some Thoughts About Higher Education for Alternatively Educated Students." In M. and H. Hegener, (eds), *Alternatives in Education*. Tonasket, Wash.: Home Education Press, 1992, 250–251.

14. Grath, "And Then What?" 250–251.

15. White, L. "Hate Speech Codes That Will Pass Constitutional Muster." *Chronicle of Higher Education*, May 1994, A48.

16. White, "Hate Speech Codes," 2, quoting C. Lawrence in the *Duke Law Journal*, 1990.

17. Muhammad, K. A. cited in C. F. Pope, "The Challenges Posed by Radical Afrocentrism." *Chronicle of Higher Education*, Mar. 1994, B1.

18. Pope, "The Challenges of Radical Afrocentrism," B1.

19. Pope, "The Challenges of Radical Afrocentrism," B1–B2.

20. Pope, "The Challenges of Radical Afrocentrism," B2.

21. Pope, "The Challenges of Radical Afrocentrism," B2.

22. Matthews, A. "The Campus Crime Wave." *New York Times Magazine*, Mar. 7, 1993, Section 6, 38.

23. Matthews, "The Campus Crime Wave," 38 and 40.

24. Siegel, D. quoted in Matthews, "The Campus Crime Wave," 40.

25. Siegel quoted in Matthews, "The Campus Crime Wave," 40.

26. Siegel quoted in Matthews, "The Campus Crime Wave," 40.

27. Siegel quoted in Matthews, "The Campus Crime Wave," 42.

28. Matthews, "The Campus Crime Wave," 42.

29. Matthews, "The Campus Crime Wave," 42.

30. Siegel quoted in Matthews, "The Campus Crime Wave," 40.

31. Matthews, "The Campus Crime Wave," 31.

32. Matthews, "The Campus Crime Wave," 40.

33. Matthews, "The Campus Crime Wave," 40.

34. Immerwahr, J., and Harvey, J. "What the Public Thinks of Colleges." *Chronicle of Higher Education*, May 1995, B1–B2.

35. Immerwahr and Harvey, "What the Public Thinks of Colleges," B2.

36. Immerwahr and Harvey, "What the Public Thinks of Colleges," B2.

Chapter Seven

1. DeAngelis, T. "Ignorance Plagues Affirmative Action." *APA Monitor*, May 1995, 1.

2. A portion of President Johnson's 1965 Howard University Speech quoted in D. Lederman, "The Special Preferences Are Not Limited to Blacks." *Chronicle of Higher Education*, Apr. 1995, A16.

3. Duster, T. quoted in A. Wildavsky, "A Question of Fairness." *San Francisco Chronicle*, May 16, 1995, A6.

4. Burd, S. "Private Colleges Try to Keep a Low Profile." *Chronicle of Higher Education*, Apr. 1995, A19.

5. Burd, "Private Colleges Keep Low Profile," A19–A20.

6. Each of the elite private university administrators I interviewed and quote here chose to remain anonymous.

7. As explained in Chapter Three.

8. Shalala, D. quoted in *Wisconsin State Journal*, Dec. 1992, D8.

9. Wildavsky, A. *Why Political Correctness in Faculty Hiring Will Destroy Higher Education.* Berkeley: Department of Political Science, University of California, Apr. 1993, 1–2.

10. Lincoln, Y. S. "Piety and Purpose: Reclaiming Elan for Higher Education." *Educational Researcher*, Mar. 1994, 37.

11. One of the extremes of the tensions inherent in academic life as set forth by J. Getman, *In the Company of Scholars: The Struggle for the Soul of Higher Education.* Austin, Tex.: University of Texas Press, 1992.

12. Getman, *In the Company of Scholars: Struggle for Soul of Higher Education.*

13. Hackney, S. "Organizing a National Conversation." *Chronicle of Higher Education*, Apr. 1994, A56.

14. Norris, in "Foreword" to *Intelligence Policy.*

15. Quoted with permission from an interview with Chang-Lin Tien, chancellor of the University of California, Berkeley, conducted by the author on July 12, 1994.

16. Karabel, *Freshman Admissions: A Policy for the 1990s*, 29 and 35.

17. Karabel, *Freshman Admissions: A Policy for the 1990s*, 29.

18. Karabel, *Freshman Admissions: A Policy for the 1990s*, 29 and 35.

19. Karabel, *Freshman Admissions: A Policy for the 1990s*, 29 and 35.

20. Karabel, *Freshman Admissions: A Policy for the 1990s*, 29–34.

21. Karabel, *Freshman Admissions: A Policy for the 1990s*, 29–34.

22. Karabel, *Freshman Admissions: A Policy for the 1990s*, 29–34.

23. Karabel, *Freshman Admissions: A Policy for the 1990s*, 29–34.

24. Karabel, *Freshman Admissions: A Policy for the 1990s*, 29–34.

25. Karabel, *Freshman Admissions: A Policy for the 1990s*, 29–34.

26. Karabel, *Freshman Admissions: A Policy for the 1990s*, 29–34.

27. Karabel, *Freshman Admissions: A Policy for the 1990s*, 43.

Chapter Eight

1. Spence, G. *From Freedom to Slavery: The Rebirth of Tyranny in America*. New York: St. Martin's Press, 1993, 80.

2. Fukuyama, *End of History and the Last Man*, 116.

3. Bateson, G. *Steps to an Ecology of Mind*.

4. Shipman, P. *The Evolution of Racism*. New York: Simon & Schuster, 1994, 271.

5. Edelman, M. Wright *A Measure of Our Success*, 54.

6. Wildavsky, *Political Correctness in Faculty Hiring*, 1; See also Wildavsky, A. "The Rise of Radical Egalitarianism and the Fall of Academic Standards." *Academic Questions*, Fall 1989, 52–55.

7. Wildavsky, "The Rise of Radical Egalitarianism," 1–2.

8. Wildavsky, "The Rise of Radical Egalitarianism," 1–2.

9. Wheeler, D. L. "The Death of Languages: Scholars Say Loss of Linguistic Diversity Is a Human and Scientific Tragedy." *Chronicle of Higher Education*, Apr. 1994, 8.

10. Kraus, M. quoted in Wheeler, "The Death of Languages: Loss of Linguistic Diversity," 8.

11. Wheeler, "The Death of Languages: Loss of Linguistic Diversity," 8.

12. Wheeler, "The Death of Languages: Loss of Linguistic Diversity," 8.

13. Smith, *Killing the Spirit*.

14. Norris, in "Foreword" to *Intelligence Policy*.

15. Bateson, M. C. *Peripheral Visions: Learning Along the Way*, New York: HarperCollins, 1994, 9.

16. U.S. Bureau of the Census. *Statistical Abstract of the U.S.: 1993.* (13th ed.) Washington, D.C., 1993, 203 and 211.

17. Census Bureau, *Statistical Abstract,* 164.

18. Census Bureau, *Statistical Abstract,* 178.

19. Zigler, E., and Susan, M. *Head Start: The Inside Story of America's Most Successful Educational Experiment.* New York: Basic Books, 1992, 226.

20. Census Bureau, *Statistical Abstract.*

21. Freedberg, L. "60 U.S. Schools to Offer College Degree Via TV." *San Francisco Chronicle,* Aug. 5, 1994, A1.

22. Miller, R. "Educating for Wholeness—A Challenge to Modern Schooling." In *Alternatives in Education,* 20.

23. Miller, "Educating for Wholeness," 21.

24. Miller, "Educating for Wholeness," 20–21.

25. Boyer, E. *College: The Undergraduate Experience in America.* New York: HarperCollins, 1987, 91.

26. Montessori, M. *The Child in the Family.* New York: Avon Books, 1956, 29 and 35.

27. As I have explained these techniques (from the metacognitive perspective) in A. Browne-Miller, *Learning to Learn: Ways to Nurture Your Child's Intelligence.* New York: Insight Books, 1994.

28. Lieberman, A. "The Meaning of Scholarly Activity and the Building of Community." *Educational Researcher,* Aug./Sept. 1992, 21(6), 8.

29. Lieberman, "The Meaning of Scholarly Activity," 8.

30. Lieberman, "The Meaning of Scholarly Activity," 8 and 10.

31. Lieberman, "The Meaning of Scholarly Activity," 8 and 10.

32. Freire, P. *The Pedagogy of the Oppressed.* (new revised 20th anniversary ed.) New York: Continuum, 1993, 65.

33. Freire, *The Pedagogy of the Oppressed,* 164.

34. See Browne-Miller (1994), where I fully explain this matter.

Index